History of Indian Philosphy

ERICH FRAUWALLNER

HISTORY OF INDIAN PHILOSPHY

VOLUME II

The Nature-Philosophical Schools and the Vaiśeṣika System
The System of the Jaina
The Materialism

Translated from Original German into English by
V.M. BEDEKAR

MOTILAL BANARSIDASS PUBLISHERS
PRIVATE LIMITED • DELHI

5th Reprint : Delhi, 2018
First Edition : Delhi, 1973
By arrangement with Otto Müller Verlag, Salzburg

ISBN: 978-81-208-0988-8 (Vol. I)
ISBN: 978-81-208-0989-5 (Vol. II)
ISBN: 978-81-208-0987-1 (Set)

MOTILAL BANARSIDASS
41 U.A. Bungalow Road, Jawahar Nagar, Delhi 110 007
1 B, J S Compound, Kennedy Bridge, Nana Chowk, Mumbai 400 007
203 Royapettah High Road, Mylapore, Chennai 600 004
236, 9th Main III Block, Jayanagar, Bengaluru 560 011
9, Panchanan Ghosh Lane, 1st Floor, Kolkata 700 009
Ashok Rajpath, Patna 800 004
Chowk, Varanasi 221 001

Printed in India

by RP Jain at NAB Printing Unit,
A-44, Naraina Industrial Area, Phase I, New Delhi–110028
and published by JP Jain for Motilal Banarsidass Publishers (P) Ltd,
41 U.A. Bungalow Road, Jawahar Nagar, Delhi-110007

THE TABLE OF CONTENTS

FOREWORD vii-x

B. THE PERIOD OF THE SYSTEMS (CONTINUED)

7. THE NATURE-PHILOSOPHICAL SCHOOLS AND THE VAIŚEṢIKA SYSTEM 3-180

The tradition of the Vaiśeṣika System, its history and literature 3. The literature of the related systems, of the Nyāya and the Mīmāṃsā 5. The place of the Vaiśeṣika in the frame of Nature-philosophical schools. The oldest Nature-philosophy. The Elements and their qualities 11. World-construction and the living creatures 21. The man. The body of the man 24 The sense-organs and their working 27. The soul. The existence of the soul 39. The constitution of the soul and psychic occurrence. The psychical organ 43. The old Nature-philosophy of the Nyāya 47. New Thoughts. The Atom Doctrine 53. The atomic-mechanistic world-picture of the Vaiśeṣika. The doctrine of movement and the oldest theory of Causality 57. The Invisible (*adṛṣṭam*) 63. The remodelling of the Soul-doctrine 67. Space and Time 72. The emergence of the doctrine of categories. The oldest three categories 79. The Realism of the Vaiśeṣika 82. The category of substance 83. The category of qualities. The characteristic qualities of the Elements 84. The common qualities 85. The qualities of the soul. Further qualities 93. The category of movement 99. Further categories. Commonness and particularity 101. The category of inherence 105. Controversial categories 108. The remodelling of the old nature-philosophy in the light of the doctrine of categories. The Indian Scholastics and its role in the Vaiśeṣika 112. Atoms and aggregates. The doctrine of the whole 115. The new form of the theory of causality 118. The doctrine of perception in the light of the doctrine of categories 123. The concluding reformulation of the Vaiśeṣika and the work of Praśastapāda 133. The degeneration of Scholastics in Praśastapāda's work 135. The classical Vaiśeṣika system according to Praśastapāda. The six categories 141. The substances 143. The four Elements. The origination and dissolution of the world 146. The ether, time and space 147. Soul and psychical organ 150. The qualities in general 152. The qualities of the Elements, Form, taste, smell and touch 153. The common qualities. The number 157. Extension and Separateness 158. Connection and Separation 159. Distantness and nearness 163. The qualities of the soul, knowledge, pleasure, pain, desire, aversion and effort 165. The remaining qualities. Heaviness, fluidity and moistness 167. Impulse or Preparedness (*saṃskāraḥ*) 168. Merit and guilt. The doctrine of deliverance 170. The sound 170. The category of movement 171. The commonness 175. The particularity 176. The inherence 177. The importance of the Vaiśeṣika System 179.

8. THE SYSTEM OF THE JAINA 181-214

The tradition 182. The system of the Jaina according to Umāsvāti and Kundakunda. The five masses of existence183. The doctrine of categories 188. The world-construction and world-occurrence 190. The living creatures 193. The man, body and the sense-organs 195. The soul. The theory of knowledge of the Jaina 199. The doctrine of deliverance 201. Appreciative estimate of the system of the Jaina 211.

9. THE MATERIALISM 215-226

The nature of the Indian materialism. Its connection with the political theory. King Paesi 216. The oldest materialistic doctrines 219. The Lokāyata system 221.

SUPPLEMENT

1. SELECT BIBLIOGRAPHY AND NOTES 229-259
2. INDEX 260-265
3. ERRATA 265

FOREWORD

The present second volume of my History of Indian Philosophy is perhaps such as is of the least philosophical interest for a larger circle of readers. Between the bold beginnings of antiquity and the grand creations of the Buddhist system, the doctrines of natural philosophy operate like a valley between two eminences and that is understandable. Only a small modest material is available for the consideration of the natural philosophy of the ancient times. The development after some beautiful beginnings soon comes to a stop. New considerations for it do not come up, as systematic research is missing. So the doctrines become stiff or lifeless or degenerate into a hollow scholastics. What has been attained and presented is for the most part primitive and inadequate. In a certain measure, Greek philosophy has also not been spared from this fate. But the Indian philosophy in this sphere has not attained to a level approaching the performance of the Greeks.

In spite of these circumstances, I have considered it desirable, nay, necessary to deal also with this part of Indian philosophy with a certain fullness. Firstly because it deals with one of the most important and original spheres of Indian philosophy. As against other philosophical creations, it was forgotten too easily that there were also other directions which did not create a philosophy out of longing for Deliverance but which endeavoured to explain the world in a scientific manner out of pure striving for philosophical knowledge. And this must be properly emphasised. Further these directions in philosophy played historically an important role. These directions have exercised influence from different sides. To him who does not know them, much in other systems would remain unintelligible—much that was created now in contrast, now in union, with other systems. Finally the Vaiśeṣika,—the most important of the systems of Nature-philosophy—brought forth with its doctrine of the categories a creation which represents an important constituent of the thought-wealth of Indian philosophy. Wide layers of later Indian Philosophy are formed through the manner of thought of the Vaiśeṣika and are dependent on it. They would be as little understood without the knowledge of this system as the scholastics of the Middle Ages without the philosophy of Aristotle.

By the way, as against Greek philosophy there appears a beautiful example of the peculiarity or originality of Indian philosophy. While the Greek philosophy rises up like a dazzling firework and produces in a short time an abundance of dazzling splendid creations, the Indian development rolls like a broad stream slowly through the centuries. But while the doctrine of categories in Aristotle remains a pretty idea, whose potentialities or possibilities are in no way worked out, in India it developed to a complete system, which far exceeds the beginnings of Aristotle's and in further stretches gets choked up in arid 'Scholastics'.

In certain particular respects, I would like to make a few following remarks regarding the present volume. As far as the Vaiśeṣika is concerned, the treatises written on it up to now are based as a rule on the later handbooks. I have, on the other hand, based my presentation on the work of the classical period. I have tried, above all, to make intelligible the origin of the system. Whoever, in the history of Philosophy, is not satisfied with a collection of mere dry statements but seeks to understand the living thoughts and the men who thought them, must needs go to their origin. The great difficulty in the case of the Vaiśeṣika is that the tradition preserved for us shows only the end of a long development. All the foregoing must be inferred. But I hope that I have succeeded to show rightly at least the broad lines. A reconstruction cannot naturally approach in its livingness an effective tradition. But an attempt must once be made. There remains a very serious lacuna in tradition which must be bridged over. In the matter of the presentation of the Buddhistic systems which will be dealt with in the next volume, the things are already incomparably favourable.

The description of the Naturo-philosophical system and of the development of the Vaiśeṣika may perhaps appear somewhat detailed. The excuse for it lies in the great importance which this system had for Indian philosophy in general. Besides I request the reader to consider that the development, which I present here, extended over eight centuries. Besides, on this occasion, I would like to remark by way of principle that my treatise attempts to meet at the same time different needs. Nevertheless, in order not to tire the reader through excessive prolixity, I have endeavoured to present the matter in such a way that the particular sections remain understandable, even if the reader skips over certain isolated parts which are of less interest to him. For example, I have considered it desirable to give in the beginning of every chapter the sources and the condition of the handed-down tradition. He, who finds these concise, necessarily dry, sections uninteresting, can turn over these pages and immediately begin with the proper presentation. He who wants only the Dogmatics of the complete system will find it presented in a nutshell at the end of the particular chapter and he can estimate the history of development. The reader can, therefore, seize that which corresponds to his wishes but has also the possibility to look up also the other, if the need be.

The weakest part of this volume is the treatment of the system of the Jaina. It lies therein that only parts of the rich material, though preserved, are published. Besides, the published material was partially available to me. What I myself possess in this sphere is already on a modest scale and the publications in the libraries in Vienna are more inadequate in this sphere than in other spheres of Indology. My presentation is, therefore, proportionately scanty. Further I have restricted myself under these circumstances to describe the things as they appear to me. I must remain here solely responsible for its justification. I could have, no doubt, presented more but it is unsatisfactory to present a work when the means to accomplish it fail, as science recognizes them. I would like to remark that according to my view, there is much scope for further research in the sphere of Jainism, especially concerning the philosophical contents.

This is all, in the essentials, what was to be remarked in regard to this volume. As for the rest, what has been said concerning the whole work in the Foreword to the first volume, holds good also here.

Concerning the reception which the first volume has received, it was gratifying. The evaluations are preponderatingly favourable ; adverse judgments have remained entirely sporadic. Especially individual reviews have occupied themselves with the work so exhaustively and the aim and the performance have been assessed with such complete understanding that I have heartily rejoiced at them. I hope this volume also will find the same approbation.

Finally I would like to thank all my scholarly colleagues who have helped me by sending the material, especially by sending the offprints which would, otherwise, have been difficult for me to obtain or would have been generally inaccessible. Above all I mention the name of my revered friend Mr. Et. Lamotte in Belgium, Messrs. H. v. Glasenapp, W. Ruben and F. Weller in Germany, Messrs P. Demiéville, J. Filliozat and A. Bareau in France, Prof. V. Raghavan and Prof. A. N. Upadhye in India. Prof. Upadhye has often most kindly helped me with his advice in the difficult constitution of the Jaina-works.

—E. Frauwallner

B. THE PERIOD OF THE SYSTEMS
(Continued)

7. THE NATURE-PHILOSOPHICAL SCHOOLS AND THE VAIŚEṢIKA SYSTEM

In the history of Indian Philosophy, as we have seen in our presentation in the first volume, two streams of Development stand out already in the ancient times. The first has its origin in the Upaniṣads of the Vedic period and is characterized by the doctrine of the world-soul—the *Brahma* or the *Ātmā* which plays in it a leading role. The doctrine of the Buddha belongs to it. Out of it arose the first great philosophical system of the classical time, viz. the Sāṃkhya which has proved of decisive influence with a series of its important and original thoughts for the whole later development. The second stream of development is of the nature-philosophical kind to which active interest in the external world has given a characteristic stamp. The doctrine of the world-soul is foreign to it. It, on the contrary, works with a very old soul-doctrine which assumes numerous individual souls. We met with this stream of development while describing Epic philosophy. To it belongs the doctrine of the Jina, the great contemporary of the Buddha. The second great philosophical system of the classical time—Vaiśeṣika—owes its rise to it; its doctrine of categories forms an important part of the Indian Philosophical thought-treasure. We shall occupy ourselves with this stream of development and no doubt, it will be the Vaiśeṣika system, which on account of its surpassing importance, shall be the centre of our consideration. However, before we begin with its presentation itself, we shall also give here, as we have hitherto done, a short review about its external history and the literature of the School under consideration.

What concerns the external history of the Vaiśeṣika, tradition unanimously names Kaṇāda as the founder of the system. He belonged to the family of Kāśyapa who was often also designated under the name of Ulūka ('the owl'). His pupil was supposed to be a certain Pañcaśikhī —a son of the Brahmin of Banaras. What is reported about both is fully legendary. What remains, then, is that we know no other well-known representative of the system of the ancient time. We only know that in the early post-Christian centuries, Vaiśeṣika was one of the leading philosophical systems besides the Sāmkhya. We hear, there were numerous schools of the Vaiśeṣika. Only out of the last period of the classical system, two men are known to us—whose works are preserved for us. The one is Candramati (or Maticandra) who belonged to about the fifth century; and the second is the final systematizer of the school, Praśastapāda or Praśastadeva, sporadically also named Praśastakāra, who lived about the second half of the sixth century. With him ends the history of the living independent system.

Like the information about the external history of the Vaiśeṣika, equally scanty is its literature preserved for us. We possess the old aphorisms of the school : The *Vaiśeṣikasūtras* of Kaṇāda[1]. Their text or wording is not testified by any old commentary. Numerous quotations in the older philosophical literature testify to a good old kernel. But much old is lost and is also variously changed; new things have also been interpolated. Besides, the language, as is generally in the case of the Sūtras, is difficult to understand and its sense often remains disputable. On that account their worth for the representation of the system is greatly diminished. An old commentary on the *Sūtras*, is, as already said, not preserved. Occasionally we hear of a commentary of one Rāvaṇa (*Rāvaṇabhāṣyam*), counted as one of the older schools. *Ātreyabhāṣyam* or *Ātreyatantram* is also quoted in the later Jaina texts; but to which time this certain Ātreya belonged, we do not know. For the rest, we possess only two independent works belonging to the later period of the classical system. The one is the short *Daśapadārthaśāstram* ('doctrinal book of ten categories'), preserved in Chinese translation, of the above named Candramati.[2] The second is the concluding short compendium of the classical system, the *Padārthadharmasaṃgrahaḥ* ('the compendium of the qualities of categories') of Praśastapāda, which is also named, on account of its close connection with the *Sūtras*, as the *Praśastapādabhāṣyam* ('the commentary of Praśastapāda') which has remained for the whole future as the authoritative presentation of the classical Vaiśesika system.[3] On the *Praśastapādabhāṣyam* three commentaries are preserved from the older time: the oldest and richest in contents is the *Vyomavatī* of Vyomaśiva (about ninth century

A.D.).[4] The second is that of the famous Nyāya teacher Udayana (second half of the tenth century A.D.) which carries the name of *Kiraṇāvalī* ('The series of rays')[5]. The third is the *Nyāyakandalī* ('the blossoming plant of logic') of Śrīdhara[6] which according to the author's own testimony was completed in 991 A.D.[7]

If we shortly summarise the facts as they are, it can be said that besides the obscure *Sūtras* and the concise handbook of Candramati, we possess only one work of the classical Vaiśeṣika system, namely the work of Praśastapāda with its commentaries, that is, a work which stands at the end of the whole development. It is, therefore, naturally clear that under such circumstances it is difficult to write a real history of the system. As things are, we are, then, thrown on our own resources, viz. on drawing inferences regarding the earlier stages of development out of the constituents of the system itself. Still other sources also come to help and they supplement, though in a modest measure, the scanty tradition of the Vaiśeṣika. In this connection there must be named the two related systems—the logical school of the Nyāya and the ritualistic school of the Mīmāṃsā.

Of both the systems, the Nyāya originated through the mixing of a dialectic with a simple natural-philosophical doctrine. It, no doubt, stands near the doctrine of the Vaiśeṣika but did not participate in its later development. Therefore, on many points, it gives a good picture of the natural philosophy of the older period. Later on, the Nyāya developed unilaterally the Theory of Knowledge and Logic and completely neglected Nature-philosophy. All the nature-philosophical views which serve as the basis of its knowledge-theory were taken over by it out of the classical Vaiśeṣika system from which it deviated only in unimportant details. In consonance with these facts, the later Nyāya hands down only sporadic supplementary features towards the picture of the classical Vaiśeṣika. On the other hand, its old nature-philosophy offers a valuable help in inferring the first steps of the classical system.

Different is the case with the Mīmāṃsā. It had originally, in general, nothing to do with philosophy. It was a school which occupied itself with the Vedic sacrificial ritual and sought, by a rigorous systematic interpretation, to bring in unison with one another the plethora of directions in the old Vedic text and to settle the standing contradictions. There was only one point which called for a connection with philosophy. For the representative of the Mīmāṃsā, the Veda was valid as a permanent infallible revelation. Now, in the duration of the philosophical development, the theory of knowledge came to the forefront and as an account was demanded of each system as to whereon its doctrines were grounded, the Mīmāṃsā was compelled to justify its appeal to the Veda and to demonstrate its permanence and reliability. So one came to be occupied with the theory of knowledge and other philosophical questions connected with it. It occurred with such emphasis and success that the Mīmāṃsā played a remarkable role beside other philosophical systems in the last period of Indian philosophy of the classical period. In that process, the Mīmāṃsā teachers joined, to a great extent, in the views of the Vaiśeṣika. Its relation to this system, however, was much more loose than that of the Nyāya. In many cases they deviated from the interpretations of the Vaiśeṣika. Besides, within the Mīmāṃsā itself, there were numerous divergences of opinion. And it could so happen that on any one point, one did not hold fast to a definite view. Because it was enough for the Mīmāṃsā to exhibit the possibilities which were permissible to defend successfully the basic views of the system about the permanence and reliability of the Veda. The philosophical knowledge had, on the other hand, only secondary interest. The multiplicity of views or interpretations, which it produced, forms, already for us, through their scantiness, a welcome supplement to the unilateral tradition of the Vaiśeṣika. Besides, it shows to us the different possibilities as to how one could consider things. Through them, we learn to understand and evaluate better and, more rightly, the interpretation in favour of which the Vaiśeṣika decided. We shall, therefore, draw upon the pertinent doctrines of the Mīmāṃsā profitably in our presentation of the classical Vaiśeṣika. It contributes, indeed, only little for making accessible the older steps of the development o the system.

The Nyāya and the Mīmāṃsā supplement, therefore, the tradition of the Vaiśeṣika on many points in a welcome way. But seen on the whole, what they have to offer is not much and, above all, they fail greatly for the older time. If we want to describe the origin and the development of the Vaiśeṣika, we are, therefore, thrown on the constituents of the handed-down system itself to infer the earlier stages of development in order to gain a picture of its history. Thereby we have a support through the fact that the knowledge of general development gives a frame in which we can arrange what can be inferred about the Vaiśeṣika. Besides, the tradition of Jinism and Buddhism comes to our help in a certain measure. The relation of both these to the Vaiśeṣika is, no doubt, entirely different from that of the Nyāya and the Mīmāṃsā. They stand in no direct relation with it. They belong, however, to the same stream of development which brought forth the doctrines of nature-philosophy. They, therefore, provide a valuable evidence for the course of development in general. It holds especially valid for Jinism. Already, in the description of the doctrine of the Jina in the first volume of this treatise, we have emphasised that its doctrine is the most important evidence, in the oldest time, for the nature-philosophical stream of development. Because in spite of unsatisfactory tradition and defective working out of the preserved material, it represents the most embracing and copious source for this stream of development. As it has preserved bulky material from the older period, we find in it much handed down and testified what we can only infer or conjecture for the older development of the Vaiśeṣika. And so we can supplement, with its help, in important points, the picture of that sector of development for which direct evidence fails on the side of the Vaiśeṣika. A similar thing holds good, though in a far restricted measure, in the case of Buddhism. The doctrine of the Buddha is based on that stream of development which issues from the Upaniṣads. But later on, as attempts were made to create full philosophical systems out of the doctrines of Deliverance proclaimed by the Buddha, the views such as were held in nature-philosophical schools were very well seized upon to a great extent. And as this development in Buddhism set in earlier, and as the old sources out of this period are preserved for us, we also find here different things which contribute to the understanding of the oldest steps of development of the Vaiśeṣika.

With the help of all these sources, we shall now try to

describe the origin and the development of the Vaiśeṣika up to its final form in the classical system. Before we begin with that, it will be profitable to name the most important representatives and their works of the other schools which we have mentioned. In the case of Jinism, it is unnecessary, as it finds its presentation already in this volume. And we have drawn upon the Buddhistic sources only in an isolated, sporadic manner. But we must repeatedly refer to the representatives of the Nyāya and the Mīmāṃsā, before we come to describe these systems themselves. Therefore, it is desirable that their names do not remain unfamiliar to the reader.

What concerns the oldest work of the Nyāya School, the oldest work is again a Sūtra-text, the *Nyāyasūtrāṇi.*[8] In it is recognizable the origin of the Nyāya through the mixture of Dialectics and Nature-philosophy, as the two sections stand out against each other distinctly and are connected only through easy touching up.

Akṣapāda from the family of Gautama is deemed to be the author of the *Nyāyasūtras*. About his person, nothing is known. What are reported are simply legends. The oldest commentary on the *Sūtras* is the work of Pakṣilasvāmī of the Vātsyāyana lineage, called the *Nyāyabhāṣyam* ('a detailed commentary on the Nyāya system')[9] This commentary presumably belongs to the first half of the fifth century. It explains, in detail, the whole *Sūtra* text—the dialectic as well as the Nature-philosophical sections and clarifies not only the wording but also deals exhaustively with all problems, and presents a precious supplement to the *Sūtras*. The whole future development stems out of it. Consequently we hear of many sub-commentaries: one sub-commentary (*bhāṣyaṭīkā*) of one Bhāvivikta and another of Aviddhakarṇa. But of all these works there is preserved to us only the *Nyāya-vārttikam* ('a supplementary commentary on the Nyāya system') of Udyotakara from the Bhāradvāja family, which may have been written in 650 A.D. [10] With it begins the later development of the Nyāya which emphasises unilaterally the Logic and Knowledge-Theory and neglects the Nature-philosophy. Another Nyāya author who is often mentioned but whose works are lost is Śaṅkarasvāmī. About 800 A.D., Trilocana wrote his works. But his works are also lost, though we possess from his pupil

Vācaspatimiśra a bulky commentary on the *Nyāya-vārttikam* of Udyotakara, called *Nyāya-vārttika-tātparyaṭīkā* ('a sub-commentary on the true meaning of *Nyāyavārttikam*'), called in short the '*Tātparyaṭīkā*'.[11] Vācaspatimiśra is one of the most fertile philosophical writers of the old times. He has written on the different systems and we have met him already in the description of the literature of the Sāṃkhya and the classical Yoga system. Still his performance in the sphere of Nyāya may be considered the most important. After Vācaspatimiśra are to be named two Nyāya authors who did not write commentaries but who dealt with the transmitted stuff independently: the first of them is Jayantabhaṭṭa who lived in Kashmir in the second half of the 9th century. His *Nyāyamañjarī* ('blossoming inflorescence of Logic',)[12] in which he, taking as his basis some select *Sūtras*, proceeds with great freedom in the shaping of the material, can be held to be the best and the most systematic presentation of older Nyāya. The second author Bhāvasarvajña or Bhāsarvajña gives in his *Nyāyasāraḥ* ('Kernel of Logic')[13] a short presentation of the Nyāya under a onesided emphasis on the Theory of Knowledge. His own exhaustive commentary on it, called *Nyāyabhūṣaṇam* ('the ornament of Logic') is still preserved for us but remains unpublished. The last great representative of the Nyāya of the older time is Udayana (second half of the tenth century A.D.), who already meets us as an author of a commentary on Praśastapāda's *Padārthadharma-saṁgrahaḥ*. He wrote a commentary on Vācaspatimiśra's *Tātparyaṭīkā*, called the *Nyāyavārttikatātparyapariśuddhiḥ* ('rectification of the true meaning of the *Nyāya-Vārttika*')[14] and many independent works. This is provisionally, in a few words, the most important that is to be said about the representatives of the old Nyāya. An exhaustive description of individual authors and their works will be given in the presentation of the Nyāya.

We are able to get still less material in the case of the Mīmāṃsā. In it also the oldest preserved work is a Sūtra text, the *Mīmāṃsā-Sūtras* of Jaimini.[15] The oldest commentary on the *Sūtras* is called *Mīmāṃsābhāṣyam* ('A detailed commentary on the Mīmāṃsā system').[16] It is the work of a certain Śabarasvāmī, who may have written it in the beginning of the sixth century A.D. Both *Sūtras* and *Bhāṣyam* contain little that is philosophical. But Śabarasvāmī, where he comes to speak of the Theory of Knowledge, quotes an old commentary and cites long fragments from it. The author of this old commentary, *Vṛttiḥ* ('A short commentary'), whom Sabarasvāmī merely names as the Vṛtti-author (*'Vṛttikāraḥ*), deals, in the quoted passages, already in details, on the questions of the Theory of Knowledge and it is his explanations on which is built the philosophy of the later Mīmāṃsā. The next great Mīmāṃsā teachers, who have remained authoritative for later times, write sub-commentaries on the *Bhāṣyam* of Śabarasvāmī, and by far the largest part on which they have to say what is philosophical is contained in their elucidations on the portions quoted by Śabarasvāmī as out of the *Vṛtti*. This holds good, above all, in the case of the greatest of all Mīmāṃsā teachers, Kumārila (first half of the seventh century). Of his bulky commentary distributed in three parts on the work of Śabarasvāmī, the first is philosophically the most important—*Ślokavārttikam* ('a supplementary commentary in verses') devoted predominantly to the clarification of the named sections. Indeed, the clarified text serves for him as only the basis on which he gives his own statements. These statements of his, exceeding by far the explained text, deal broadly with all pertinent questions and discuss exhaustively the points raised by the opposing schools. It was Kumārila who gained, by fighting arguments for the Mīmāṁsā an equal place beside other great philosophical systems. He has always remained the most pre-eminent representative of the Mīmāṃsā. Besides Kumārila is to be named in the second place, his pupil Prabhākara, who also commented on the work of Śabarasvāmī in a long commentary called *Bṛhatī*, also called *Nibandhanam*).[18] He also wrote a short commentary called (*Laghvī*, also called *Vivaraṇam*). Prabhākara, as against Kumārila, shows great independence and has achieved important things though he does not approach his teacher in his stature. The third great Mīmāṃsā teacher of the same time who entirely goes his own way is Maṇḍanamiśra. The whole later Mīmāṃsā depends on these three great teachers. Kumārila as well as Prabhākara have become the heads of respective Schools which cultivated their own doctrines and explained their works. Only Maṇḍana has not founded his own school. Of the successors and the commentators of Kumārila and Prabhākara, we need only mention here a few. The oldest exponent of Kumārila is Uṃveka (first half of the eighth century) who wrote a commentary on the *Ślokavārttikam.*[19] The same works were commented upon by Sucarita Miśra (about tenth century) in his *Kāśikā* (commentary from Banaras)[20] and by Pārthasārathimiśra (about the eleventh century) in his *Nyāyaratnākaraḥ* ('a mine of jewels')[21]. Of the commentators of the School of Prabhākara is to be named, above all, Śālikanātha (eighth century A.D.) who not only commented on the work of Prabhākara but also wrote an independent work called *Prakaraṇapañcikā* ('Elucidation in the form of an independent work').[22] This work represents for us the most important source for the doctrines of Prabhākara, because the works of Prabhākara himself are preserved in fragments which also have been only partly published. This is all what we need provisionally say about the literature of the Mīmāṃsā. At the same time, we have concluded what was to be said about the external history and literature of the system. We can now go over to the presentation of the doctrines. But we shall still preface it with a few general remarks.

The Nature-Philosophical Schools : We have already said that the stream of philosophical development, with which we are now dealing, is, above all, characterized by two things: the heightened interest in the external world and the assumption of numerous individual souls. Of these the second point requires to be supplemented with additional remarks. Though the plurality of the souls is, no doubt, a striking external sign, what gives a decisive stamp to this stream of development is not this plurality but the place which the souls have assumed in it. In the stream of development which issues out of the Upaniṣads, the world-soul—the *Brahma* or the *Ātmā*—represents a world which, being of a different nature, stands different from this world of phenomena. This world of *Brahma* is the only important thing. Metaphysically, it gives the 'ur-ground' for explaining the world and, in ethics, represents the highest of goal for which striving holds good. It is the centre of interest. Entirely different is the position of the soul in the stream of development with which we are now concerned. The souls stand on a stage beside the elements as one of the factors out of which the world of phenomena is built. There is no fundamental contrast. Also with the assumption of the souls is in no way connected the necessity of ethical inferences or conclusions. This is shown clearly by the fact that there were also materialistic doctrines which recognized the existence of a soul. The soul-doctrine serves, in the first place, the explanation of the world. It forms only a part of what is essential and predominating in this stream of development i.e. of nature-philosophy which seeks to understand and explain the world out of pure philosophical striving for knowledge.

This Nature-philosophy appears in different forms and in different relations with other doctrines. On the one hand, the recognition of one individual soul rendered possible a union with the doctrine of Deliverance, however, external or mechanical it may occur—e.g. in the classical Nyāya where simply a knowledge of the sixteen dialectical categories was explained as a pre-requisite for Deliverance or in the finished classical Vaiśeṣika, where, in an entirely similar way, Deliverance was allowed to depend on the knowledge of the six categories without changing, on that account, anything of the system; more still, in the whole presentation, in general, the aim of Deliverance could not receive strong importance. On the other hand, light materialistic doctrines which considered their chief aim as one of contesting the belief in the beyond and the ethical inferences arising out of it, could find support in this nature-philosophy. In fact, the information preserved for us in spite of its scantiness shows to us the different sub-varieties of such doctrines. As we have already occasionally remarked,[23] the Indian attempt after systematization and numerical understanding of things led early to the fact that the representatives of several doctrines put together, in well-arranged enumerations, the factors out of which the external world was formed according to their views. And such enumerations, at the place itself where they are preserved, allow us to know well the basic attitude of different doctrines. Thus we hear of the contemporary of the Buddha—Ajita Keśakambala who recognized only four elements : Earth, Water, Fire and Air and represented a gross materialism. Another, Kakuda Kātyāyana enumerated as factors of existence, besides the four elements, Pleasure, Pain and Soul. As his statements and the acceptance of ideas of Pleasure and Sorrow in the lists show, his doctrine was materialistic-hedonistic. The series of six elements (*dhātavaḥ*) which we find mentioned in oldest Buddhism [24], clearly emanated out of pure nature-philosophical circles and recognized besides Earth, Water, Fire and Air, also Space and Knowledge, Knowledge taking the place of the soul according to the basic views of Buddhism. An old enumeration of the Jaina shows a mixing with the doctrine of Deliverance; it allows after the soul (*jīva*) and the inanimate ((*ajīva*), also the instreaming of *Karma* (*āsravaḥ*), its warding off (*saṁvaraḥ*), its elimination (*nirjarā*), entanglement in the circle of existence (*bandhaḥ*) and the release (*mokṣaḥ*). Thus it counts, among the factors of existence belonging to nature-philosophy, the basic ideas of the Deliverance-doctrine. The interest in Deliverance completely dominates the old nature-philosophy of the Nyāya which puts forth the following enumeration : the soul (*ātmā*), body (*śarīram*), senses and organs (*indriyāṇi*), the sense-objects (*arthāḥ*), knowledge (*buddhiḥ*), psychical organ (*manaḥ*), activity (*pravṛttiḥ*), defects (*doṣāḥ*), continuance after death (*pretyabhāvaḥ*), fruit of works (*phalam*), sorrow (*duḥkham*) and deliverance (*apavargaḥ*).

If we now ask the question as to what position is held by the Vaiśeṣika in the frame of these doctrines, we can say that the classical system knows a doctrine of deliverance. The doctrine of deliverance, as we have already mentioned, was introduced into the Vaiśeṣika system externally, without any inner connection with the rest of the system. As a matter of fact, it shows itself to be a later supplement which had originally nothing to do with the system. It was, on the contrary, a purely Nature-philosophy. With the Vaiśeṣika we stand before a philosophical system— a phenomenon rare in India—which sets before it as its final goal not Deliverance, but the attempt to understand and explain the phenomenal world. We stand before a system which developed to a considerable height and which therefore merits our attention in a special measure.

How did this system originate? What was its oldest form? This question cannot be answered with certitude; we may assume, as a starting-point, a doctrine similar to the philosophical doctrines of the old Epic. Its subject formed, with greater probability, the four Elements, Space (*ākāśaḥ*), and the Soul (*jīvaḥ*), to which the psychical organ (*manaḥ*) was added. As regards the formulation of this doctrine, we may think that it is similar to the one as in the dialogue between Bhṛgu and Bharadvāja (See Vol. I). It embraced presumably the doctrine of the elements, and described how the world was constructed out of these elements and by what beings it was peopled. Above all, it dealt with men with regard to their bodily and mental constituents. Accordingly, we shall describe the oldest form of the Vaiśeṣika so far as it can be inferred from later tradition. I, therefore, begin with the doctrine of the Elements which occupies a large place in all Nature-philosophical theories.

The Elements and their qualities (guṇāḥ) : The natural-philosophical theories know as a rule four Elements: Earth (*pṛthvī*), Water (*āpaḥ*), Fire (*tejaḥ*) and Air (*vāyuḥ*).[25] We may assume the same also for the oldest Vaiśeṣika. The elements are characterized by definite qualities. To earth was ascribed solidity and hardness (*saṃghātaḥ* and *kharatvam*), to water humidity and fluidity (*snehaḥ* and *dravatvam*), to fire heat (*uṣṇatā*) and to the air movement (*īraṇā*). But soon there emerged besides this series of qualities, a second series of qualities which soon pushed itself to the forefront and finally crowded out the first completely. They were namely the series of qualities which formed the objects of sense-perception : form (*rūpam*), taste (*rasaḥ*), smell (*gandhaḥ*), touch (*sparśaḥ*) and sound (*śabdaḥ*).

We have seen (in Vol. I) that form, taste, smell, touch and sound played a special role in the Indian Deliverance-Doctrine as objects of sense-perception. Because desires are aroused by their perception and it is desires which are the chief causes of the entanglement in the misery of the cycle of births. Especially the Buddha emphasised repeatedly the fateful influence of the qualities towards which the desires directed themselves (*kāma-guṇāḥ*). In his doctrine of Bondage and Deliverance, they assume an important place.[26] It was now the next step to connect these qualities with the Elements and it did occur. How it occurred is characteristic for different doctrines.

If we recall the doctrines which belong to the stream of development that has its origin in the Upaniṣads, they give the following picture. In the doctrine of the Buddha, the five objects of sense-perception and the four elements are still unconnected with one another. In the doctrine of the Epic, however, the connection is already carried through and, no doubt, in the following way: [27] Form, Taste, Smell and Touch could, without further ado, be ascribed to the four known elements because the form was explained as the quality of fire, taste as the quality of water, the smell as the quality of earth, and touch as the quality of air. The sound created a difficulty because there was no fifth element which could be its bearer. Now help was sought in such a way that the old idea of world-space (*ākāśaḥ*) was seized upon. It had already played a role in the doctrines of the Upaniṣads and in the ancient way it was considered as material ; later on, as was similar in the case of the elements, a quality was ascribed to it—viz., non-hindrance (*anāvaraṇam*) or allowing space (*avakāśa-dānam*). It could, therefore, be made, without any hesitation, the bearer of sound. The fact, that in many Upaniṣadic texts there subsisted a connection between space and quarters and the sound, helped the development. Finally, it was not far to connect the sound, which penetrates far and wide and recurs in echo from far away, with space. This moved on or occurred on the same step with the other remaining elements. And we have in our presentation experienced that we designate it, in the role of the bearer of sound, not as space but as Ether. Thus was secured a series of five Elements as the bearer of the five objects of sense-perception which corresponded with the five sense-organs. This doctrine has found wide dissemination. Above all, it was taken over by the Sāṃkhya system and has penetrated everywhere where the influence of the Sāṃkhya reached.

Essentially different was the development among the Schools of Nature-philosophy. Here also the connection of the first four qualities (*guṇāḥ*) with the four Elements offered no difficulty. But the connection of sound with Space aroused doubts. Finally, the positing of the five Elements corresponding to the five objects of sense-preception and the five sense-organs was a pure schematic-theoretic construction. Still, though the parallelism gave an impetus towards seeing in the sound the quality of one element just as in the remaining objects of perception, the sharper consideration such as was peculiar to the nature-philosophical schools could not escape the conclusion that the sound was, in essential points, of a different kind from the rest. While the rest adhered fast to definite things of matter, the sound now emerged here, now there and rose again quickly to disappear. So one was induced to decline the acceptance of the fifth element as the bearer of sound in general. Where they decided to make Space or Ether as the bearer of sound, a special place remained conceded to it. A schematic coordination with the remaining elements as in the Sāṃkhya never ensued in the circles of thinkers of these doctrines.

Each one of them came to the following views : The Jaina could not decide in favour of assuming a special element as the bearer of sound. On the contrary, they considered the sound as an independent entity. It was done so far without any scruples, as, in ancient time, there was an inclination to regard the quality as material. [28] For example, the speech consisted of small parts which issued out of the mouth of a speaker. So far as the sound was considered as quality, it was considered as the quality of the aggregate formed of other elements[29]. The Buddhists also came to similar ideas, though these appear to have been formed differently under the influence of other views.[30]

In contrast, the Vaiśeṣika decided to follow the prototype of the Sāṃkhya and to posit ether as the bearer of sound. For them, the thought was not foreign that the bearer of a quality can itself be invisible and must be inferred; e.g. they thought that the air is itself not perceptible but is inferred out of the perception of touch. So in the case of sound, one was inclined to conclude an invisible bearer and to find it in the ether. But as distinguished from the Sāṃkhya, it was made clear that this bearer according to its constitution must be different from the other elements. Because the sound can arise everywhere, it was taught that the ether is unlimited and is everywhere and the view was presented that because the sound spread on all sides, it was assumed that the ether was all-penetrating. The ether is, therefore, different from the other four elements with their special limitations and impenetrability. This special place of the Ether was expressed as follows : In the development-stream to which the Sāṃkhya belongs, the accumulation theory, according to which qualities were ascribed to the elements[31] in rising number was widespread. According to it, the ether possessed only one quality viz. the sound, the air the sound and the touch and so on further, the last being the earth which possesses all the five qualities. This theory was taken over by the Vaiśeṣika but they restricted it to the four traditional elements. It was, therefore, taught that to air was ascribed touch, to fire the form and touch, to water, form, touch and taste and finally to the earth all the four, viz. the smell, taste, form and touch. The sound is only restricted to the ether which thus possesses only one quality.

Again, the doctrine of sound gained a somewhat different shape in the Mīmāṃsā. In the Mīmāṃsā, the dogma that sound is permanent, held ground and it was unwaveringly and firmly held. Because it was the basis for the doctrine that the Veda is a permanent Revelation. On this doctrine depends the whole Mīmāṃsā which is intended to serve the exclusive purpose of explaining the Veda. From this dogma of the permanence of sound, it follows that in the clanking of a sound, the sound does not arise at this moment. But on the contrary, the sound which exists from eternity is audible temporarily. But as it is now heard here, now there, it had to be assumed that like its bearer Ether, it also must be present everywhere and all-penetrating. It became, therefore, the general doctrine of the Mīmāṃsā. Indeed, the relation of the sound to its bearer suffered again a shift and in the Mīmāṃsā School of Kumārila one went so far as to the length of denying the existence of any such bearer in general and of explaining the sound as an independent entity.

To summarize what has been said : the oldest Element-doctrine of the Vaiśeṣika gives a picture which is somewhat as follows; First of all there are four elements : earth, water, fire and air, and these are characterized by definite qualities, the earth by firmness, the water by fluidity, the fire by heat, and the air by mobility. Besides, these elements possess a second series of qualities which are the objects of sense-perception and which belong to the elements in an ascending manner in a decreasing number. 'The earth possesses form, taste, smell and touch, the water possesses form, taste and touch, the fire possesses form and touch, the wind possesses touch.'[32] The object of the fifth sense-sound has ether as the fifth element as its bearer which only possesses this one quality. "The remaining qualities are not existent in Ether."[33] Though with these propositions the basic features of the Vaiśeṣika doctrine of the elements have been given, they, however, did not end therewith. Rather in conjunction with it, there was ushered in a further comprehensive development. It was, no doubt, the doctrine of qualities of the Elements which was built out of it. Thereby, this development took a course in a way which in different cases always recurs so that they proved typically valid for Indian philosophy. When new ideas were found and new ways discovered of which men became conscious, the discovery was sought to be fully employed. All things of like sort—everything that was found to behave in the same way—were sought to be systematically understood and put together in a complete enumeration as far as possible. But this insight was not sharpened enough for new things at first. As one enrolled in a series involuntarily what appeared to belong together with one another, and as one rejoiced in the abundance of such a discovery it might still appear as accumulated together arbitrarily. Then came the critical reflection. One began to arrange the assembled things and to prove it. And much or most of it was differently arranged or separated until finally a satisfactory solution was found which could hold its ground on the basis of a more rigorous proof.

The course of development was similar in the case of the doctrine of the qualities of the elements. Here also, one sought, first of all, to understand the total qualities of the elements as far as possible and arranged, in so doing, the most different things with one another, only in order to separate them later to a great extent by a thorough-going proof. How motley such an assemblage of the qualities of the elements looked is well shown by the list of these qualities with which we have been acquainted in the description of the Sāmkhya system.[34] Now the Natural-philosophical schools would not have, indeed, enumerated such a variegated list. Here, one account of a thoroughgoing occupation with the external world, the way of looking at things appears to have become more pointed so that at least to a certain extent, the related things were grouped together. In doing so, one collaborated also with what had been chosen as the starting point of the traditional elements, viz. form, taste, smell, touch and sound. Then one attempted to define the five qualities more exactly, distinguished their different sub-varieties and included in them other sub-varieties also which appeared to be in any way related and belonging to it. And thus the unplanned arbitrariness was at last subjected to certain restriction.

How the lists, which came into existence, appeared, we can well imagine. We are acquainted with such an ancient list, for example, in the philosophy of the Epic in the dialogue between Bhṛgu and Bharadvāja.[35] Among the Buddhists and the Jainas, we find also equally lists which exhibit right ancient features. Put together, they would present approximately the following picture :

Relatively simple was the enumeration of the sorts of taste (*rasaḥ*): Mostly, six kinds of taste were assumed : sweet (*madhuraḥ*), sour (*amlaḥ*), saltish (*lavaṇaḥ*), bitter (*tiktaḥ*), pungent (*kaṭuḥ*) and acrid or astringent (*kaṣāyaḥ*). Temporary attempts to widen the group did not succeed. Some deviations are unimportant e.g., the Jainas recognize only five sorts, as they explain the saltish as a sub-variety of sweet.

Greater was the vacillation in the case of smell (*gandhaḥ*). People differentiated, above all, fragrant (*surabhiḥ* or *sugandhaḥ*) from obnoxious smell (*asurabhiḥ* or *durgandhaḥ*). But other varieties were also added such as sweet-smelling (*madhuraḥ*), stinking (*kaṭuḥ*), itching (*rūkṣaḥ*), pure (*viśadaḥ*) and such others.

A pretty motley list was compounded of the kinds of touch (*sparśaḥ*). One distinguished between hot (*uṣṇaḥ*) and cold (*śītaḥ*), heavy (*guruḥ*) and light (*laghuḥ*), hard (*kaṭhinaḥ or kharaḥ*) and soft (*mṛduḥ*), raw or crude (*rūkṣaḥ or karkaśaḥ*) and smooth or sleek (*snigdhaḥ or ślakṣṇaḥ*). The Buddhist doctrinal system added also hunger (*jighatsā*) and thirst (*pipāsā*).

By far the most manifold was the list of the kinds of form (*rūpam*). It, first of all, embraced the colours first, no doubt the basic ones : white (*śuklaḥ*), black (*kṛṣṇaḥ*), red (*lohitaḥ*, *raktaḥ*), blue (*nīlaḥ*) and yellow (*pītaḥ*) as also their different mixtures. Besides, there appear also under form different kinds of shapes: long (*dīrghaḥ*), short (*hrasvaḥ*), high (*unnataḥ*), low (*avanataḥ*), gross (*sthūlaḥ*), fine (*sūkṣmaḥ*), quadrangular (*caturasraḥ*), round (*vṛttaḥ*), smooth (*cikkanaḥ*), slippery (*picchilaḥ*) and others. Still other entire things were included in this list : smoke (*dhūmaḥ*), cloud (*abhram*), shadow (*chāyā*), darkness (*andhakāraḥ* or *tamaḥ*), hot rays (*ātapaḥ*), brightness (*ālokaḥ* or *uddyotaḥ*).

Finally, concerning the varieties of sound, there was no uniform comprehension. One either enumerated the seven sounds or notes on a gamut or one distinguished the sounds as stretched (*tataḥ*), relaxed (*vitataḥ*), settled (*ghanaḥ*), hollow (*suṣiraḥ*) and rubbing (*gharṣaḥ*), each according to the constitution of the objects, which produced the sounds or the distinction was based on whether the sound was produced by living beings or inanimate objects and also whether it dealt with the sounds of the alphabet or not.

We must also imagine, in a similar way, the list of the qualities of the elements. Their varieties grew further and were formulated among the Nature-philosophical schools, out of the circles of thinkers from which the Vaiśeṣika arose. The further development followed in the above-mentioned way : things or properties not belonging together were gradually separated. It occurred, for example, in the cases in which further reflection gave rise to the view that one dealt not with the qualities of the Elements but with phenomenal forms of the Elements themselves. Of these new and better explanations were attempted. Light or brightness was explained as an apparent form of fire. It arises, it was said, when small particles of fire arise from the source of light. These parts are more loose and are equally distributed and their palpability or perceptibility is not distinct (*anudbhūta-sparśaḥ*) so that they are not perceived. Thus arise circles of light particles which offer no opposition to the penetration of moving bodies. [36] The heat of rays (*ātapaḥ*) was also similarly explained. Vapour and clouds were understood as apparent forms of water. Darkness (*tamaḥ or andhakāraḥ*) and shadow (*chāyā*) presented greater difficulties.[37] Shadow could not be explained as the apparent form of a known element. Therefore, one came to the popular view of the existence of the shadow as an independent element. It was therefore, first of all, explained as an independent stuff beside the element. A proof was adduced that it moved like a real thing and possessed quality—especially the quality of colour. But it was only a provisional solution. Gradually, a conviction dawned on the Vaiśeṣika that the shadow is nothing else than the absence of light. This absence of light could not naturally move as it is a mere non-existence. Its movement is only apparent. In fact, the object, which bars the light, moves. Through that appears the absence of light, i.e. shadow in different places and it arouses the impression that as if it is itself moving. In a similar way, the colour of a shadow or darkness, which was considered as dark blue, was explained. A non-existence cannot naturally be the bearer of a colour. And one still believed that he saw the dark colour in the shadow or the darkness. It was, therefore, said that here there was a transfer or transmission. For that, one referred to the example of the blue colour of the heavens for which the following explanation was given:[38] It was said that when looking at the heavens, the rays of the eye which emanate from the eyes are held up[39] by the stronger light-rays and that they are thrown back and return back to the eyes. Through that they perceive the dark colour of the pupil. But when one looks at the sky, he ascribes the colour to the heavens. A similar transference lies, it was thought, in the case of darkness. The dark colour is only ascribed to it; it really does not belong to it. This discussion about the nature of darkness continued by the way in the Vaiśeṣika until the time of the formulation of the complete classical system; in the Mīmāṁsā school of Kumārila, however, the old view still asserts itself which understands darkness as an independent entity.

That may be provisionally enough to show in which paths the further development of the doctrine of the qualities moved. In general, the following can be said with regard to it: The described development continued for a long time, extending over a long period. In Buddhism and Jainism in which the doctrine of the qualities of the elements early took firm root, we find much old material preserved regarding the doctrine of the qualities of the elements. The Vaiśeṣika shows, on the other hand, a much advanced or progressive stage. But it reached that position only late. In it the doctrine of the qualities of the Elements found its final form only during the formulation of the doctrine of categories. Therefore, for the present we shall restrict ourselves to what has been said here. We shall return to this subject during the description of the categories. With this whatever most important was to be said about the doctrines of the elements has been already said.

The Construction of the World and the Creation of living creatures:— The Elements provide the most important building stone out of which the world is built. The origin of the world appears to have been thought somewhat like this:[40]

As the first one of all the Elements rises the air or the

wind which fills the space. In the air originates water and it forms a mighty sea. In this sea, the earth forms itself into a conglomeration. Finally out of the water, likewise, is formed fire as a gigantic mass. When these four elements originate, they form together into a world-egg in which the God Brahmā appears and creates the worlds and creatures.

About the construction of the world, we hear little in the Vaiśeṣika. The mythological interest was here still less than in the Sāṁkhya. Especially the later system of categories-doctrine had left nothing worth to be said for the same. In the traditional writings there have been preserved only a few isolated interpretations. And as the philosophical worth of the phantastic world-pictures such as were customary in India is in itself so very little that we shall abstain from putting together these interpretations into a total picture. It is all the more justified from our point of view, when we have already got acquainted with a similar world-picture during the presentation of the Sāṁkhya system. Besides we shall return to this topic when we shall describe Jainism and Buddhism in which the world-construction and world-occurrence have been delineated especially at length. It may be enough if we say here that the Vaiśeṣika presupposes a similar world-picture like the Sāṃkhya.

More important and more suitable to the natural-scientific spirit of the system is how one attempted to define more exactly and restrict the distribution of the Elements in the construction of the world. Three functions of the Elements were distinguished so far as they formed the objects, i.e. the external world, the bodies of living creatures, and the sense-organs. Concerning the external world, the earth appears in a threefold form as earth in the strict sense i.e. loam or clay, as rock and as the plant-world In contrast to the Sāṃkhya, the plants were not enumerated among living creatures. Of water, different forms were distinguished; e.g. streams or rivers, sea, snow and hail. The fire is of four sorts: the earthly fire in fuel, the heavenly fire in the sun, moon and stars and in lightning. Further, metal was considered as the phenomenal form of fire. Also the fire in the abdomen which cooks and digests food was also enumerated under fire, as one did not know to accommodate it in any other category.[41] The air exhibits no different phenomenal forms. According to the Vaiśeṣika, it is itself not perceptible. It makes itself perceivable when it moves the leaves or carries the clouds. Under it, the breath was also included—the breath which works in the body in different ways.

Besides the elements in the construction of the world, it must be mentioned that people in older times occupied themselves with all possible scientific questions, as, for example, the origin of the seasons. It was allowed to be dropped in the later system. We hear of them only as isolated, scattered pieces of information.

With regard to the living creatures which inhabit the world, the tradition is equally scanty. There are rich sources available for anthropology. Beings who people the world are named as gods, men and animals. There is little interest in the mythological elements, so that nothing further about the classes or groups of gods is reported. Only occasionally there is a mention of eight groups of gods like Brahmā and spirits like ghosts (*piśacāḥ*). Among animals are distinguished tame and wild animals (*paśavaḥ and mṛgāḥ*), birds (*pakṣiṇaḥ*), reptiles (*sarīsṛpāḥ*) Of men, there is only one group. Thus there is the same distribution of beings with which we have been acquainted in the Sāṃkhya.[42] Only plants are missing, as they have been reckoned by the Vaiśeṣika among the surroundings.

Besides this classification of creatures, there is also in the Vaiśeṣika the popular distribution, according to the kind of their origin. But it deviates to a great extent from the Sāṃkhya. First, two groups of creatures are distinguished : such as are born out of the womb (*Yonijāḥ*), and those which are not so born (*ayonijāḥ*). Gods, many holy seers of the past and the smallest living creatures such as flies, gnats and lice are not born out of the mother's womb. Of those beings born out of the mother's womb, men and tame and wild animals are born out of the outer skin of the embryo (*jarāyujāḥ*), birds and reptiles are born out of an egg (*aṇḍajāḥ*). Further sub-groups are not recognized.

And now regarding the doctrine of men, it was worked out in the most detailed way and for the later times it had great importance. Still in it, the natural-scientific i.e. the physiological treatment about it was left, in the later times, very much in the background.

According to the Vaiśeṣika, man consists of body and soul. The system does not know of a fine body, from the beginning. It is quite natural. Because the stream of philosophical development, to which the Vaiśeṣika belongs, presupposes, as we know, a soul-doctrine according to which there are a number of individual souls spatially limited, who are not only the bearers of knowledge but also of the wishes and human actions. Under such presuppositions, a psychical organ and a fine body such as were taught in the Sāṃkhya, are superfluous. The soul itself is the bearer of the mental personality and it is what goes after death from one body to another and wanders from existence to existence in the beginningless cycle of births. There is no place for any other bearer of soul-transmigration.

The Man and his Body—Thus, in the Vaiśeṣika, besides the soul, there stands only the gross body, of which it is said that it is composed of earth. [43] In this the Vaiśeṣika differs from the popular view, which also the Sāṃkhya follows, according to which the human body is constituted out of all the five elements. But this difference or deviation is proved and justified in the system in the course of its development.

We, already, meet with those popular views which are already in the philosophical doctrines of the old Epic, especially in the dialogue between Bhṛgu and Bharadvāja. [44] They are there put forth at length and justified in details. There, the qualities of five Elements, viz. allowing space, movement, heat, fluidity and firmness or solidity serve as the proof. Because all these qualities are firmly established in the bodies of men, animals as well as of plants, it follows therefrom that all the elements also must be present in them. This was the authoritative proof of the doctrine in the Epic and it has remained so in the later period. This proof, however, was soon considered weak by the Vaiśeṣika, as it was based on a series of the qualities of the elements which very soon fell in the background in the Vaiśeṣika and as we shall see later, entirely given up by them. Thus, their ground-basis had been lost. It, therefore, so happened that the Vaiśeṣika decided for another doctrine that the human body is formed only out of earth.

In the Vaiśeṣika, as we have already seen, in place of

the old series of the qualities of the elements, a second row stepped in—viz. smell, taste, form and touch which likewise distributed themselves among all the elements. Now it would have been possible to infer the existence of all these elements out of the existence of all these qualities in the human body. But the Vaiśeṣika showed, from the earliest times, a disinclination against the assumption of a mixture of elements. It has, therefore, early taken over the accumulation theory which ascribes the named qualities to the elements in a mounting or rising number. And it explains the existence of several such qualities with the help of this accumulation theory and allows the mixture to hold good, where the accumulation theory does not suffice to explain. The existence of smell in the human body makes it necessary to assume earth as one constituent of the human body. Thus, however, according to the accumulation theory, the existence of the remaining elements would also be assumed in the same way. The assumption of other elements was, therefore, unnecessary. Therefore, the body was explained as consisting of earth only. It was granted that there appeared other elements in the human body. But the body itself, it was taught, was formed only out of earth. Besides, in the course of the further development of the system, a still more forceful reason to stick to this doctrine came up. The Vaiśeṣika has, for example, in later times, created the doctrine of the Atoms, of which we shall learn in details in the sequel, according to which all things were formed out of Atoms. Thereby it was taught that the aggregates, thus formed, are something new, different from their parts. The qualities of the aggregates originate out of the qualities of the parts. But that presupposes that the aggregates which thus arise are formed out of parts of like sort which possess all the concerned qualities. Because it was impossible for the heterogeneous or opposite qualities to produce a uniform or homogeneous constituent. Consequently it was concluded in the case of the body that it also must have been formed out of homogeneous parts which possess the same qualities as itself. That is to say, the same qualities of the element must also belong throughout to its parts. They must therefore consist of one element and this element can be only earth.

Regarding the origin of the body and its functions, the Vaiśeṣika considerably participates in the views usually customary in Indian philosophy. Man is begot through the union of father and mother. From father comes the semen, from mother the blood. These form together into coagulated matter in the womb of the mother. Besides, the nourishing juice which streams forth out of the body of the mother gathers itself. When it is gathered or assembled enough, there ensues the formation of the embryo under the influence of the fire in the body of the mother. This develops itself, through the stages of small knots (*arbudaḥ*), small lumps of flesh (*māṃsapeśī*), a small ball or globule (*kalalam*) [45], gradually into a body with all its limbs. Nourished by the juice of nourishment which flows to it through the navel-string, it grows further on and is finally ripe for birth. With the birth is the form of man completed; he later on matures into manhood, through boyhood and youth. As regards the construction of the human body, it consists of six limbs : head, trunk, arms, and legs. Its constituents are sinews, skin, bones, arteries, muscles and ligaments. [46]. The metabolism is carried out in the following way : Through the human body, there extend a series of hollow spaces : mouth, heart, throat, the space for undigested nourishment, the space for digested nourishment and the openings of the body leading downwards. The food, which is received, reaches into the space for the undigested food. Then, chiefly in sleep, it is digested by the digestive fire. In this way there is gained, out of it, the sap of nutrition (*rasaḥ*) which is carried to the whole body through a net of arteries (*nādyaḥ*). The sap of nutrition is the basis of life and well-being, of strength and soundness or health. Out of it are developed serially the different basic stuffs of the body (*dhātavaḥ*) : Blood, Flesh, Fat, Bones, Marrow and Semen.[47] Separated matter and residues of nourishment are emptied as urine and excreta through the downward openings of the body.

Besides the metabolism, the activity of the corporeal winds (*prāṇāḥ*) is of special importance. They penetrate, through the network of arteries, the whole body and operate everywhere in it. Five winds are distinguished : the out-breath (*prāṇaḥ*), the down-or-away-breath (*apānaḥ*), the together-breath (*samānaḥ*), the up-breath (*udānaḥ*) and through-breath (*vyānaḥ*). The out-breath is the breath which streams through the mouth and the nose. The through-breath (*vyānaḥ*) distributes the sap of nutrition in the various arteries. The together-breath (*samānaḥ*) leads it likewise to the different parts of the body. The up-breath (*udānaḥ*) causes its mounting up in certain arteries. The down-breath (*apānaḥ*) finally drives the separated matter out of the body. In reality, however, there is only one corporeal wind. The distinction of five winds depends only upon the difference of activities already described, which, in reality, are the operations of one corporeal wind.

Finally is to be mentioned the medical doctrine of the three saps which plays its part occasionally in the Vaiśeṣika. The human body, according to it, contains three juices or saps (*doṣāḥ*)[48] : wind(*vātaḥ*), bile(*pittam*), phlegm (*śleṣmā* or *kaphaḥ*) which have their seat in definite places, above all, in the vessels (*koṣṭhāḥ*). On their right distribution and mutual relation or behaviour depends the health of the body. For instance, if their relation is disturbed, different illnesses emerge, according as this or that sap preponderates. Not only, however, health and disease but also moods and the behaviour of a man, why, his whole character is determined by the distribution of these saps (*doṣāḥ*) in his body. It is the one widespread doctrine which, in ancient times, was pursued from India through Persia to Greece. And when we speak today still of melancholy or phlegmatic temperament, it is to be traced to this theory.

Up to this time, we have described the processes in the body which go on mainly unconsciously. Essentially greater was the interest of the system in those processes which lead to knowledge and consciousness. We shall now, therefore, next turn to them and begin with the doctrine of the sense-organs.

The Sense-Organs and their Work: In the description of the ancient period of Indian philosophy, as we have already seen, the idea of the sense-organs arose gradually out of the doctrine of the different life-forces in the human body. This development was carried out in the Vedic period and in the period directly following. In the philosophical texts of the old Epic, it is already concluded. The idea of the sense-organs is already a firm idea in the Epic. The same holds good also for the oldest form of the Vaiśeṣika which belongs to the same stage of development. And no doubt it is already a completely definite and advanced doctrine, a doctrine which forms the basis, which counts a fixed number of sense-organs and has a clear and definite idea of their constitution.

The beginnings, which ascertain the number of sense-organs, are found in the older Upaniṣads. In the time of the Buddha, we meet with the usual number five, and against the five sense-organs are juxtaposted the five qualities of things as objects: for the eye—the form, for the ear—the sound, for the nose—the smell, for the tongue—the taste, and for the skin—the touch. The next step was that these five qualities were brought into connection with the elements. It has occurred in the philosophy of the Epic. Above all, in the dialogue between Manu and Bṛhaspati[49] it is fully carried out where the five elements and the five qualities of the Elements correspond in strong parallelism to the five sense-organs. The same view has been further taken over in the oldest Sāṃkhya.

In the natural-philosophical schools and, above all, in the Vaiśeṣika, the number five of the sense-organs also holds good. The strong parallelism effective in its clarity between the sense-organs, the qualities of the elements and the Elements, has, as we have already seen in the description of the doctrine of the elements, influenced them also. The Vaiśeṣika, therefore, besides the traditional qualities, held also the fifth viz. ether, though it was confronted with various scruples. Because, according to the natural-scientific attitude of the system, one could not overlook the fact that ether, as it was assumed, differed in essential points from the remaining four elements. The same view-point compelled them, as we shall still see, to assume for the corresponding sense-organ, the ear, another constituent as in the case of the remaining sense-organs. But one put up with it and held fast to the once assumed number five of the sense-organs and the Elements. The Vaiśeṣika did not participate in the attempt to widen the number of sense-organs, like the attempt which we have seen in the Sāṃkhya[50] and which we shall still see in the Buddhistic doctrinal systems.

Concerning the constitution of the sense-organs, we have already seen likewise during the description of the Epic philosophy[51], how at the moment when men began not only to ponder over the nature of the Ātman but also to discuss the surrounding world in a thorough-going manner, the question arose how the sense-organs are to be arranged, whether they were to be placed on the side of the Soul or Matter. The choice was preponderatingly in favour of Matter—especially among the nature-philosophical schools. One had been too long accustomed to consider the sense-organs as independent entities, so that one would hardly enrol them without any distinction under the rest of the Matter. The Buddhistic doctrinal system in its own way, derives them out of peculiar sorts of atoms. The Vaiśeṣika did not go so far. They taught that they were formed out of the Elements like the remaining things of the surrounding world. But a special position was still conceded to them. That is indicated by the already mentioned classification into three of the products of the Elements as objects, body and sense-organs, the sense-organs having been enumerated separately. But in the Vaiśeṣika as also in the other schools, the proper sense-organs or sense-faculties are sharply distinguished from the gross bodily organs. They are by their nature somewhat of a completely different kind. The bodily organs are only their carriers.

The relation between the sense-organs and their bearers (*adhiṣṭhānāni*) is as follows: The bearer of smell is the nose, of taste the tongue, of eyesight the pupil of the eye (*kṛṣṇasāram*), the bearer of the touch is the skin and the bearer of hearing is the ear (*karṇacchidram*). Of these smell, taste and touch have the same extension as their bearers. Of touch, it is to be marked that not only the external skin is the bearer of touch but also the internal as e. g. when we feel cold inwardly when we drink cold water. As we shall still see, the sight is greater than the pupil of the eye; it leaves the body in the form of the rays of the eye.[52] The ear consists of the ether which is infinitely great. But the ether restricts itself to the body as it is able to perceive under the influence (*saṃskāraḥ*) of the human body.

Now the constitution of the sense-organs, viz. its composition: At the moment when it was decided to consider the sense-organs as products of the Elements, it was the next step to confront the five sense-organs with the five elements with their qualities, to allow every sense-organ to consist of the element, the quality of which it perceives. It was also the doctrine of the Vaiśeṣika. The opinions fluctuated, no doubt, in a certain degree. Partly, it was taught that every organ consists of only one element. Partly, it was also held that parts of other elements participated in mixing with it. But it was said that the one element fully overwhelms and is not impaired in its work by the remaining.[53] This doctrine thus, nevertheless, had a deeper basis. For instance, the view was represented that the qualities of the Element which formed the objects of perception were known only through the fact, that the same quality exists in the sense-organ, that this quality in the sense-organ renders possible the knowledge of the same quality in the object. The necessary inference out of this was, however, the doctrine that the sense-organs in their essential constituents must be composed of the like element with a like quality as the object which they perceive.

But, indeed, in the case of the Vaiśeṣika, the doctrine required a supplement. We have already said in the description of the doctrine of the elements that the Vaiśeṣika had taken over, in the earlier period, the accumulation theory, according to which the elements possess qualities in an increasing number, and that not merely one Element possesses one quality. But that implied that in the elements which form the sense-organs, there are present, besides their own proper qualities, also other qualities. So the question came up why only one of these qualities was effective and not the others. Why, e.g. the smell-organ consisting of earth perceived only the smell and not also the remaining qualities, as still to the earth belonged all the four qualities.

As an answer to this question, the Vaiśeṣika introduced a new idea. It was taught that the characteristic quality of an element alone is, no doubt, able to permit the manifestation of this same quality (*vyañjakatvam*). The same quality (*guṇa*) may also exist in other elements and appear in manifestation there (*vyaṅgyatvam*). But only as the quality of the element for which it is characteristic, it can bring into manifestation the same quality in a similar element or also in any other element. A good example of this is the form (*rūpam*) which is present in water or in earth but is able to illuminate other objects and to make their form visible only in light i.e. in fire, i.e. in its own proper element. The same holds good also for the sense-organs. Only in the eye which is essentially formed out of fire, the form is able to permit the knowledge of the forms of objects—but not in other organs. Accordingly also, in the organ of smell which is chiefly made of earth, the characteristic quality of the earth—the smell is able to perceive the smells of the surrounding world. Taste, form and touch, no doubt, are also present but they are not able to bring perception into effect.

Among all, only the ear takes a special position.[54] The special position lies in the difference which separates the ether and its quality the sound from the rest of the elements and their qualities. The sound is not a permanent quality (*guṇaḥ*) of ether; it arises only in a ringing sound. It was also not therefore possible to regard it as a permanent quality of the ear. The ear by itself is only ether without its characteristic quality. Further the sound, when rung or clanked, propagates or transmits itself immediately and reaches the ear which is only a part of the infinite ether. It is perceived in the ear itself. Thus the relations during the perception of sound through the ear are represented. The quality of the objects will not, as in the case of the remaining senses, be perceived by the sense-organ with the help of its own qualities. The sense organ itself, on the contrary, perceives its own quality which arises in it temporarily. A difference of the form of sound which brings into manifestation and another which appears in manifestation, is omitted under these circumstances.

This is how the Vaiśeṣika imagined the constitution and the composition of the sense-organs. But how did they think about their operation? Here was a decisive question which separated the different systems from one another and which was debated for a long time in the liveliest possible way—the question, viz. whether the senses during perception entered into contact with the objects (*prāpyakāritvam*) or whether perception was possible without contact.[55] In the case of the feeling of touch and taste, there was no doubt. Here the contact was evident. Also in the case of smell, there was unanimity that the perception comes about through the particles of fragrance streaming into the nose. But what is the position with the eyes and the ears?

The Buddhistic doctrine, above all, taught that the eye and ear are able to perceive their objects without contact—especially the eye.[56] As proof, it was adduced that we can see distant objects and objects which are larger than the eye—which would be impossible in case there was contact. The Vaiśeṣika asserted that here also a contact with the objects takes place. In its favour it was advanced that we cannot see a covered object. It becomes, then, understandable, when the covering object prevents the contact between the eyes and the objects. If, on the other hand, the eye is able to see an object with which it has no contact, then it is not explicable why the covering of the objects shall prevent the perception. Likewise, the dependence of perception on nearness or distantness of objects is only explained if a contact takes place which is there though facilitated or made difficult. Finally, an analogical inference was put forth, viz., that all tools or instruments operate through direct contact and that this must also hold good in the case of sense-organs which are the instruments of the soul.

When one attempted to refute the opponent's objections, the following theory was put forth.[57] The sense-organ of the eye is not the pupil in the eye (*kṛṣṇasāram*) but fine particles of fire or light which dwell in the eyeball. During perception these go forth from the eye in the form of the so-called fine rays (*cakṣūraśmayaḥ*) and enter into contact with the perceived object. As a matter of fact, a contact between the sense-organ and the object thus does take place. As the rays of the eye, after leaving the eye spread out further like a cone of light, they are able to perceive the objects which are incomparably greater than the eye. That the eye-rays are not seen implies no difficulty. The existence of a perceptible quality does, in no way, lead to the conclusion that it is also perceived. It must, on the contrary, be existing in a clear, clear-cut form (*udbhūta*); e.g., Fire possesses the qualities of heat and brightness. In the rays of the sun both are clear-cut and are, therefore, both perceived. In the rays of the lamp, on the other hand, only the brightness is clear-cut or marked, the warmth remaining concealed. In the case of the particles of fire which penetrate water and heat it, it is only the heat that is marked; particles of fire are not seen in the case of the eye-rays, neither heat nor brightness is marked and therefore they cannot be perceived but only inferred. Only among nocturnal animals, they are occasionally visible.

The dependence of perception on the distance of the objects is explained by this doctrine of the eye-rays as the rays of the eyes come into contact with it and therefore the eye-rays must travel over the corresponding stretch or extent. That we believe to be perceiving the near and far objects simultaneously does not go against it, because it is explained by the error or illusion which is caused by the immense rapidity of the eye-rays. If the object is covered, the contact of the eye-rays is cut off and it becomes imperceptible. That we can see through glass, depends on the special constitution of these things which allow the eye-rays to pass through. The same things offer no resistance to the solar rays or the rays of the lamp.

A special constitution of many things explains also certain phenomena such as reflection.[58] The Vaiśeṣika had broken with the old idea which assumes the existence of a real image on the surface of the mirror. On the other hand, the Vaiśeṣika doctrine teaches that the surface of the mirror, on account of its clearness, possesses the ability to throw back the rays of the eyes so that the latter move in the opposite direction and through them touch the reflected object. The perception, which the cone of the tip of the eye-rays brings about, is further led or transferred to the organ of the eye and is brought to consciousness by the latter. One is deceived by the situation of the eye and believes that he sees the object in that direction in which originally the eye-rays moved — i.e. in that distance which the eye-rays collectively covered. Again one sees the object from that side on which the eye-rays meet it, i.e. reverse to its real position.

This doctrine of the eye-rays deserves special consideration as it offers a good example of natural-scientific interest of the old Vaiśeṣika, which has come into currency in the preserved tradition only in a restricted measure. It finely shows how one employed the modest observations which he had made and the explanations were offered which need not shun comparison with the corresponding doctrines of Greek philosophy.

To the doctrine of seeing and of sense-perception in general, remain to be added a few things : For bringing about perception, not only the operation of the sense-organs is necessary but certain conditions from the side of the object also must be fulfilled so that it can be perceived. In many cases, the qualities of the elements and things made out of them are perceptible without much difficulty, in other cases they require aids from outside.[59] The brightness of light i.e. its form (*rūpam*) is seen off-hand. The form of other things is, however, only seen when it is illuminated or according to the Indian way of expression it is brought into manifestation (*vyaktiḥ*). We have already touched this idea when we talked about the composition of the sense organs and have mentioned that a quality, only in that element for which it is characteristic, possesses the ability to allow the same quality to appear in other things.

In cases where a quality is perceptible by itself, its perception is bound up with the presupposition that it is not overshadowed (*abhibhavaḥ*).[60] The light of the lamp is seen, only when it is not outshone by the sunlight. A sound is only heard when it is not drowned by a louder sound. But the following definition or regulation is above all important :

The theory of the elements and of their qualities and the views about the composition of the surrounding world out of these elements brought with itself or implied that behind the composition of several things, the existence of definite qualities must be presupposed. But as a matter of fact, the reality did not too often agree wtth these claims or demands. In water whose distribution in the atmosphere was supposed to cause the cold of winter, the cold was quite distinctly experienced but not seen. The same holds good of the fire which brings about the heat of summer. In order to circumvent these and similar difficulties a new idea was introduced : the idea of clear-cutness or markedness (*udbhavaḥ*)[61]. A quality, when it is supposed to be perceived, must not only exist but also be marked in a clearcut manner (*udbhūtaḥ*). We have already met with this idea in the description of the eye-rays, where it was employed to prove the invisibility of the eye-rays. There we have already cited a few examples. The Vaiśeṣika could not give a more exact clarification of this idea. They defined it as a special constituent (*dharmaḥ*) of the quality of the Element.[62] Still in future, markedness (to become '*udbhūta*') was fixed as one of the most important conditions for the coming into existence of Perception.

A further condition for the perception by the eye is the size of the perceived object. An object, if it is too small, cannot be perceived. This condition gained special importance especially, since the Atom Theory was developed ; an important place was conceded to it in the system and it was later emphasised. But entirely new ideas began gradually to penetrate. Until now, the qualities of the Elements were reckoned as objects of Perception. But the size belongs not to the qualities but to the things. Do we perceive, therefore, not only the qualities but the things themselves? It was a far-reaching question which here newly emerged. Were things and qualities perceived necessarily together? Or is it possible to perceive the qualities without the objects and the objects without the qualities ? Why, under which conditions, in general, is the perception of things possible ?

Thus were raised important questions whose answers presented many difficulties to the system and they were bound to involve it in lively discussion with the opposing Schools. But we must here break off and postpone the consideration of this discussion to a later occasion. For here we have reached a point which lands us into the second great section of the history of the Vaiśeṣika, the section which is characterized by the formulation of the Doctrine of Categories.

It still remains to describe how the Vaiśeṣika thought about Perception through the ear. Here operated the special place of the Ether and its quality the sound (*śabdaḥ*) The Buddhist doctrinal system taught that in this case also the perception took place without contact. On the other hand, the Vaiśeṣika had to assume, according to their basic views, a contact of the organ with the perceived object. But the conditions at bottom were here completely different from those in 'seeing'. As we have already described, the ear-organ is, according to the doctrine of the Vaiśeṣika; a part of the all-penetrating Ether. Therefore, every movement of the organ is eliminated or out of consideration. On the other hand, the activity of the organ is also restricted to the body. This must be assumed because otherwise in the illimitability of the Ether, it would not be possible to explain the spatial limits of the ear-perceptions. From the side of the ear, therefore, the contact cannot be established. Nothing else, therefore, remains than to assume that the sound reaches the ear. As a matter of fact, they decided in favour of this assumption. But though it sounded so simple, it, in reality, was confronted with many doubts. This will be especially evident, when we consider the propagation of sound during speech—an interesting case for the doctrine of knowledge.

About speech, there prevailed ancient ideas as we still find them preserved in the Jaina. According to them, the speech consists of the small parts of the elements which are uttered during speech and spread themselves from the body in the form of a thundering sound and are able to reach the limits of the world. The Vaiśeṣika could not naturally reconcile themselves with the doctrine of Ether and its quality—the sound and they rejected it. For them another prototype held valid—the doctrine of speech as it was worked out amongst the circles of Grammarians.[63]

In these circles, it was early known that during speech, the uttered breath-air is moulded by the instruments of speech and becomes a word and reaches, in this form, the hearer's ear. The Vaiśeṣika made an allowance for it or accommodated themselves to it so far that they took over at least the role of breath-air during the speech-process. It was therefore said[64] that the breath-air during speech moves upwards and touches the articulation-points of speech-instruments. But now it was asserted that through this contact the sound is produced in ether—the sound which moves towards the ear of the hearer. The oddness of this doctrine and its vulnerability to criticism are obvious. But it will be evident especially if we compare this doctrine with that of the Mīmāṃsā which is very closely connected with the views of the Grammarians.

For the Mīmāṃsā, there was a completely different starting point for the formulation of their theory of sound and its perception, from that of the Vaiśeṣika. That was, no doubt, due to their doctrine of the permanence of sound. According to them, the sound is not an evanescent and spatially limited quality of the Ether but it is permanent and all-penetrating. One may consider it as a quality of ether or as a self-standing entity. Its perception ensues through the fact that this permanent and, in general, inaudible sound is temporarily brought into manifestation and is made audible through that. Corresponding to these presuppositions, the question of the perception of sound is represented by the Mīmāṃsā in the following way : It is not necessary to clarify how sound produced in one definite place comes in contact with the ear, because the sound exists everywhere. The question, on the other hand, was how the one all-pervading sound, when it is brought into manifestation in a particular place through any cause or occasion, appears not everywhere but only resounding in this one place and which processes affect our ears, so that we believe that we hear it in this particular place.

In order to answer this question, a theory leaning upon the theory of the grammarians was thus formulated.[65] During speech, breath-air mounts from the abdomen upwards. It hits the speech-organs and is formed through their openings and shuttings (*saṃskṛtaḥ*). The air thus formed is called sound (*dhvaniḥ or nādaḥ*) and moves from the mouth of the speaker through the surrounding unmoved air, until it reaches the ear of the hearer. It is not itself heard but affects the ear and lends it the ability to perceive temporarily the permanent sound (*śabdaḥ*) which it, otherwise, would not be able to hear. That we thus believe that we are hearing in a particular place the sound in spite of its omnipresence, depends on the fact that we ascribe to the (*śabdaḥ*) permanent sound the spatial limitations of sound and remove it to a place where the sound (*dhvaniḥ*) thrusts itself into our ears.[66]

The assumption that the qualities of the temporary sound (*dhvaniḥ*) are ascribed to the permanent sound offered the possibility to circumvent the different difficulties which the permanence of sound presented. By the idea of the one permanent sound (*śabdaḥ*) the differences in the sounds of the different speakers—the differences in the (high) pitch of sound and its volume could not be explained. These were now seen to be the qualities of the temporary sound (*dhvaniḥ*), they being merely carried over to the permanent sound (*śabdaḥ*).[67] But the greatest advantage of this whole Mīmāṃsā Theory was as follows : it allowed the origin and propagation of sound (*dhvaniḥ*) in the air and not in Ether and was, therefore, able to explain a series of phenomena which had confronted the Vaiśeṣika as insurmountable difficulties. If the permanent sound (*śabdaḥ*) is a quality of Ether, which propagates itself in it, then the weakening of the permanent sound (*śabdaḥ*) by a wall and other hindrances is hard to explain. Because, according to the doctrine of the Vaiśeṣika, the ether is all-pervading and is not hindered and held up in any way by corporeal (*mūrtaḥ*) hindrances. The same holds good for the weakening of the sound which comes distantly from its place of origin. Under these presuppositions it is also as little explained as to how a favourable wind facilitates the hearing of a sound, while the unfavourable one makes it difficult. All this becomes intelligible easily in the Mīmāṃsā doctrine of sound (*dhvaniḥ*). Because the breath-air which is the carrier of sound (*dhvaniḥ*) is corporeal and can be held up by hindrances. The impulse, which it gains during speech, becomes gradually weaker, as it moves through the unmoved air. That it can be furthered or retarded by the wind is directly evident.

The advantages of the Mīmāṃsā Theory are obvious and they enable us to know with full clarity the weakness of the Vaiśeṣika doctrine. But that the Vaiśeṣika as nature-philosophy held fast, in spite of all difficulties, to the doctrine of the Ether as a bearer of sound to which man had arrived out of pure theoretical considerations, and that it stuck to the forced explanations[68] rather than depart from its theory, is characteristic of the system and of Indian philosophy in general.

With the description of the sense-organs and their work we have concluded the theory regarding the body and now come to what together with the body makes up man, animates his body and directs it i.e. the Soul.

The Soul :—As we have repeatedly said, the Vaiśeṣika, regarding the doctrine of the soul, is based on the old popular views which regarded numerous individual souls as carriers of life. The starting-point, in all probability, was the belief in a soul in the form of a small, shadowy nature in the human body, the soul which is of the size of a thumb (*aṅguṣṭhamātraḥ puruṣaḥ*).[69] It has its seat in the heart. From there it directs the body, as the charioteer a chariot.[70] The life depends on it. When it departs from body, the man dies.

These old views were soon remodelled in the frame of the philosophical doctrines and were adapted to the governing views and ideas. In place of the shadowy nature of the soul, it was taught that it is subtle (*sūkṣma*) and cannot, therefore, be perceived by the sense-organs. But above all, the view regarding the size of the soul changed, as soon as man tried to gain clearer views about its collaboration with the body. It was observed that the perceptions and sensations are possible in all parts of the body and that the driving force of the soul works itself in all limbs. It was, therefore, assumed that the soul is as big as or of the size of the body. The Jainas have continued to stick to this view and we may suppose it to be the view, in all probability, of the oldest Vaiśeṣika. The oldest Vaiśeṣika knew a soul of fine matter, of the size of the body, which is the bearer of life. Simultaneously, it is the bearer of the transmigration of the soul and it represents, in contrast to the perishable body, the permanent in man.

The further occupation with the problem of the soul led to a further formulation of this oldest soul-doctrine in two directions. On the one side, one was compelled to prove the existence of the soul against the opponents' attacks. On the other side, one investigated thoroughly into the constitution and the working of the soul.

The existence of the Soul : We have already said in the beginning that in the Vaiśeṣika, the soul does not occupy a prominent place ; it is only one of the factors besides the rest out of which the world is built. But when it came to the formulation of the Deliverance-Doctrine, one naturally joined in the soul-idea and it became the object of attack by the materialistic schools which denied the reward and retribution of good and bad deeds in the life beyond. Further, in the course of peculiar development in Buddhism itself, schools were formed which denied the existence of the soul and it led to a lively discussion with reference to their theory. In this way the question regarding the existence of the soul had become one of the most disputed ones. Thus the Vaiśeṣika were induced to take up a position with regard to this problem.

The basis which was brought in for the existence of the soul was connected with the old idea that the body resembled a chariot, which the soul directs as a charioteer. The body is, therefore, like a tool, from the activity of which one concludes about somebody who handles it. Now this idea is executed further in particular details. The in-and-out-breathing of the body is like the activity of the bellows which presupposes somebody who activates it. The opening and shutting of eyes resembles the movements of a wooden machine which somebody sets in motion. The healing of injuries, ruptures and wounds reminds one of the repairing done in the case of damages of a house which a master of the house gets repaired. Especially one invoked the activity of the sense-organs in this sense. They are, it was said, tools like other tools which somebody uses. Particularly, they are the instruments of knowledge. There must, therefore, be a knower who knows through them. He can be none else than the Soul. Other considerations were joined to it It can happen that one sees and feels simultaneously the same object. While so doing, one is conscious that it is the same object. Therefore there must be something which joins the knowledge of both the sense-organs with each other. And it is the Soul which stands above all sense-organs. A similar case is found, when an activity of the sense-organ affects another e.g. seeing affects the organ of taste and causes secretion of saliva. It proves the existence of a central factor which connects the activities of the sense-organs with one another. And this central factor is the Soul. Thus continually new proofs for the existence of the Soul are enlisted and that continued during the whole history of the Vaiśeṣika. As the Category-Theory was created and the whole system was remodelled after it, new proofs based on the category-theory were put forth and the progress of logic reflects itself in the different formulations of the proof. And we shall, therefore, in the course of our treatise find still many more occasions, to return to this topic later on.

Though the question of the existence of the Soul was debated in a lively manner, essentially more important and interesting still was what one wanted to know and to say about the constitution of the Soul and its working.

The Constitution of the Soul :—As upto now we have already said, according to the view of the nature-philosophical schools, the Soul is spatially restricted and numerous individual souls were assumed. It showed or implied a basic difference as against the all-pervading world-soul which was taught in the schools which had their origin in the teachings of the Upaniṣads. But ultimately this difference between the world-soul and individual soul is only external. Far more important is the difference in their nature. In our presentation of the doctrine of the world-soul in the first volume of our work, we have described how one early came to the idea, according to which the world-soul was considered as something standing high above everything which is earthly and remaining incomprehensible to our knowledge, because all earthly definitions do not prove true in its case.[71]

Entirely different are the individual souls in Nature-philosophical Schools. The individual souls belong to this world, because they are the bearers of all total psychical occurrences. The doctrine of Yājñavalkya in the Upaniṣads has, no doubt, characterized the world-soul as the knowing one. But the consistent carrying out of the old ideas in the Sāṃkhya had led to the conclusion that the soul is nothing else than an undefined, unrestricted spirit. So it was believed that the proper psychical occurrences occurred to a psychical organism which belonged to the world of matter. This psychical organism is the bearer of soul-transmigration and entanglement in this existencc and freedom from it are conditioned by it. On the other hand, the nature-philosophical schools taught that the soul itself is the bearer of all psychical processes and that, therefore, it itself wanders in the cycle of births. There is no psychical organism, according to the nature-philosophical schools.

The constitution of the individual souls determines also the position which they occupy in the doctrines of nature-philosophical schools. It shows a pronounced earthly character. The sublimity of the world-soul is lacking in it. It is, therefore, as we have already said, only one of the factors, like the elements, out of which the phenomenal world is built. But on account of this, all the greater importance is attached to it. It is a decisive factor in men. Among the already cited proofs for the existence of the soul, this factor comes to be expressed most distinctly. The body and the sense-organs are mere dead instruments. It is the soul, on the other hand, who rules over and directs them. Again, it is the soul as the bearer of all psychical processes and the qualities, which constitutes the human personality and determines it in all features in a decisive way. The self-evident importance which the psychical organism claimed to win in the Sāṃkhya and has, in fact, won in Buddhism is something which would never occur in the frame of the nature-philosophical schools. Here everything clings to the soul itself and is exclusively conditioned by it.

These are the essential features which characterize the general picture of the soul in the Vaiśeṣika and in the remaining nature-philosophical schools. Concerning the constituion of the soul, there were made two distinctions. The soul, on the one hand, is the bearer of the entire psychical occurrences. It is therefore, the knower (*jñātā*). Simultaneously, it is also the director of the body and is that organ which causes the whole activity of man. It is, therefore, the doer (*kartā*) also.

The further formulation of the soul-doctrine followed first of all in this way : one occupied oneself thoroughly with the soul in its quality as the knower, as he attempted to comprehend the psychical occurrences more exactly. Thus ensued a stage in the course of development which we already know.[72] One tried to comprehend, before all other things, all psychical processes in a comprehensive enumeration. Then an attempt was made to arrange and simplify the plethora of phenomena; the related things were joined and those which did not belong together were separated until one finally was able to give a clear and coordinated picture of all psychical occurrences.

Of the several stages of this development, so little is preserved that we cannot follow them in details. But it does not matter, because the development, as it is already said, is typical. We have got acquainted with it in the Sāṃkhya and shall also find it in a detailed form in Buddhism. We, therefore, lose nothing if we pass lightly, in short, over the development in the Vaiśeṣika. Because what is most important is that the concluding result lies clearly before us. The concluding result shows that the Vaiśeṣika has understood it better than any other Indian system to bring clarity and order in the plethora of psychical occurrences. The total psychical phenomena were summarized in fairly big groups which organized the psychical phenomena in a suitable way. These groups are as follows : Knowledge (*buddhiḥ*), Pleasure (*sukham*), Pain (*duḥkham*), and Desire (*icchā*) and Aversion (*dveṣaḥ*).

Regarding this arrangement of groups it should be marked that it does not embrace merely the knowledge-processes, so that the old description of the soul as the knower turned out to be too narrow. And as all the groups, in contrast to the creative activity of the soul, summarized those processes which dealt with the making up of external impressions, another general designation for the soul was chosen in its place, viz. the enjoyer or the consumer (*bhoktā*). In particular, of the named groups, the knowledge-faculty (*buddhiḥ*) which participates in gaining right or false knowledge embraces all knowledge-processes. The group of pleasure and pain embraces all feelings and experiences. Desire and aversion embrace all wills and desires. Thus the total psychical processes are broadly ordered in a well-arranged manner. No doubt, the composition of the group gives an impression of its being motley or variegated. Thus, there appear, for example, in the group of desire, besides craving, also compassion, passionlessness, intrigue and dissimulation. But the appropriateness of arrangement in itself cannot be denied.

This arrangement and distribution of psychical occurrences in the Vaiśeṣika implies a valuable advance in the sphere of Psychology and represents, especially in comparison with other systems, a performance which must be recognised. It is particularly gratifying that the Vaiśeṣika did not, as is unfortunately the case in India, restrict itself to external or mechanical distribution in columns and classifications but attempted to comprehend more precisely the course of psychical processes which led to new kinds of knowledge and remarkable theories.

Among such is counted the assumption of a psychical organ, *manaḥ*. In order to avoid misunderstanding, it must be emphasised that the psychical organ of the Vaiśeṣika has nothing to do with the psychical organs with which we have been acquainted in the Sāṃkhya, though the same word is employed for naming what in the Sāṃkhya designates a thinking organ (*manaḥ*). In the psychological organ of the Vaiśesika, knowledge-processes play no part. These belong, as already said, exclusively to the sphere of the soul. The psychical organ, on the other hand, in the Vaiśeṣika, is, like the sense-organs with which it is placed on the same level or stage, a mere tool i.e., a mediating organ. This role explains how one came to the assumption of such an organ. As soon as a doctrine was formulated to the effect that the soul is of the size of the body, the question arose as to why all perceptions did not take place at the same time, although the soul stood in connection with all sense-organs in the same way. To answer this question, one seized upon the assumption of a mediating organ which restricts the activity of the soul to a particular sphere. It was said that the soul did not enter into connection with the sense-organs directly; it rather required its own organ. As this organ is small and tiny, the activity of the soul can only extend always to a small sphere. This organ, it was further said, lacked the quality of touchability. It can, therefore, move unhindered everywhere.[73] The great rapidity of its movement explains the quick alternation of the knowledge-processes. As a name for this organ which stands between the soul and the sense-organs, the name of the thinking organ (*manaḥ*) was chosen, which in other schools, especially in the Sāṃkhya, has its place as a central organ directly over the sense-organs.

On this occasion, we shall also mention a second doctrine which presumably belongs to a later period but which best finds its place here. During the precise consideration of psychical processes the question of recollection or remembrance naturally arose. How is it possible, it was asked, that things which are not present but belong to the past, are known? To answer this question, the following way, which was also followed by most other systems, was chosen.[74] It was said that every perception is able to call forth an impression (*saṃskāraḥ* or *bhāvanā*)[75] which may be able later to bring forth a similar knowledge. This impression, according to the Vaiśeṣika doctrine, clings naturally to the soul itself and not to a psychical organ. This assumption led on to further conclusions. Such an impression, it was taught, is specially impressive or effective when it is called forth by an unusually lively perception or by a perception which one looks forward to with great interest; further by practice or study, as is the case in learning a craft or scientific knowledge, similar inpressions strengthen themselves. But an impression can lose its force, may-be through opposite perceptions, through excitement, sorrow, drunkenness or similar other things. That such an impression finally releases the recollection at a particular time, can depend on several causes—, that a man himself tries to remember and muses with exertion, but, above all, on different sorts of associations.

With the help of all these different assumptions an attempt was made to sketch the clearest possible picture of all psychical occurrences. Thereby the assumption of a psychical organ turned out to be especially of great importance and fixed, in a far-reaching manner, the features of this picture. Originally the psychical organ was a mediating organ which brought about the connection between the soul and the sense-organs. Now its activity was extended to all psychical processes and the temporary appearance of particular psychical phenomena with their operation was proved. When now this, now that recollection is awakened, now this, now that desire becomes awake and enters into consciousness, the psychical organ is its cause. But, as the function of the psychical organ consists in directing and restricting the activity of the soul to a particular point, it follows from it that every time only one psychical process, especially only one knowledge is possible; it may be of a compound or composite nature. When, occasionally, we have an impression that several perceptions are simultaneous, it depends on an illusion and on the rapidity with which they follow one another. As two knowledge-processes cannot stand beside each other, every new knowledge crowds out the preceding, in order to make a place again for the following. Thus all psychical occurrences are reduced to a quick succession of individual knowledge-processes and one in conjunction with the Buddhist Schools went so far as to assert that every knowledge-process has the duration of a moment. When we believe that we are holding on to a perception or idea longer, it is a succession of homogeneous moments of knowledge flowing, as it were, in a stream (*dhārāvāhinyo buddhayaḥ*) which appear to us as a unity erroneously, on account of their similarity.

The doctrine of the psychical organ not only made it possible to prove how man is able to direct his attention always only on a single psychical process but it also offered a possibility for the explanation of the rapid change of the psychical occurrences. But beyond that it also proved fruitful and drew into its orbit the explanation of different phenomena. In the period of the

Upaniṣads, sleep and dream were explained[76] by the fact that the soul which has, during working state, entered into the sense-organs with its subtle parts, withdraws itself out of them and consequently man goes to sleep. When the soul sees the different sights in the cavity of the heart or in a self-created (dream—) world, then this appears as a dream. The soul-doctrine of the Vaiśeṣika with its presuppositions did not hold to these ideas; it gave a new explanation. It was said, that the sleep ensues, when the psychical organ withdraws from the sense-organs and its connection with the soul is interrupted. When, however, the impression of an earlier perception is awakened in the soul and consequently lively memory-pictures appear, then a man dreams.

From all this we see that the natural-philosophical schools and especially the Vaiśeṣika have created a highly developed psychology; they have, above all, designed or sketched a picture of the psychical occurrences, which appears to agree with observed facts and explains them in an illuminating way. We have, however, so far considered only one side of the psychical occurrences, viz. the soul as the knower and the enjoyer. But according to the doctrine of the nature-philosophical schools the soul is also a doer and is as much the cause of total human actions and behaviour. This part of psychical occurrences was also included in the sphere of consideration.

A distinction, first of all, was made between the conscious and unconscious actions of men. The first is dependent on the will and rests upon the desires (*icchā*) and aversion (*dveṣaḥ*). Under the second category, were understood mere life-expressions or life-forces which were also traced to the activity of the soul. Among these expressions of life were counted, above all, the breath during sleep, as also the first connection of the psychical organ with the sense-organ after waking, which ensues involuntarily and causes the first perception. Consequently it is also to be marked that during the activity of the soul, an important role is, as it is directed, played by the psychical organ. It was taught that every act of the soul is released through its connection with the psychical organ. Thus is explained the spatial and temporal limitation of the momentary activity. The psychical organ, thus, gained an immensely vast field of activity.

Finally in this way, not only all psychical processes but all the life-forces of men are conditioned, somehow, in general by its operation. Finally one went so far as to teach that life itself depends on the connection of the soul with the psychical organ.[77] This is how the doctrine of the soul is presented which developed itself in the soil of the old nature-philosophy of the Vaiśeṣika. But we must at the same time mention that it did not conclude with this. On the other hand, later on, the Vaiśeṣika made important changes in the soul-doctrine. One of the changes was that infinite bigness was ascribed to the soul instead of spatial limitation and restriction. These changes belong, however, to the later stages of development of the system, in which the total world-picture of the Vaiśeṣika gained new characteristic features. We must describe them, therefore, connectedly. Before we go oyer to that, we shall enter into another subject, in all conciseness, which deserves at least a short presentation, viz, the old nature-philosophy of the Nyāya.

In our attempt to understand the stages of development of the Vaiśeṣika, we were dependent on inferring what had been lost and such an attempt can always lay claim to a greater or less probability for itself. It is, therefore, all the more valuable that for us, in one case, a nature-philosophical doctrine is fairly preserved from out of the circle of the old Vaiśeṣika. That is also the case with the Nyāya. As we have already said, the Nyāya system arose through the mixture of a dialectical doctrine with an old nature-philosophy which approximately stands on the same stage as the oldest Vaiśeṣika. This nature-philosophy is further joined with a Deliverance-doctrine and is rounded into a closed unity. In this way, it represents a good example of an independent doctrine, as we need presuppose such ones in greater number, before the great systems gained their supremacy and we are still intensely reminded of the doctrines which are preserved for us in the old Epic. As an example, we wish to set forth one such doctrine in short.[79]

The Deliverance-doctrine of the old nature-philosophy of the Nyāya depends on a simple basic thought which is confided to us by the teachings of the Epic. The cause of entanglement of creatures in the cycle of being is false knowledge (*mithyā-jñānam*). That consists in the fact that one cherishes false views about the most important things. e.g., one believes that there is no soul or regards something, which is not the soul, as soul. One regards what is sorrowful, perishable and detestable as joyful, permanent and worth striving for. One does no more believe in the force of good and bad works or such like things. Through this false knowledge, arise desire and aversion and all the vices connected with them. Under their influence, the creatures act and do good and evil in thought, word and deed. The base or good action leads as its consequence to birth in a bad or joyful existence. There is, thus, produced an entanglement in the sorrow of existence which endures from birth in endless succession until finally the right knowledge puts an end to the whole chain of causes. Then "the Deliverance follows, as of sorrow, birth, action, vices and false knowledge, through the repeal of the following one, the previous one disappears."[80]

Corresponding to this Deliverance-Doctrine, the subjects for the knowledge of which one is supposed to endeavour, are enumerated in the following manner: "soul, body, sense-organs, objects, knowledge, psychical organ, activity or effort, vices, continuance after death, retribution, sorrow and deliverance are the subjects of knowledge."[81] Of these, the soul, the body, sense-organs, objects, knowledge and psychical organ are the foundation of existence in the cycle of births. Activity or effort, vices, life after death, retribution, sorrow and deliverance are the most important ideas of the Deliverance-Doctrine.

In particular, the following explanations are given: "Desire, aversion, toiling, joy, sorrow and knowledge are characteristic of the soul."[82] "The body (*śarīram*) is the bearer of the activity of a being, of the sense-organs, and of joy and sorrow as the result of its action."[83] "The sense-organs (*indriyāṇi*) are smell, taste, eyes, skin and ear. They are made out of the Elements." "These are Earth, Water, Fire, Air and Ether." "The qualities of the Earth etc. viz. smell, taste, forms, touches and sounds are the sense-objects (*arthāḥ*)"; "*Buddhi* is the same as Perception and Knowledge." "The sign of the psychical organ (*manaḥ*) consists in the fact that knowledge cannot originate at the same time."[84]

All this stands in consonance with what we have heard about the oldest Vaiśeṣika and is understandable without more ado. Still simpler are the explanations of the ideas of the doctrine of deliverance. Thus it is said, "application or effort (*prayatnaḥ*) is the operation through speech, knowledge and body." "The vices are characterized by the fact that they cause application" (*prayatnaḥ*): "Under continuance of life after death is to be understood rebirth in the cycle of being." "Retribution is brought about as the result of application or effort and vices." "The deliverance (finally) consists in full freedom from sorrow."[85]

After these short explanations, there follow detailed discussions which serve as the clarification clearing up different points and the refutation of opponents' doctrines. The sequence corresponds to the enumeration of the topics of the doctrine given in the beginning. At the head stands the problem of the soul and, doubtless, there is here an attempt to prove the existence of the soul. The proofs brought forward are similar to those made use of by the Vaiśeṣika. The central place of the soul plays a special role, the soul being the factor which unites the knowledges of the different sense-organs with one another.[86] The grounds which support the doctrine of the transmigration of the soul are new.[87] The mental impulses of a new-born child, which we deduce from its movements and gestures, depend, it is said, on the memory of joy and sorrow which the soul has experienced in earlier births. Also instinctive actions, like the striving of child towards the mother's breasts, are explained in the same way. So also, the inborn talent or aptitude, above all, the inborn passions are considered as the inheritance of earlier births. From all these arguments, one concluded the existence of a permanent soul transmigrating in the cycle of births.

About the body, little was said. One satisfied himself with only saying that the body was composed of the Element earth and not of all Elements.[88] More detailed is the treatment of the sense-organs. Above all, the perception through the eye with the help of the eye-rays is thoroughly described. The presentation corresponds to the doctrine that we have already described, so that we need not enter into it again.

Then follows the proof of the number of sense-organs.[89] It turns out in the following manner: As the sense-organs are found in different places of the body, their multiplicity could be assumed. On the other hand, an extended unity or wholeness could be extended to all the places of the body; so the multiplicity of the organs appears doubtful. As a matter of fact, we find in the older texts a doctrine repeatedly mentioned that there is only one sense-organ, viz. the skin which stretches over the whole body and of which the remaining sense-organs are merely parts. On the other hand, the following should also be taken into consideration. If there would have been only one sense-organ, all sense-objects—: forms, sounds, etc.—, would have been necessarily perceived at the same time. Besides, if the view be valid that there is only one sense-organ, then one must assume that only one and the same organ perceives a part of the sense-objects through direct touch, others from a distance. But one is involved in a contradiction. In the last resort, it was demanded that five sense-objects should have five sense-organs. One cannot invoke the innumerableness of sense-objects, as the same are of five kinds. Again finally the sense-organs must be different from one another from the point of their seat, shape, manner of working and the kind of mediate knowledge. Besides, every sense-organ must consist of one element because it knows the special quality of this element.

Next follows the description of the sense-objects i.e. the qualities of the Elements.[90] Here is the question which stands in the forefront, namely the question regarding the distribution of the qualities among the elements. With regard to it, the same views hold good as in the full-fledged Vaiśeṣika and they are formulated in the following way: "Of the qualities smell, taste, form, touch and sound, the first four upto touch are ascribed to earth." "To water, fire and wind are allotted the same qualities, omitting, however, respectively the preceding; to the Ether is allotted the last namely, the sound."[91] An opponent, however, raises an objection: "If it be true that some elements possess several qualities, it cannot be understood why the sense-organs which are formed out of the elements, perceive only one of the qualities and not all." It would be, therefore, better to assume that every element possesses only one quality. If we believe to have observed many more qualities in many elements, it depends on the mixture; during the world-creation, as the holy writings of the Purāṇas describe, every earlier created element enters with its quality in the following Element. This assumption is contradicted by the fact which is hinted, namely, that the perception of several qualities in the elements is not explained in this way. Thus, to take only one example, the taste of the earth is six-fold; that of water, on the other hand, is exclusively sweet. The quality of the earth can, therefore, not be explained by the mixing of water. In the case of the elements, therefore, which possess more qualities, qualities belong to them naturally. If in spite of it, the sense-organs formed out of the elements are at any given time only able to perceive one quality—the special quality of the element concerned, some other explanation must be sought for it. It consists in the fact that the special quality of the element concerned is present in the sense-organ in a particularly clear-cut, marked form and it is therefore able to know this same quality alone in the object. The question joined along with it arises as to why the concerned quality in the sense-organ itself is not perceived. The answer is that this quality in the sense-organ is shared together in the perception of the object and cannot itself be perceived. The ear, however, forms an exception, but as we know, it represents a special case.[92]

Especially comprehensive is the following description of knowledge (*buddhiḥ*).[93] At the beginning, there is the justification of the doctrine of the evanescence of knowledge as against the Sāṃkhya which recognized knowledge (*buddhiḥ*) as a psychical organ and regarded it as enduring for some time.[94] As this discussion, however, does not play a great role, we can skip over that. The next is the proof that knowledge is a quality of the soul.[95] The proof is put forth in such a way that one exhausts all possibilities so that only the proper assumption remains as the only way. The knowledge can neither be a quality of the sense-objects nor of the sense-organs because it also continues to remain, though others are destroyed. It cannot also be a quality of the psychical organ. If it be, then it would cease to be a mediating organ between the sense-organs and knowledge and therefore all perceptions would be simultaneous. In contrast to that, in the assumption that knowledge (*buddhiḥ*) is the quality of the soul, this difficulty falls away, because the psychical organ mediating between the sense-organs and the soul allows only one perception. Further objections against this assumption are refuted and finally it is concluded : "Because only this possibility remains and cited reasons stand the test of rightness, the knowledge (*buddhiḥ*) is, therefore, the quality of the soul."[96]

Now it is briefly justified why the knowledge (*buddhiḥ*) has only the duration of a moment.[97] It must be momentary because the things, which it may comprehend, stay only for a moment. Despite the fact that a man is able to distinguish only indistinctly the forms through the fleeting illuminations of lightning, the knowledge, in spite of its being momentary, is not indistinct because the homogeneous moments of knowledge can connect themselves with one another and render a distinct knowledge possible, just as the continually renewing flame of a lamp shows the illuminated objects distinctly.

Lastly, the special composition of knowledge as the quality of the soul in contrast to the quality of the body is described.[98] There are three points on which both differ from one another. The qualities of the body are like the qualities of the Elements in general, somewhat of an enduring nature and stick to the body as long as it stays, while knowledge originates only temporarily and again vanishes. Further, the knowledge (*buddhiḥ*) penetrates through the whole body because feelings or sensations emerge forth in the whole body and in all its parts. Were it to be a quality of the body and of all its parts, there would have been produced a plurality of knowledges and consciousnesses. Besides, the knowledge distinguishes itself from the qualities of the body through the fact that the qualities of the body, so far as they are perceptible, are perceived only through the external senses, while knowledge is brought into consciousness with the help of the psychical organ.

In conclusion, there is a short description of the psychical organ.[99] It is proved why there is only one psychical organ in the bodies of men. The psychical organ had been assumed, as we have heard,[100] in order to explain how at any given time only one knowledge can emerge. Along with it, however, it is presupposed that it has the unity and smallness. It was therefore, explained : The psychical organ is one, because knowledges are not simultaneous. It is tiny and small for the same reason already given.[101] This also found opposition from the opponents who asserted that as many activities of a man are possible at one and the same time and as the psychical organ mediates in the working of the soul, there must follow a plurality of psychical organs. But this objection is refuted by the argument that the apparent simultaneity of these activities is only an illusion, which depends on the rapid succession of the same, just as a rapidly swung or revolved torch appears as a circle of fire.

With this, the description of the subjects of old nature-philosophy are concluded and there follows the discussion of the doctrine of Deliverance. This is, however, essentially concise and contains little that is remarkable[102] so that it can remain unconsidered. What has been already said is, however, quite enough in order to give sufficient idea of the old nature-philosophy and of the old doctrines of the same stream of development. We shall, therefore, allow the matter to rest there and proceed to describe the further development of the Vaiśeṣika itself.

The old nature-philosophy of the Vaiśeṣika which we have already described forms a compact unity and could be easily rounded, as the last section of nature-philosophy of the Nyāya has shown, into a self-sufficient system through the connection with a Deliverance-doctrine. The Vaiśeṣika, however, did not remain stagnated. It included, in course of time, new important subjects in its orbit of consideration. Why, it worked out new valuable points of view which made larger parts of its teaching appear in quite a new light. We shall now occupy ourselves with these innovations.

One of the most important doctrines which thus found entrance into the system is the Atomic Doctrine. What led to its formulation, escapes our knowledge. Because it falls in a period for which the sources are denied to us. As firm starting-points fail, it is idle to make presumptions. In a later period we find the thought-process as follows.[103] "When a man divides something, the division goes on until it reaches the atom. It is spoken of as an atom (*paramāṇuḥ* i.e. extremely small), because the succession of continually smaller and smaller things during the division has an end, as, at last, there is nothing smaller. If we divide, for example, a lump of earth into its parts, the part following in our division becomes continually smaller. When the succession of continually smaller and smaller parts has an end, as there is nothing smaller, we name it the atom. If the division of parts would continue endlessly, it would follow that the motes or dust-particles in the sun would be unmeasurable as regards their number, extension and weight. It would be impossible to say: so great is a mote or a particle of dust in the sunlight, so much is its weight and so many are the atoms which form a mote in the sun through their union. Why ! As for instance the Himālaya consists of an accumulation of numerous atoms and according to the number, extension and the weight, is unmeasurable, so also is the case of the particles of dust in the sun, on account of the endlessness of division." The proof of the atom rested on the supposition that the division of matter must have a limit. Whatever similar or other thought-processes there might have been, which have led to the formulation of the Atom-doctrine, the fact at any rate is that the Vaiśeṣika represented in fairly early times the view that the elements consist of atoms i.e. the smallest parts which cannot be further divided, and that out of these atoms, the world of matter was built. It holds good for the old traditional elements : earth, fire and wind or air. The ether (*ākāśa*) assumes a special position, water, as usual.

This doctrine, as it soon found wide dissemination, met, however, a lively opposition or contradiction. The attack of the opponent was based, above all, on the contrast between partlessness or indivisibility on which the theoretical idea of the atom rested and the extension which its practical application absolutely demanded. It was shown, for example, that it was impossible for the formation of an aggregate to take place, if the atoms are partless or indivisible. It was said, for example,[104]: "During a simultaneous connection with six atoms from all six sides, there arises a six-partness of the atom, because in the place of one atom, there can be no other. If, on the other hand, the place of one atom be simultaneously the place of all six, then all would be in one place and the entire aggregate would only be of the size of one atom, because one would not extend beyond the other. No aggregate would then be seen." Or it was said : "What is organized according to parts of space, cannot be a unity. One is the eastern space-part of the atom, another is the western, others the northern, the southerly, the upward, the downward space-parts. How can the atom which is composed of these parts, when an organization according to space-parts is present, form a unity? If, on the other hand, in the case of single atoms, there is no organization according to space, how is it seen that during the entry of the sun's rays, there is on one side a shadow and on the other, light? Because it has still no other part into which the light could not come in. How can an obstruction of one atom by the other take place, if no organization according to space-parts is assumed? Because the atom has still no other part, the one, when it moves thither, would knock against the resistance of the other. If the atom knocks against no resistance, then, as we have already said, all atoms would assume the same place and every accumulation would have only the size of one atom."

It was difficult to meet these attacks. An attempt was made to meet them in a different way but it did not bear any clear result. For the most difficult task viz., the bridging over of the gulf between the partless atoms and the gross things composed out of them during the formation of aggregates, the Vaiśeṣika later made use of the idea of the 'Schematik' or the scheme of the Category-Doctrine. We shall come to describe it during the presentation of the Category-Doctrine.[105] Still, in this way, a real solution was not available and the artificial sophistry was scarcely satisfying.

But the significance of the Atom-doctrine in the Vaiśeṣika lies not so much in the theoretical discussion of the atom-idea as in its practical application in the formulation of the World-picture. As we have already said, the atom-doctrine quickly got a wide circulation. Besides the Vaiśeṣika and the Nyāya, the Jaina and the most important Buddhist Schools are familiar with it and it found acceptance in the Sāṃkhya towards the end of the classical period. It was respectively remodelled according to the views of the system concerned and was formulated in such a way as to suit them. Now it is important that this formulation in the Vaiśeṣika ensued in an entirely definite sense and, no doubt, in such a way that it can scarcely be a matter of chance; but we need regard it as a definite way of consideration which expresses itself therein. According to the Vaiśeṣika doctrine the atoms are infinitely small and according to the exact expression used for them, they are globular (*pari-*

maṇḍalaḥ). By shape or form they are all alike. They possess definite qualities—the characteristic qualities of the respective elements and these qualities are permanent and unchangeable. There is, no doubt, one exception. Of the earth-atoms, it was taught that they could change their qualities under the influence of heat and they named the new qualities as generated through cooking or heating (*pākajāḥ*). As the most frequent example, they cited the change which clay undergoes during the baking of a pot. But it appears here that a concession was made which one was compelled to make as he knew no other alternative to help him. It is, in any case, remarkable that there were two different views inside the school on this point. According to one the change is undergone by the qualities of the atoms into which the pot is dissolved during the temporary baking. According to the other view, the change ensues in the pot as a whole. I hold the view which is not unlikely that in the second view, an attempt is to be seen to remove the change at least out of the sphere of the atoms, an attempt which was given up by the orthodox schools because it went against the different basic tenets of the system.[106] In any case, this deals with a sporadic exception, as otherwise the basic view of the unchangeability of the atom was strongly held. Where, otherwise, changes in the elements appeared to exhibit themselves, e.g. during the heating of water, they were explained through the mixture of the elements, as when the fire atoms penetrated in the water.

This doctrine that the atoms are permanent and fixed and unchangeable in their qualities is of the greatest importance. Because the Atom-doctrine provided for the Vaiśeṣika of that time, who created it, an entirely definite comprehension of the world-occurrence. According to it, the whole world of appearance is built out of the permanent and unchangeable constituents to which it is again reduced. For the Vaiśeṣika holding the Atom-doctrine, there is no origin and destruction through continual change and transformation of a permanent Ur-matter as in the Sāṃkhya, no appearance and disappearance of fleeting and perishable things as in the most important Buddhistic Schools. In the Vaiśeṣika, on the contrary, the whole world-occurrence is a play of the imperishable atoms which conglomerate and again separate but themselves remain permanent.

This view is so consistently maintained that there can be no chance or doubt about it.[107] We may, therefore, assume, although in the preserved works, it is not more or less clearly expressed, that in the old Vaiśeṣika, the atom-doctrine served for designing a world-picture, which traced all origin and end back to the movement of permanent, unchangeable atoms, which was, therefore, dominated by a pure, mechanistic interpretation.

That shows also that we here in the Vaiśeṣika and for that matter, no doubt, in the whole sphere of Indian Philosophy find a thorough preoccupation with the problems of a mechanistic view. This view dealt with a whole series of pertinent questions and it is subsumed and dealt with as a doctrine of movement (*karma*). One tried to ascertain what causes a movement (*karma*), how it runs its course and attempted to explain the different nature-processes in this way. No doubt, one came to the following ideas in their essentials:

The movement is, as a rule, called forth by an impulse (*nodanam*) or a stroke (*abhighātaḥ*). Such an impulse can be directly but also indirectly effective. The propagation of movement was also known. When a body is set in motion by an impulse, an impetus(*vegaḥ*) is thereby communicated to it, which keeps it further in motion. This impetus can gradually relax. Otherwise, the movement finds its end, when it impinges against a resistance i.e. when the moving body hits against another. In this case, a back-movement can ensue, because the swing or the impetus is given in the opposite direction. As the first cause of a movement there comes into consideration the heaviness (*gurutvam*)when the hindrances working against it fall away. The flowing of water is traced back to its fluidity (*dravatvam*). It, therefore, appears among the causes of movement. In many cases, a movement also can be caused by the influence of the soul. It is here seen distinctly how the old nature-philosophy of the souls and their work is dealt with on the same level with the other factors of the surrounding world. In consequence, the most different life-processes in human bodies are included in the doctrine of the movement, above all, in the working of the psychical organ. It is also to be marked that one, when an occasion arises, reckoned with the co-operation of many more causes.

One or two examples will explain how things present

themselves under such a view-point to the representatives of the Vaiśeṣika; e.g. when an arrow is discharged, first of all the impulse of the string calls forth a motion, during the flying (with a jerk) of the arrow from the bow. This movement begets, on its part, a swing or a flight which either keeps the movement going until it gradually vanishes and the arrow falls to the earth through its own heaviness.[108] When a man pounds rice in the mortar with a pestle, in order to unhusk it, the following process occurs : A movement originates in the hand under the influence of the soul. This movement of the hand communicates itself to the pestle which it holds and raises it as far as one wishes. A new influence of the soul causes the falling down of the hand and of the pestle, by which a swing is called forth in it. As the pestle now rebounds on the floor-mortar, this impact together with the swing dwelling in the pestle causes the movement of the pestle in the opposite direction which the hand also follows. In this, neither the movement in the hand is caused by the influence of the soul, nor the movement of the pestle by the hand but both are simply called forth by the impact. In a similar way, further movement runs its course.[109]

In order to gain a survey of the different processes of movement and their causes, an attempt was made to arrange them according to their bearers—the elements and the psychical organ. [110] The heaviness as cause falls away in the case of the fire, the fluidity in the case of the wind, stroke and thrust in the case of the psychical organ. [111] In this connection, the explanation of different nature-processes was classified, Thus e.g., the absorption of water by the sun's rays was explained through a connection with the wind, the thunder through the knocking together and separation of water in the clouds. [112] Some may occur to us as self-intelligible and superfluous when a movement of the grass or herbs is traced back to the contact with the wind. [113] Still we must consider in this case that the wind according to the Vaiśeṣika is not perceptible but is only inferred. An independent group is formed by the processes in the human body. We have already dealt with these while describing man in the presentation of the old Nature-philosophy. It will suffice, here, to hint that the processes are placed also in this frame.

Besides the doctrine of the movement, the Vaiśeṣika of

that time further created a Theory of Causality which is, no doubt, simple but deserves a short mention in this connection. Corresponding to the theory which allows all things to originate through the connection of the atoms, a distinction was made between two kinds of causes : the atoms were considered as cause positive (*kāraṇam*) and everything that contributes to the connecting together of the atoms as an occasional cause (*nimittam*) ; e.g., the clay out of which the pot is formed is the positive cause in the production of the pot. The potter and his tools are the occasional causes (*nimittam*). The positive cause corresponds to the material cause of the Sāṃkhya. Thus, one was well conscious of the fundamental difference of views between the Sāṃkhya and his own doctrine. The causality theory of the Sāṃkhya, according to which everything originates through the transformation of permanent Ur-matter, was designated as the doctrine of transformation (*pariṇāmavādaḥ*), while the Vaiśeṣika doctrine, which allowed all things to come out of the meeting together of the atoms, was called the doctrine of composition or synthesis (*ārambhavādaḥ*).

Regarding the Causality-Theory, the following should be marked. Outside the Vaiśeṣika, one was accustomed to posit the decisive cause (*Sādhakatamaḥ*) which lets out the effect directly, in order to distinguish it from other causes. In a similar way the Vaiśeṣika also distinguished between dependent (*sāpekṣa*) and independent (*nirapekṣa*) causes, that is to say, such causes (*sāpekṣa*) which require the cooperation of other causes for producing forth the effect, and such others (*nirapekṣa*) which entail or derive the effect directly. Finally, it is to be mentioned that space and time were counted among occasional causes (*nimittam*), as general presuppositions of every occurrence.[114]

If we now sum up all that we have said about the Atom-doctrine, the doctrine of movement and the theory of causality, a mighty picture of the world in a uniform view unfolds itself in its broad features. In our presentation of the Sāṃkhya we have seen[115] that it summarized the idea of a world-occurrence in a compact picture—the picture of the one Ur-matter which, itself permanent and imperishable, allows the world to arise out of itself through continual transformation in a thousand forms, and to return to itself. Now we meet, in the Vaiśeṣika, a picture similarly viewed on a larger scale but a picture of an entirely different sort. The prime cause of all the phenomenal world is not the Ur-matter but the permanent, unchangeable atoms. There is no change of matter, no arising and reverting to its fine, incomprehensible Ur-form. Only the law of mechanics is supreme. Every occurrence depends upon movement, on impulse and counter-impulse, which are caused by permanent nature-forces. Also every visible rise or appearace and disappearance go back to it. It is the movement which brings the atoms together and allows the things to originate. It is again the movement which breaks the holding together of the united atoms and destroys things. Here is, therefore, developed a uniform, great thought and has been carried to its conclusion to explain the total phenomenal world. And this explanation stands equal in rank beside the great attempt of the Sāṃkhya to explain the world.

We, therefore, see that the Indian nature-philosophy did not restrict itself to giving an explanation of nature sporadically and to erect a few thought-processes and further formulate them. On the contrary, it has advanced in the Vaiśeṣika towards designing a uniform grand world-picture by a consistent logical working out of thoughts. In this world-picture which seeks to explain the total phenomenal world on the atomistic-mechanistic foundations, they have succeeded in bringing forth a creation which need not shun comparison with the system of Greek Atomism.

With this atomistic-mechanistic world-picture, the Vaiśeṣika reached the peak of its development. But it did not remain and stop at this point. The change of the times led to new thoughts which crowded out the old world-picture, so that it is reflected in the tradition more indistinctly and must be inferred through research. This change is now conditioned by the general development-process. To the Indian mind, the pure natural scientific attempt at knowledge is not enough in the long run. The religious talent or aptitude and the overwhelming drive for Deliverance penetrated gradually into the circle of the Vaiśeṣika and drew it into the stream of development. This development led finally to the acceptance of the Deliverance-doctrine and of a belief in the highest God, in the system. Above all one idea entered early into the Vaiseṣika, where it worked like a foreign body and disturbed the compact edifice of the old nature-philosophy. The idea was as follows :

In the presentation of the Sāṃkhya we have seen[116] that in the course of development, a period was reached in which the question arose as to what force brought forth the world-occurrence, what impels the Ur-mattar to bring forth out of itself the phenomenal world. As the souls in the Sāṁkhya were held to be completely inactive, the prime cause could not be sought in them. The reply which was given on this question was ancient and unsatisfactory. One did not know to say anything else but that the Ur-matter worked of itself (*svabhāvataḥ*) and this was elucidated by analogy instead of by argument. The same question must have confronted all other systems which knew no first cause, when they offered something like a belief in a higher God and it was quite natural that they did not rest content with the solution of the Sāṃkhya and sought for a better answer. One such answer was now, in fact, found and that answer agreed with the predominating inclination or direction of the mind so much that it found the widest circulation. The answer ran as follows:

The force which keeps the world-occurrence in process is the good and bad actions of men. The belief in the good and bad actions of men is very old. We have seen that it already emerges in the Upaniṣads.[117] It was taught that the actions fixed the fate of creature in the cycle of being or transmigration. How one thought of its effect sporadically, we have already been acquainted in the example of the Yoga system.[118] This idea of the force of actions widened itself beyond its original sphere and extended to the whole world occurrence. It was said that, as the action individually fixes the fate of the individual, so the works of all creatures together determine the world-occurrence on a large scale. They occasion the origin of the world, fix its constituents, and create as necessary presuppositions the frame in which an individual accomplishes his works and enjoys their fruit.

A difficulty which had not been thought of, had, indeed, in the time of the Upaniṣads, to be solved with regard to the doctrine of actions. It had to be explained, how good and bad works of men could produce effect at a much later time, when they themselves had long perished. The solution of the difficulty which was attempted was different. We shall get to know, before all, one such interesting attempt to resolve this difficulty in the Buddhistic systems. In the development-stream to which the Vaiśeṣika belonged, the assumption held good to the effect that the works first of all call forth an invisible force which was named, in short, 'the invisible' (*adṛṣṭam*) and that this latter produces the effects later. This force embodies itself each time according to the constituents of the work and merit (*dharmaḥ*) as well as demerit (*adharmaḥ*) and operates favourably or unfavourably accordingly.

The idea to trace the whole world-occurrence to the driving force of action or work corresponded entirely with the tendency which ruled Indian philosophy to the greatest extent. We have repeatedly emphasised that it was determined largely by the striving after Deliverance. It saw in the fate of men and of all other creatures a painful wandering through the cycle of births, directed by the moral power of works and saw the last end of human endeavour, to which it was desired to point out the way, in the deliverance out of the sorrowful entanglement in births. It was, therefore, alluring to conceive, with this aim, the whole surrounding world as one created and called forth by the same force, a stage on which this occurrence was enacted. And a doctrine which represented it and explained the whole world with a uniform point of view, was bound to be of the greatest success.

This doctrine of works or actions as a cosmic force found widest circulation and its effect was so enduring that it found entry where it need not have,—why—and where its entry was confronted with difficulties. The Jaina system offers the most striking example. It had already early formulated its doctrine of the works or actions in an entirely definite form and the view was presented that through the good and bad works of men, fine matter streamed into the soul and entailed its further entanglement in the cycle of being.[119] One could not well explain this matter as the driving force which keeps the entire world-occurrence going. On the other hand, one did not wish to renounce that cosmic force which was of such importance for world-explanation in other systems. And so two independent entities were assumed under the names of merit (*dharmaḥ*), demerit or guilt (*adharmaḥ*) : merit which causes a driving movement and demerit which hinders a movement and brings it to rest. Both these entities have lost their connection or relevance to the good and base actions of men and with it also their ethical character as this place in the system was filled up by another doctrine. They became pure nature-forces and only their name reminds us still of its descent or origin.

Any such remodelling of the doctrine of the cosmical power of works was not necessary in the Vaiśeṣika. It was simply assumed that the good and bad works of men as merit and guilt bring forth the Invisible (*adṛṣṭam*) and it was taught that this not only determines the fate of souls in the cycle of being but that it also works like a nature-force on the world-occurrence. It could be added to the system without much ado and created no further difficulties. The doubtfulness, however, lay in the fact that with it was introduced, into the system, something which contradicted its original spirit.

In particular, the doctrine of the working of the Invisible (*adṛṣṭam*) looked thus : The Invisible determines the course of soul's transmigration because it brings to end a life when old actions are exhausted and bring forth a new life corresponding to the works done in between. It influences further the course of every life; it does not abrogate the natural causes but it influences in a definite way (*niyāmakaḥ*) and directs to such paths as are demanded by the works or deeds of the beings concerned. When for example, a man's senses are damaged, if he is blind or deaf, the Invisible is the cause of it. It also works in individual processes. When knowledge (*buddhiḥ*) fails, when a man doubts or errs, its cause lies in the Invisible.[120]. Even where there is no question of the retribution of good or bad works, where no other cause could be stated, it was ultimately seen as the effect of the Invisible. Thus one traced back all unconscious life-forces—falling asleep, breathing in sleep, dreaming—to its influence[121]—Further as far as the Invisible is concerned as a cosmic power it causes in the beginning of every world-period the movement and gathering together of atoms which leads to the origin of the world. It is named as the cause of all these processes in nature, of which explanation was not known. Thus it concerns the flaming upward of fire, the sideward movement of the wind, the movement of iron towards the magnet, etc.[122] It was finally said, "Every other process in the great elements for which no cause can be pointed out through perception or through inference is caused by the Invisible."[123]

Therein lies the rub, the dubiousness. With the doctrine that the Invisible provides the impulse to the origin of the world, an intrinsically foreign element was introduced into the old nature-philosophical system; it was taken out from the religious-moral sphere and thereby broke through the fundamental attempt to explain the phenomenal world from natural causes. This step had two immediate results : Where no reason could be discovered for a phenomenon, resort was had to the convenient explanation through the Invisible (*adṛṣṭa*) which was no explanation at all and one became accustomed to the renouncement of a penetrating explanation of things. This extinction of the natural-scientific spirit was one of the causes which made the system later grow stiff in the scholastics of the Categories-Doctrine.

Still that is the item to which we shall again return. Here we wish to deal with the other effect of the doctrine of the Invisible—especially on the sphere of the Soul-doctrine. On this occasion, we shall give expression to the other important changes through which the soul-doctrine of the Vaiśeṣika passed during this period.

The Transformation of the Doctrine of the Soul : The manner of the Vaiśeṣika, with which we shall always continually meet during our consideration of the system, namely, to think out every assumption clearly and consistently and to shape it in consonance with the presuppositions of the system, brought with it the fact that they attempted to formulate clear ideas about the nature of the Invisible (*adṛṣṭa*) and its effects.[124] Thereby, they came to the following result. To see an independent entity in it, as the Jainas did, one was confronted with a difficulty that the system did not recognize independent entities which are created out of causes and are again later destroyed. It could not be permanent, because otherwise it was bound to always operate. The same difficulty still remained, even though an atom or a psychical organ would be made its bearer, as the qualities of the Atom are permanent. Because one did not desire it to be considered as a precedent, the exception was conceded unwillingly in the case of the Earth-atom changing under the influence of Fire. The next alternative assumption remained, namely, that the Invisible clings to the soul. In fact, it was this alternative which was assumed—namely, to connect it with the personality by the force of actions—the personality which has done the works and must bear its consequences. But this assumption led to further consequences.

When this Invisible (*adṛṣṭa*) was looked upon as a cosmic force which worked on the total world-occurrence in the most diverse ways, it meant that its operation can affect any place in the world. But now, the assumption of influencing from a distance or from afar went against the strict materialistic-mechanistic way of thought of the older Vaiśeṣika. On the contrary, every influence was explained by direct contact. We have seen how, for example, in the doctrine of perception, the Vaiśeṣika held stubbornly to the view that the sense-organs operate through direct contact (*prāpyakāritvam*). In the case of the Invisible, the same point of view was firmly adhered to. As a result, one was bound to explain, if not the Invisible itself, at least, its bearer, as ubiquitous or omnipresent. One was, therefore, compelled to give up the old doctrine of the restricted size of the soul and assume it as infinitely great.[125] According to my view, it was the starting-point for the radical remodelling of the soul-doctrine in the Vaiśeṣika, which ensued about this time. Thus, in essentials, the conclusions were drawn out of the presupposition of the system but partly also they might have been determined by the prototype of the soul-doctrine in the Vedānta and the Sāṃkhya.[126]

On account of this, therefore, the following doctrine was arrived at: The soul possesses infinite dimensions or size (*parama-mahattvam*), that is to say, it is unlimited or as it is there expressed, formless (*amūrtaḥ*). Therefore it is all-penetrating (*vibhuḥ*), and omnipresent (*sarvagataḥ*). It also exists there where other things are; it is, as it is said, in the same place like all things connected with it (*sarvasaṃyogi-samānadeśaḥ*). It follows further from this that it cannot be impenetrable and offers no resistance to other things. They, therefore, spoke of the fineness or subtleness (*saukṣmyam*) of the soul. This expression is, indeed, only occasionally used. It appears to have been used rather unwillingly, as it was connected in other systems with other ideas. Also otherwise in the Vaiśeṣika, one was accustomed to derive the impenetrability of things from the quality of touchability (*sparśaḥ*). The want of this quality was enough in the case of the soul, in order to prove that it offers no resistance to the existence of other things in the same place. Further, the soul is not composed of isolated parts. The position is logical and consistent. Because the construction of the elements out of the atoms presupposes their (-of the atoms-) impenetrability.[127] From the lack of parts one seems to have inferred the partlessness of the soul. As it appeared to stand in contradiction with the spatial extension, the Vaiśeṣika did not fight shy of asserting that the soul stands outside the conditions of space.[128]

Thus there began to be sketched gradually quite a new picture of the soul. Hitherto, according to the teaching of the system, the many wandering and active souls together with the elements had built or formed the world. They operated on the same level with them with the exception that the difference of their nature from the elements preponderated. Now the permanent all-penetrating souls stood out against the elements with the restless multiplicity of their atoms as something completely heterogeneous. The essential difference between the two began to make itself valid and was expressed, in particular, continually more and more.

The next obvious inference which arose out of the valid consideration that the soul was infinitely great concerned the transmigration of the souls. The souls of infinite size cannot naturally migrate from one body to another, as they are everywhere. On what, then, depends the embodiment of the soul and how does transition ensue from one body to another ? For answering these questions, the Vaiśeṣika held to the prototype of the Sāṃkhya; because the Sāṃkhya also in the beginning regarded soul as of infinite size and had the same question to answer. In the Sāṃkhya, the bearer of soul-transmigration was the psychical organism.[129] It causes the entanglement of the soul and contributes, through its migration from one body to another, to rebirth. These ideas were seized upon by the Vaiśeṣika, because they, on their part, made the psychical organ (*manaḥ*) as the bearer of the migration of the soul. In this context the

Sāṃkhya had found it necessary to assume a body of fine stuff as a support for the psychical organ in its transmigrations. Of course, opinions were, no doubt, divided on it. Partly it was held by some that this fine body endures throughout the whole world-period; partly it was held by others that it originates after death and mediates only the transmission from one body to another. The Vaiśeṣika followed the prototype of this particular view and taught that after death, a transmitting body (*ātivāhikaśarīram*) makes possible the transition of the psychical organ from one body to another.

But it was not only this obvious external inference that was drawn out of the change in the soul-idea. With the consistency of thought peculiar to the Vaiśeṣika, an advance was made towards the fundamental general problem and the question was raised, how under these pre-suppositions, in general, an activity of the soul is conceivable. As we know, it was one of the essential features of the soul-doctrine in the old Nature-philosophy that the soul was regarded as actively efficient. But how can any such activity be thought of, in the case of a soul of infinite size? On account of its mechanistic manner of thought, the Vaiśeṣika was inclined to understand every activity as movement, that is, no doubt, as change of place. Any such thing is not possible in the case of the infinitely great things. It was, therefore, taught that limitedness (*mūrtatvam*) of a thing is the presupposition of movement. That was why, as we have already seen, the transmigration of the soul was no more allowed to be valid. But not every activity of the soul was thought as change of place. The activity which a man had before his eyes, when he spoke of the doership (doing activity) (*kartṛtvam*) of the soul, was its role as director of the body and the organs. And this could not be interpreted simply as change of place. Another sort of movement viz. Atom-movement, was known as a kind of vibration or swinging (*parispandaḥ*). Any such movement was thinkable in the case of a soul of a limited size consisting of parts. And thus the activity of the soul could be thought of, in so far as it sets the body and organs in movement. This idea, as a matter of fact, has been held to be valid. We can prove it at least in the case of the Jaina,[130] and it may also be presupposed, in my view, in the older Vaiśeṣika also. But in the case of an omnipresent, fine, partless soul, as was just assumed, this sort of movement was excluded. Under these circumstances, how should one comprehend the activity of the soul?

As an answer to this question, there stand at our disposal two circles of thought of that time. The first was developed by the representatives of the science of Grammar, which in India had attained high blossoming very early and had with their thoughts begun to penetrate into philosophy, while the Grammarians on their side seized the philosophical ideas, employed them in their sense and developed them further. According to them, the subject of every occurrence is a doer (*kartā*). For example, the Mīmāṃsā teacher Kumārila could say[131]: "Activity for us is not merely the movement of the atoms as for the adherents of the Vaiśeṣika. By the doer (*kartā*) not only one activity is accomplished—activity which inheres in them[132]. Activity is, on the contrary, what the root of a verb expresses. Doership (*kartṛtvam*) can also consist, when somebody is the bearer of the activity. In the activities of existence, knowledge etc., the soul itself is directly the doer. During the movement of the elements it is also the doer so far as it causes the same (*adhiṣṭhānataḥ*)". Such thought-processes lay far from the Vaiśeṣika; they belonged to the thought-complex which had no interest for the Vaiśeṣika. The Vaiśeṣika found useful suggestions in the second circle of thoughts which considered doership (*kartṛtvam*) from the moral point of view and sought to fix it in the sense of responsibility in a moral action. This was, for example, the case in Buddhist Schools. They saw, in action, the decisive factor of the will and taught that the moral action of man consists of will and actions depending on it.[133] In a similar way, the Vaiśeṣika interpreted the activity of the soul as the will-impulse which leads to action, as it sets in movement the body and organs. This will impulse was called by them as effort (*prayatnaḥ*).

Thus was found a form of activity which was different from movement and which could be ascribed to the soul of infinitely great size without much ado. As a matter of fact, it is quite right when the Mīmāṃsā teacher Maṇḍanamiśra in consideration of this doctrine says that there are two sorts of activity: Atom-movement (*parispandaḥ*) and effort (*prayatnaḥ*).[134] The representatives of the Vaiśeṣika with regard to the old thought-habit of the School which joined every kind of activity with the idea of movement, preferred, indeed, to describe effort (*prayatnaḥ*) not as any activity but allowed this expression to occur in general, when it concerned the soul and therefore explained effort (*prayatnaḥ*) as a condition or a quality of the soul. Thus it was moved back to the same level as that of the remaining conditions of the soul—knowledge, feelings and desires. Then also these were consistently looked upon not as processes but as conditions or qualities. So the old doubleness or duality in the comprehension of the soul, as knowing and doing, vanished and only a great uniform unitary group of the qualities of the soul was recognized.

With this we have in no way described all the changes which the soul-doctrine of the Vaiśeṣika underwent in the part of the period we have dealt with. It must yet be mentioned that the comprehension of the mentioned group of qualities of the soul in their totality underwent a shift which was as follows: Until now the view had held good that every soul possesses qualities. This view confronted no difficulties so long as the soul was regarded as limited and restricted to the body. When, on the other hand, the souls were considered as omnipresent, consistently the question would arise, whether the same would hold good for the qualities also, whether they also were omnipresent. Nothing remained except answering the question in the negative. Because all qualities which were known—the knowledge-processes as well as feelings were considered only in the sphere of the body and it is therefore hardly possible to assume them outside the same. Consequently, it was taught that the qualities of the soul emerge restricted in a place.[135] (*pradeśavṛttitvam*). But this doctrine reacted back on the idea of the relation of the qualities to the soul. The connection between both was loosened therethrough and they appear no more as absolutely belonging together. This impression was besides strengthened still by the following circumstances: From antiquity, the view was held that the qualities or conditions of the soul are not enduring, that they, on the contrary, change rapidly.[136] This view was further held strongly. Even it was more sharply worked out and, no doubt, under Buddhist influence.[137] According to the Buddhist teaching the doctrine had been considered that things, which are perishable by nature, must vanish immediately; they need not wait for an external impulse and it is therefore not considered why they should not pass away immediately. The Vaiśeṣika had assimilated this interpretation and had come to assert that the qualities of the soul which are transitory by nature have only a duration of a moment (*kṣaṇikatvam*). Thus the qualities of the soul are held to be limited not only spatially but also temporally limited to the shortest period. On account of that, they were bound to appear as something external beside the omnipresent, permanent soul—something that does not belong to its nature. And at bottom, they play no other role than that of the psychical organism in the Sāṃkhya as fully different from the Soul. But that means that they are not the qualities which determine the nature of the individual souls and give them a special character—an interpretation to which one, in the case of the older soul-doctrine, could be easily inclined. They have rather nothing to do with the nature of the soul itself.

With this, the individual soul in the Vaiśeṣika completely lost its individuality. Earlier it had been said: The Sāṃkhya doctrine runs as follows: "The souls are not different; difference lies, on the contrary, in the objects, the body, the sense-organs and mind and their temporary causes." The Vaiśeṣika, on the other hand, taught that the souls are characterized by their qualities."[138] Therefore, the essential feature of the system had been regarded as lying in the individual definiteness of the souls through their qualities. Now it was said : "The nature of the soul is free from all qualities."[139] In this way, the soul-idea of the Vaiśeṣika approximated towards the *Ātmā*-idea of the Upaniṣads. This becomes particularly evident, when we consider the condition of the Released, as it is represented by the doctrine of Deliverance taken over later in the system. According to it, the Deliverance consists in the cancellation of the embodiment; it follows through the fact that the psychical organ which is the bearer of the soul's transmigration and which forms the foundation of all psychical processes, enters into no new body and suspends its activity for the soul. Therewith also vanish all the qualities of the permanent, omnipresent soul which now remains free from all limitations, calm and unchanged, untouched by all material things. It reminds us involuntarily of the descriptions of the *Brahma* as we find it in the Upaniṣads.[140] Thereby, in the condition of Deliverance, there is no consciousness, as with the vanishing of the qualities of the soul, the knowledge also ceases. That agrees with the doctrine of Yājñavalkya in the Upaniṣads, according to which there remains no consciousness after death.[141]

Thus it was gradually a completely new picture of the souls that arose. While earlier, the souls were considered beside the elements as a fundamental homogeneous factor in the construction of the world of phenomena, they were now recognized as something essentially different. In place of the body-sized souls wandering in the cycle of births, there emerged the idea of their infinite size and permanent immovability. And through the fact that the qualities had lost their firm connection with the souls and had become like something accidental and external, the picture of the soul gained a feature of undefinedness and incomprehensibility which is reminiscent of the soul-doctrine of the Upaniṣads.

In spite of it, however, a fundamental difference continued to remain and the development in the Vaiśeṣika leads to no complete assimilation with the soul-doctrine as depicted in the other great stream of development of Indian philosophy. After all, the decisive last step was not taken by the Vaiśeṣika. The world of souls did not become the only sphere which, as in the Sāṃkhya, would have been placed in juxtaposition, and of equal value with the world of matter or would have become a decisive factor of explaining the world. The similarity with the doctrine of the soul of the Upaniṣads is, finally, only outward. In reality, there lies a chasm between the attributelessness of the souls in the Vaiśeṣika inferred from bald logical considerations and of the *Brahma* against which all earthly definitions fail. On the one side there is the rationalistic vacuum ; on the other side there is the mystic incomprehensibility and inexhaustibility. The Indians were conscious of this contrast. The opponents of the Vaiśeṣika had marked the contrast with a sharp eye and had brought to the forefront the deathlike stiffness in the condition of the Deliverance as found in the Vaiśeṣika. So the Buddhists flung the contemptuous verse at the adherents of Vaiśeṣika : "Rather I would like to be born in the charming Jaitavana as a jackal than get Deliverance in accordance with the Vaiśeṣika."[142]

Space and Time—In conjunction with the described changes in the Soul-doctrine, we shall deal with still two new ideas which were taken into the system about the same time—the ideas of space (*Dik*) and Time (*Kālaḥ*). The mere fact that these in and by themselves were included in the orbit of consideration would deserve no detailed treatment. But the manner in which it occurred is so characteristic that it is worthwhile entering into it somewhat more closely. Because it is a good example, which indicates with unusual distinctness, how a philosophically gifted people like the Indians felt it hard to work through to pure general ideas, how tenaciously the once cherished old ideas and thought-processes asserted themselves and how much trouble and detour it cost them to reach a uniformly satisfactory result.[143]

The idea of space (*ākāśa*) is very old in Indian philosophy. It appears already in the Vedic texts, above all, in the Upaniṣads and is counted as one of the Nature-forces with which one continually reckoned. The doctrine of space has undergone a special formulation : during the confrontation of the macrocosm and the microcosm, the space in the heart has become the counterpart of the world-space and we have seen how this idea was employed in an original way in the doctrine of dreams.[144] Partly, the space (*ākāśa*) was even placed in connection with the *Brahma* and was explained as the spring of all things.[145] But, in general, this thought did not turn out to be fruitful. One remained stuck up in the start which was not further utilized. A new development ushered itself when the space was made the bearer of sound and was enrolled as Ether among the Elements. We have already spoken about it and need not speak about it again.[146] In this enrolment, it gained a special place. As it was assumed to be unlimited and all-penetrating, it appeared as something of quite a different kind from the remaining limited and impenetrable fixed Elements. This its special place remained enduring and was rather strengthened. This was, no doubt, the case during the introduction of the Atom-doctrine. That doctrine remained restricted to the four remaining elements and was not extended to space. Thus there was produced a fundamental distinction between the ether and the remaining Elements. But that did not alter the fact that it had, as a bearer of sound, become an Element and could not play, besides, the entirely different sort of the role of space. In this way, there was created a lacuna in the system. This lacuna was especially felt in comparison with other systems like those of older Buddhism and the Jaina where it had retained its original character as space (*ākāśa*), and as such was reckoned not only in the list of factors of existence but it also assumed its place, otherwise, in the presentation of the systems. Therefore, one was compelled to fill up this lacuna.

It is characteristic that with this aim in view, the idea of pure space was not juxtaposed against Ether but an old traditional idea was seized upon involuntarily, namely the idea of the quarters or directions (*diśaḥ*). In the Vedic period, we find Time and Space and almost more frequently than these we find ideas closely related to them and graphically employed. Thus in the speculation of the sacrificial priest, there appear, besides the Time as a cosmic power, year and seasons, months and days. So also besides the space there appear the quarters : East, South, West, North, the intermediate directions : South-East, South-West, North-West, North-East, the above and the below which are also reckoned as directions. They are also put as cosmic powers in relation with others, and are included in ponderings about macrocosm and microcosm and definite divinities are brought into connection with them.

The Vaiśeṣika, therefore, seized back these ideas, as it turned out to be necessary to create a new idea of space. The old word for World-quarters (*diśaḥ*) was given a general meaning of space.[147] Thus, however, not merely a new word was given. All ideas, which originally clung to the idea of quarters, appeared therewith. Formerly, one had designated space (*ākāśaḥ*) as that which allows space. Now space (*dik*) was explained as what determines the spatial layout of a thing. But one did not comprehend it in general but referred it to the directions and said : "The space is the cause of the ideas of East, South, North and West".[148] Thereby one determined the quarters in the old traditional way according to the course of the Sun : "The region in which the Sun rises is the eastern direction. The region, in which it sets, is the western direction. The region in which the sun wanders is the southern direction, the region, in which the sun does not wander, is the North."[149] Later on, the expressions were changed. The word rising and setting were avoided. The world-picture, which the Indian mythology created in course of time, knows no rising and setting of the Sun, but only a circle around the divine mountain Meru. The formulation was finally chosen as follows : "Out of the first connection with the Sun—it may be past, present, or future,—the easterly direction arises." "Accordingly the Southern, Western, Northern".[150] The determination of directions is made dependent on an order of sequence in which the Sun enters into connection with them, as it may be now the case with the time when one speaks about it or one may think of the past or future.

An important change which the new coming of the old idea of quarters produced on the space-idea was as follows : The quarters are many, a plurality. The space, on the other hand, was considered a unity. One held fast to this idea and it was said that one only speaks metaphorically of a plurality of directions, with respect to the different connections with the Sun ; in reality only one space is dealt with. Still more important was the following : One soon came to the knowledge that it is only relative when one speaks of the layout of things according to directions, that the same thing which appears out of the east from one standpoint, can appear out of the west from another. One adjusted himself to this knowledge. Up to this time, space was explained as the cause of the ideas of the East, South, West and North. Now it was added that these ideas must refer to particular stand-points; it was said that the space is the cause when something from a given stand-point appears as in the East, South, West or North. Therewith one was accustomed to consider the layout of things relatively in their relation with one another. This occurred not only with respect to the direction in which things are, but also with regard to their distance. The latter also was traced back to the cause of space. Thus a new definition of space was arrived at : One said : "The sign of space is that through it one knows that this is nearer or further than that."[151] This definition appeared gradually as more important and was finally predominant so that the cause of the ideas of nearness or distance was seen, above all, in the space.

One had come so far, when the classical Vaiśeṣika system

gained its final form, and the development came to a provisional conclusion. The idea of quarters was thrown in the background but one stopped with the ideas of nearness and distance. One had not gained the general idea of spatial layout as the characteristic of space. Thereby we need not think that there lay therein a conscious knowledge of relativity of all spatial relations. On the other hand, space as something permanent was fast adhered to. Only through the accidents of development, one had stopped with these ideas and did not advance to any further generalization.

Similarly inconclusive remained the development of the idea of Time. But it ran its course on an entirely different path. It lies at the basis of every thing. In the mythological and the religious sphere there is the idea of Time as the world-ruling power which brings forth everything and again destroys it— immensely impressive and capable of lasting development. To the philosophical thought, on the other hand, the idea of Time creates great difficulties. One begins, therefore, to discuss it comparatively late and the problems connected with it give rise to protracted and toilsome discussions. Thus it is to be understood that in the Iranian neighbouring region where the religious streams predominated, the idea of Time gained overwhelming importance and found its embodiment in the form of the God Zurvan who was long considered as the highest Godhead. In India, on the other hand, where in the attempts to explain the world, philosophy assumed the lead, the things developed differently.[152]

In the oldest times, we find sporadically the idea of Time (*Kālaḥ*) as the highest principle and Power governing all things. There is, in the Atharvaveda, a hymn which extols it, as the basis of all things, in ringing words full of ardour and mystery. It begins with the following words :[153]

"Time the steed runs with seven reins (rays), thousand-eyed, ageless, rich in seed. The seers, thinking holy thought, mount him, all the beings (worlds) are his wheels.

"With seven wheels does this Time ride, seven navels has he ; immortality is his axle. He carries hither all these beings (worlds). Time, the first God, hastens onwards.

"Time begot yonder heaven, Time also (begot) these worlds.

That which was and that which shall be, urged forth by time, spreads out.

"Time created the earth, in Time the Sun burns. In Time are all beings, in Time the eye looks abroad."

This idea of Time has further asserted itself. We hear continually again and again of a doctrine of time (*kālavādaḥ*) which traces all things back to Time and in the mouth of whose representatives, for example, the following words are placed : "The Time brings all creatures to ripeness, the Time again destroys all things. The Time keeps awake among the sleepy. It is hard to transgress Time."[154]

"Without the time, not at all, not even a bean is cooked, even when a man has placed the pot in the Fire ; therefore, a man knows that it has occurred through Time."[155]

But in general, this doctrine remains in the background. Apart from an occasional mention, the leading philosophical systems take no knowledge of it. On the contrary, they discuss the question of Time in quite a different way.

First of all we can say that the idea of Time vanishes where the proper philosophical thought comes in; it emerges only comparatively later. It was considered by the nature-philosophical schools; it only emerges, as it appears then, when one attempts systematically to understand all factors of existence and was persuaded to discuss the question of Time. It came about in this way that one was compelled to put the question anew—what is to be understood by Time. The reply ran as follows : Time is a permanent, ubiquitous entity which brings forth everything, but which is not itself visible but is only inferred as cause from its effects. In spite of the bald, matter-of-fact formulation of thought, here the influence of the doctrine of Time as the prime ground of all things—the only one on which a man could lean—is obvious. But is Time really the cause of all things ? Does it produce everything ? The nature-philosophy of the Vaiśeṣika in their atomistic-mechanistic world-picture had sufficiently proved the origin of all things so that there was no room for Time as the World-cause. But still there is a case in which the influence of Time is palpable. When in spring, the flowers bloom, when in autumn, the fruits ripen, it is the work of Time.[156] But is it also right ? On more exact consideration, one must say that it is not the things which Time brings forth. On the contrary, it only conditions the moment of its origin that they emerge in appearance earlier or later. So one came to the doctrine that Time causes the 'earlier' or 'later' of things.

In the formulation of this doctrine we come across a remarkable thing. This 'earlier' and 'later' is referred only to the present, not to the past or future; that is to say, of two simultaneous things, the older is to be understood as the earlier, the younger as the later. "The earlier and the later are produced out of the earlier of the causes and the later of the causes"[157] The older is therefore, on that account, the earlier because it originated earlier, the younger, later because it originated later. But both are present at the same time. With it the questions about the past and the future and their character which have troubled the Buddhistic Schools so much[158] are shoved away. Has it occurred intentionally? Has the cause of it been put forth? We are unable to say anything about it. According to the aim-conscious and consistent manner in which the Vaiśeṣika have otherwise formulated their doctrine, one could like to believe it. But our sources are silent. The discussions regarding it must belong, according to a process of development, to a period which still lies before the formulation of preserved knowledge. The sources, which lie before us, know nothing to say about it.

One thing need not be lost sight of. The doctrine of Time is perceptibly fashioned after the doctrine of Space. Finally, it was easy or proximate to lean upon the simple prototype of space while working out the difficult Time-problem. It, therefore, happens that in India the earlier and the later are expressed by the same words as the further and the nearer. So it is said: Just as far (*paraḥ*) and near (*aparaḥ*) express the relation of two things which lie in the same direction, so also earlier (*paraḥ*) and later (*aparaḥ*) express the relation of two things which lie in the same scale of time.[159] The 'earlier' and 'later' have also been always looked upon as the most important signs of time, in agreement with the doctrine of space. No doubt, in course of time, what otherwise expressed a time-relation—simultaneity and non-simultaneity, slowness and speed, was included. It is said: "earlier, later, simultaneous and non-simultaneous, slow, quick are the signs of time."[160] But the idea of 'earlier' and 'later' have always remained the most important.

A further point in which the doctrine of Time in the Vaiśeṣika agrees with the doctrine of space is as follows: There is only one, single Time. When one speaks of the parts of Time such as moments, hours, days and years, it is only a metaphorical way of expression and serves a practical aim. Again one thing remains to be mentioned. A question with which Indian philosophy much occupied itself is the origin, duration and the disappearance or passing away as the constituents of things. Especially the Schools of the Buddhists and the Jaina have endeavoured to understand the nature of phenomena and have developed interesting thought-processes in that connection. On the other hand, the Vaiśeṣika teaches only that the rise, duration and disappearance of things are an effect of Time. This question has not been discussed exhaustively but they have chosen to make short ad hoc small comments in regard to the discussions of other systems.

This is all what the classical Vaiśeṣika system has to say on the question of Time. The essential thing about it is that the time is considered as a permanent, all-penetrating entity which is the cause of simultaneous things, of the one appearing earlier and the other later. We miss here the whole problem which other systems have developed in all its richness.

In conclusion, if we want to summarize the results of our considerations so far, we can say thus: We have seen in the example of Space as well as of Time, how the development issues out of simple ancient ideas, how the thought again and again involuntarily comes round in a once trodden path and only slowly works itself out forward. In the period in which the classical system gained its final form, only a certain stage is attained which is far distant from a satisfactory solution of the raised question. The result of the development for the classical system of the Vaiśeṣika for philosophical purposes can be summarized thus: Space and Time have become firm ideas of the system by the end of the classical period. They, as such, hold good as permanent all-penetrating elements, the importance of which before all lies in the fact that all relative spatial and temporal relations are conditioned by them.

When the development of the Vaiśeṣika had advanced so

far, once again new thoughts were of quite a different sort. They directed the development of the system into fully new paths; on the strength of these thoughts the system was recast, the recasting finding its expression in the doctrine of categories. Up to this time, everything new had only contributed to widen the sphere of considered topics and to deepen the insight gained in that consideration. Now they dealt with a completely new way of reflection. Up to this time, one had deemed all objects of the phenomenal world on the same level as things of the same sort. Now one learnt to distinguish different forms of their existence and that, through the distinction of different categories.

The Emergence of the Doctrine of Categories—How this new knowledge came about and who was the first to express it, we cannot say. Because this development falls in the period in which our sources cannot be traced back. But, nevertheless, its course is at least clear in the basic features. The first step lay in the distinction between substances and qualities. It occurred thus: The thought of the oldest period cared to imagine all things, with which it occupied itself, as things, objects, objectively.[161] We see it especially in the Brāhmaṇa-texts of the Veda. What the priestly thinker of those times included in the orbit of his thought—year and seasons, sacrifice and metres, belief and penance—everything of all these appeared to him in the form of particular, independent entities. The same held true originally in the case of the things and their qualities. Not that no distinction was made between both. They were distinguished in an intuitive manner, as it was already conveyed by the genius of the language. But where one attempted to give a more exactly mathematical account about their constituents, the objective way of thought automatically appeared forth. We are already acquainted with the characteristic examples in this connection in the history of the Sāṃkhya. As one formulated the doctrine of the three qualities and inquired into their constitution and into the way of their working, he saw in them involuntarily independent entities.[162] This character showed itself so distinctly in the tradition that the best knowers or scholars of the Sāṃkhya doctrine fought shy, during the presentation of the system, to speak of the qualities of the Ur-matter but chose the expression constituents. Another example of the same manner of thought is offered by the old psychology of the Sāṃkhya system in the doctrine of the fifty ideas. As we have already seen, all psychical conditions were considered as something material and were explained by the streaming-in of matter in the psychical organism.[163] The singularity of these ideas must have, however, made them doubtful and must have led to a setback. Then finally one came to the view that things and their qualities need not be comprehended in the same way as independent entities but that their sort of existence is something basically different and that two essentially different forms of existence confront each other. Thus was gained the knowledge of the first two categories substance (*dravyam*) and quality (*guṇaḥ*).

Indeed, one was not able to give a clear definition of the nature of substances and qualities. What one knew to say was that substances possess qualities[164] and qualities have substances as their bearer which meant that they themselves possessed no qualities.[165] Therein was always contained the essential knowledge that qualities cannot occur independently but they require a bearer. Thus there was a break with the old objective manner of thought. Besides it was recognized that a substance cannot occur without qualities, that both emerge necessarily connected with each other. "Qualities without a substance and a substance without qualities are not possible. Substances and qualities, therefore, never occur separated."[166]

Thus was gained a new basic insight and the first step on a completely new path was taken. Indeed this insight would never have won such importance, as was really the case, if it had not been employed with the genuine Indian thoroughness and a flair for systematic action. It is a case where the Indian originality shows itself with special distinctness. Whereas in the philosophy of Aristotle and his schools, the categories-doctrine has only somewhat an episodic character, in India, however, all the potentialities, latent in it, are exhausted and thought out to the last conclusions until finally, on this basic foundation, was created a full system compact and self-sufficient in itself, which influenced the total later Indian philosophy of India in an authoritative way, nothing being left out of thought. We shall, indeed, nevertheless, later on, get acquainted with the disadvantage with which this method was attended.

The Oldest Three Categories—The next step in the development of the doctrine of categories consisted of the addition of a further category. It was in itself evident that one would go beyond both the categories of substance and quality. We see it in the Jaina who have a beginning of the doctrine of categories common with the Vaiśeṣika. They observed that a thing also undergoes changes, without the disappearance of old qualities and with the coming in of new ones. So they distinguish besides the qualities, a third category—the condition of things (*paryāyaḥ*, *P. pajjayo*). The Vaiśeṣika proceeded quite differently and it is characteristic, viz. the way they chose. Among them at that time the atomistic-mechanistic way of considering things was predominant and the idea of movement played a decisive role in it. So it was movement (*karma*) which was posited as the third category.[167]

In this way a group of three categories was gained, which formed a close unity and remained as such in the system for a long time.[168] The 'systematic' or systematization already set in and an attempt was made to utilize the knowledge gained to the fullest extent. One sought to delimit and fix the orbit of individual categories, everything whatever that falls within the given frame. One proceeded in such a way that, first of all, he arranged, in the frame of the categories, the topics dealt with by the old Nature-philosophy and supplemented it by new ideas as circumstances demanded it. In this procedure, earlier features which are characteristic of the Vaiśeṣika method of thought, stepped forth and they defined decisively the picture of the classical system. We must turn to that and enter into it, in brief.

Among these features, above all, belongs the fundamental realism of the system. This realism is occupied with understanding things in a way which goes back to an ancient way of viewing things and which resulted, as one was compelled in the course of development, in taking up a fundamental attitude or position towards this manner of viewing things. In the beginning of philosophical thought, a man is inclined to consider all objects of knowledge as real; that is to say, it is presupposed involuntarily that to every content of knowledge, there corresponds a real object in the external world. It is a naive realism, naive so far that this assumption ensues as a result of what one felt sentimental about it, becoming conscious of the problem lying before him. The further development in such cases follows as a general rule in such a way that a moment comes when a man sees himself compelled to take up conscious, intellectual, intelligent attitude towards an interpretation which until then was arrived at emotionally or by way of feeling and to decide for or against it. The inclination shows itself most in affirming, first of all, the hitherto existing accepted interpretation. But the decision which confronts man constrains him to think out through the things more exactly. Through that, man becomes conscious in general of the problem before him. With that the requisite conditions are made available to overcome gradually the old views which have become untenable in course of time.

In the Vaiśeṣika, there arrived now the moment for taking up a fundamental attitude towards the old naive realism, when one proceeded to classify the subjects of the old nature-philosophy into the frame of the categories. The doctrine of Categories had taught that the different kinds of existence should be distinguished and that everything should no more be considered as material. But one still saw in everything an existence which was called as something peculiarly real. The question now forced itself whether such a view was also justified. Because, among the things which were classified under various categories, there were also such as were in no way independently existing, whether they were considered as independent entities or not—e.g. Time and Space and the different qualities. With the classification into categories, one was, however, bound to decide which view he wished to profess. The Vaiśeṣika fundamentally decided in favour of realistic comprehension and executed this view with their peculiar consistency down to the last possibility. According to the doctrine of the classical Vaiśeṣika there exists, corresponding to every content of knowledge, a real correlate in the external world and this view was held to firmly as far as it was somehow possible. Especially clearly it comes, among other things, to be expressed when one explained this during the definition of different things with a preference, as the basis, of corresponding ideas and of words belonging to them. Characteristically the Indian word for a category (*padārthaḥ*) has also its own peculiar meaning—"object of a word." Through the oversharpened execution of extreme realism, its critical attitude also became evident and served as the starting-point for its later being overcome by the logical-epistemological school of Buddhism.

On this occasion, further, an equally critical feature of the development, described above, may be mentioned by the way, namely, its favourite inclination towards external systematization. The attempt to classify all things in the frame of categories and to summarize all and everything under a few ideas, and that too, under the presuppositions created by the extreme realism, brought with itself the fact that quite heterogeneous things were placed near each other as homogeneous. With this, its speciality receded into the background as against the general character of the group. One forgot the particular and the individual against the general idea. Thus there opened gradually a chasm between the living view and the empty world of the ideas of the categories—doubly dangerous in a school which started with explaining nature and understanding it. One continually got accustomed more and more merely to working with the ideas which were offered by the categories and ended in this way finally with an unnatural scholasticism in which the system gradually grew rigid and stiff.

Still, we shall have to return to it later on. We shall now return back to our proper subject—the further development of the doctrine of categories through the classification of the objects of the old nature-philosophy in the frame created by the Vaiśeṣika.

In the case of the category of substance (*dravyam*), it was not difficult. Only one needed to survey the factors out of which the old nature-philosophy built the world-picture and to gather them, which were suitable, together. Thus there was no possibility for much doubt. It was self-evident that the Elements together with the Ether were explained as substances. There was also no fluctuation or wavering with regard to the souls and the psychical organs. One could be uncertain only with regard to Time and Space. But here the realistic attitude of the system proved decisive so that they were also enrolled as substances.

Thus one arrived at a series of new substances which were arranged in the classical system in the following way : Earth, Water, Fire, Air, Ether, Time, Space, Souls and Psychical Organs. There were hardly differences of opinion with regard to them—not also among the related schools. Only the Jaina shared the view whether Time should be regarded as substance or not.[169] In the Mīmāṃsā School of Kumārila, as we have already heard, the sound and darkness were regarded as substances.[170]

Though things with regard to the category of substance were simple, it was different to get at a clear decision with regard to the category of qualities—what were to be regarded as the qualities and how were they to be arranged. Let us, first of all, consider the qualities of the elements. The old nature-philosophy had formulated lists of these qualities. But these lists were not employable or usable without much ado. They were exceedingly manifold and in spite of many simplifications, which ensued in between, were composed of the most diverse constituents.[171] The formulation of a list of all the qualities which could dwell in the substances required, on the other hand, a far stricter selection, a restriction to the essentials and a well-arranged marshalling together of the same. One had, therefore, to proceed very systematically—more than hitherto. It resulted in bringing about decisive changes.

Above all, the old series of the qualities of the elements fell a victim to this great systematization. While describing the qualities of the Elements in the old Nature-philosophical doctrines, we have seen that the elements had been first characterized by a definite series of qualities such as hardness, moistness or liquidness, heat and movement and only later on were placed beside them the lists of qualities which correspond as sense-objects of sense-perception.[172] The older series was now bound to fall away. As long as more than one or several lists were tolerated beside one another or as long as the qualities of individual elements were enumerated in a motley or promiscuous series, it could easily happen that the same sort of homogeneous qualities would be repeated in various places. In the formulation, on the other hand, of single uniform lists, such repetitions were bound to disappear. Now in the present case, on a more exact examination, it was seen that hardness, which was taken as the quality of the earth and the heat, of fire also occurred in the second series, namely, as sub-varieties of touch and that they were there in a better place. The movement of the wind was naturally classified under the category of movement (*karma*). Thus, of the whole first series, there remained only the moisture and fluidity of water, for which a proper place had to be found in the new list which was formulated.

Regarding the assessment of the qualities of the Elements, other view-points, besides the greater systematization, also were taken into consideration. Through the Atom-doctrine one had learnt to distinguish between atoms and the aggregates formed out of them. It led to the knowledge that certain qualities occur to the aggregate but not to the atoms. This knowledge was, above all, employed by the Jaina.[173] In the Vaiśeṣika, the following also came up. According to the mechanistic manner of thought of the Vaiśeṣika, the atoms and therewith also their qualities were considered as fundamentally unchangeable.[174] So it was obvious to differentiate the qualities which were firmly bound with the substances from those which were not. Thus finally one came to the conclusion that there were qualities which are bound up with definite substances and are characteristic of them (*vaiśeṣika-gunāḥ*), as against those which can be common to different substances (*sāmānya-guṇaḥ*).

Under the influence of this point of view, the doctrine of the qualities of the Elements was formed in this way: It was natural that the qualities, which, according to the older doctrine, form the objects of sense-perception and which had been connected with the individual elements, namely, form, taste, smell, touch and sound, should be considered as the characteristic qualities of these elements. But the accumulation theory, which had been taken over, went against it, as according to it individual qualities occur in more and more elements.[175] But one, however, resolved to lightly pass over these difficulties because he was of the view that, in spite of the accumulation theory, every quality lends its special character to every element. With this assumption, form, taste, smell, touch and sound were received into the list of qualities to form the category of quality and they were explained as the characteristic qualities of Fire, Water, Earth, Air and

Ether.[176]

Next, in conjunction with it, there arose the necessity to examine the sub-varieties of these qualities and to fix them finally. In this respect, taste, smell and sound presented no difficulties. Besides, the things were made more easy; with the formulation of the doctrine of Categories, the proper natural-scientific interest stepped back continually more and more. Of taste the customary six varieties were formulated: sweet, sour, saltish, bitter, pungent and acrid. Smell was simply divided into good and obnoxious smells. As for sound, one was satisfied with differentiating it as sounds of speeeh (*varṇāḥ*) and unarticulated sound (*dhvaniḥ*).

In contrast to the above, form and touch served to give occasion for basic important decisions in the field of the doctrine of the Categories. The extensive group of the sub-varieties of Form, after singling out the obvious things not belonging together such as Light and Shadow, organized itself distinctly into two sub-groups, of which the first embraced all colours (form in the strict sense), while the second contained what concerned the shape (*saṃsthānam*) of things. Now it was clear that of these two, clearly only colour could be valid as the characteristic quality of Fire. The shape according to the Vaiśeṣika played rarely a role in the fully uniform atoms ; only it played its part in the aggregates. Besides, a view could not be shut out that the shape could be well attributed to all other substances as well like the fire. The result was that the shape was separated from the old quality of Form which was now defined as merely colour.

Similar results accrued on a more exact examination of the varieties of touch. Heaviness and lightness were also counted among them. In the meanwhile, however, in the mechanics, heaviness was known as something different from the other qualities of the elements. Before all, it could not be reckoned as a sub-variety of touch among the characteristic qualities of air to which the old nature-philosophy attributed no heaviness. It was, therefore, to be excluded. Again, to ascribe hardness and softness, roughness and smoothness to the atoms went against the doctrine of the atoms of the Vaiśeṣika. Rather they were attributed only to the aggregates and were traced back to the kind of their compounding. And so finally of all the sub-varieties of touch, only heat and cold remained.

In this way, by the time of the final doctrine of categories in the Vaiśeṣika, the doctrine of the qualities of the elements and their sub-varieties had the following result : There are five characteristic qualities of the Elements : form, taste, smell, touch and sound. Of these, form embraces different colours white, etc. The taste is six-fold : sweet, salt, bitter, pungent, sour and acrid. The smell can either be good or bad. The touch is three-fold—cold, hot and neither hot nor cold. In sound, finally, sounds of speech and inarticulate sounds are to be distinguished.

Thus with regard to the first group of qualities which was enrolled under the category of quality, namely the characteristic qualities of the elements, there came about clarity. But the reflective thought bound up with it gave rise to a formulation of a further group of qualities. As we have seen, one had found it necessary to separate from 'form' (*rūpam*) what concerns the shape of things. But how should this shape itself be judged? The realism of the system demanded that it should be explained as something real. But then if one comprehended something real as such, it could only be considered as a quality. Then arose the question, as to what place among the qualities should be given to it. As an answer to this question it was decided that the shape (*saṃsthānam*) was not to be regarded as the characteristic quality of a substance but that which is ascribed to all substances—to the atoms as well as the aggregates. It was therefore explained as a common quality (*sāmānya-guṇaḥ*).

Regarding the precise constituent of this quality, the essential of shape (*saṃsthānam*) was seen in the extension. Evidently the thought conjointly gave the idea that the shape was ascribed to the atoms as well as to the endlessly great substances. This quality was therefore named extension (*parimāṇam*). As sub-varieties, distinction was made between smallness (*aṇutvam*), largeness (*mahattvam*) and shortness (*hrasvatvam*) and length (*dīrghatvam*). The sub-varieties which the old nature-philosophy had assumed e.g. quadrangularity, roundness etc. were rejected, because it was believed that they only occur to the aggregates and could be traced to the bigness and to the arrangement of the parts. To the permanent substances which have atom-form, comes infinite smallness, and to those which are unlimited, comes unending infinite bigness (*mahattvam*). Both become summarized as an independent variety of extension under the name of spherical roundness (*pārimāṇḍalyam*).[177]

The perishable aggregate could be small or big, short or long.[178] It could, indeed, not be overlooked that smallness and bigness are relative ideas and that their respective knowledge is directed to the relation to other things. Therefore, it was firmly laid down that only aggregates, which are formed out of two atoms, are really small and short, while everything else is big and long. If in spite of it, it is designated as small or short, that is due to a figurative usage of speech.

Extension (*parimāṇam*) gave the first common quality of the substances. While examining the qualities of the Elements, hard ness, softness, roughness and smoothness were separated from the sub-varieties of touch because they were traced to the kind of the composition of things. But what is this composition of things? The simplest answer was: thc connection of its parts. With it there emerged a new idea, the connection (*saṃyogaḥ*) and the question arose with regard to its character.

The reply to this question could not be doubtful in the given situation of things. The fundamental realism of the Vaiśeṣika demanded that it should be understood as a real entity. Thereby one was confronted with old, already existing ideas. In the older period, it was a natural thought to see an independent entity, when two things were seen connected together, in those which it binds and which distinguishes it from the unbound things. We meet consequently with corresponding views in Jinism as well as Buddhism.[179] They, therefore, need be presupposed in the older Vaiśeṣika. This entity appears to have been originally imagined as material, as a body which holds together the connected things.[180]

With the emergence of the doctrine of Categories, this was no more tenable. In it, the connection was bound to become a quality which dwells in the connected things and allows them to appear as connected. As this quality can indwell in different substances, it was naturally explained as a common quality.

It may be remarked here that this quality of connection

(*saṃyogaḥ*) played a fairly large part in the doctrine of Categories of the classical Vaiśeṣika system, as during the incorporation of the old Nature-doctrine in the scheme of the ideas of the Categories, different important processes were understood as connection (*saṃyogaḥ*). According to the atomism of the old Nature-philosophy, every origin or product ensues through the coming together of permanent atoms; this coming together was explained as connection (*saṃyogaḥ*). In the Mechanics it was known that a movement is called forth through a push (*nodanam*) or stroke (*abhighātaḥ*). In an attempt to define these two in the sense of the doctrine of Categories, the best solution appeared in understanding these as a sort of connection. The idea of connection was also worked out otherwise. The cooperation of the soul and organs was traced back to their connection. The temporal and spatial layout of things was derived from their connection with the substances Time and Space. To it were also finally attributed different individual cases like the origin of sound which is caused by the connection of the drum with the stick. Thus the quality of connection gained an exceedingly wide sphere of validity. It joined itself with the issue of living discussion, particularly with the Buddhistic Schools—to which we shall return still on a later occasion.[181]

As to the nature of the quality of connection, it was defined as the uniting of two things, which until now were not united (*aprāptayoḥ prāptiḥ*). It is possible in the case of limited (*mūrtaḥ*) as well as unlimited (*amūrtaḥ*) substances, indeed with a limitation. The limited (*mūrtaḥ*) substances can well be conjoined among themselves, as well as the limited and the unlimited. But the conjunction of unlimited substances among themselves is impossible. These unlimited substances exist since eternity without entering into a conjunction. Because, according to the mechanistic manner of thought of the Vaiśeṣika, it can occur only through a movement, that is, a change of place which is not possible in infinitely big substances. According to the Vaiśeṣika doctrine there exists no connection (*saṃyogaḥ*) between Ether, Time and Space and the infinitely great souls. It remains to be marked that connection, in contrast to the other qualities described up to now which always cling only to one substance, is a quality which dwells at the same time in many substances (*anekāśritaḥ*)—i.e.

the substances which it connects. Further it was taught that it does not wholly penetrate its bearer but extends itself only on a part of the same (*pradeśavṛttiḥ*). As it was seen, an extended object can enter into a connection only with one of its parts. Finally, the following should still be considered. The hitherto described qualities, with the exception of sound to which always a special place is assigned,[182] permanently cling to their substances. On the other hand, connection is a perishable quality which rises in its bearer and again vanishes. Its cause is, as a rule, a movement i.e. a movement which leads to the union of the objects concerned. Its destruction depends finally on movement, i.e. a movement which drives the connected objects asunder. In between, comes in or interpolates, according to the Vaiśeṣika, a further idea and with that we already come to the next quality, which we must describe in connection with connection (*saṃyogaḥ*), that next quality being separation (*vibhāgaḥ*).

It suited the formulation of the Vaiśeṣika to place an independent quality, separation, in contrast to connection. Because, during the systematic summing up, one was accustomed to put together the pairs of opposite ideas. The positing of this quality (separation) occurred after good deliberation and with full consciousness. Objections were not wanting: it was said that the mere abrogation of connection is something purely negative and a positing of a special quality was not justified. Against that, the adherents of the Vaiśeṣika represented that the idea: 'These things are separated', just like the idea : 'These things are united', expresses something positive and, in a logical execution of their fundamental realism, assumed for this idea also a positive correspondence in the external world. In one case, at least, they believed to have been able to show distinctly 'separation' as a special, independent real entity. Just as a stroke —a connection of two things, generates a sound, even so the breaking of a stick i.e. a separation, occasions a sound; they therefore, felt themselves justified in the positing of 'separation' as a separate quality. Finally, there was mixed in it an attempt to carry out as symmetrically as possible the fundamental maxim according to which the doctrine of categories was built up.[183] Now, in general, the rule was considered valid that the qualities are destroyed by qualities which are opposed (*virodhī*). It appears, therefore, desirable to infer the abrogation of connection through one such opposed quality. 'Separation' (*vibhāgaḥ*) turned out to be suitable for that. The process was thought out as follows: The movement which disturbs the connection (*saṃyogaḥ*) brings forth separation (*vibhāgaḥ*). This destroys the opposing quality of connection (*saṃyogaḥ*). And the things connected hitherto loosen themselves from one another.

Concerning the constituent of the quality of separation, the same held good, in general, as in the case of connection. It is a common quality which dwells in limited as well as un-limited substances. It extends itself simultaneously over more substances, namely the substances which it separates. And it penetrates the things not entirely but only partially. It is further called forth like the connection through a movement, that is, a movement which drives asunder the previously joined or connected substances. Only with its destruction the position becomes different. In the case of connection, it was clear that it was destroyed by separation which drives asunder the hitherto connected things. In the case of separation, on the other hand, it cannot be said, that it is first destroyed when the separated things again unite with one another. Because it need not so occur in general. But the idea which considers the things as separated and on which the assumption of the idea of separation is based considers the things only in view of their earlier union as separated, as soon as the consciousness of their earlier union vanishes. It lasts, as a rule, only for a short time and the same must hold good for the quality of separation. In order to establish it the following assumption was made: The movement or action, which separates the connected things, causes also a change of place of these things. But a change of place consists in a connection with another place. Now it is this connection, it was said, which destroys the separation in the separated things. As a change of place follows immediately after separation, the quality of separation is also destroyed immediately and lasts only for a moment. In this way, the destruction of the quality of separation without a new connection of separated things is explained. The explanation corresponded simultaneously with the fundamental concepts of the system as it allowed the destruction to follow through another opposite quality.

With the formulation of the three qualities—extension (*parimāṇam*), connection (*saṃyogaḥ*) and separation (*vibhāgaḥ*) there emerged, beside the group of the characteristic qualities of the elements—a second group, and that is the group of common qualities (*sāmānyaguṇāḥ*). It correponded with the Indian attempt at systematization—which we have already described in connection with the old Nature-philosophy—to complete this group further and seek to make it as consummate as possible. Towards that end, the following possibility offered itself.

The development of the old Nature-philosophy, of which we have just spoken, led to the fact that space and time were included in the sphere of dealt-with subjects and both ideas had been incorporated into the system. A cause was seen in them, whereby something appears as further or nearer, earlier or later. This 'Further' or 'Nearer', 'Earlier' or 'Later' must now appear, seen from the stand-point of the doctrine of Categories, as the qualities of things, in consonance with the consistent realistic attitude of the Vaiśeṣika, qualities which are called forth through their connection with Space and Time. Thereby, in them were necessarily seen the common qualities, as they occurred in all things which are in Space and Time. As the ideas of 'distant' and 'earlier', 'nearer' and 'later' were expressed in India through the same word and fell under a similar idea, two such qualities (*guṇaḥ*) were posited viz. the spatial and temporal distantness (*paratvam*) and nearness (*aparatvam*).

But with the positing of these two new ideas, there arose a new problem. On a more exact reflection, it could not be overlooked that distantness and nearness are something relative and depend on the stand-point of the observer. Thereby one was confronted with the question how qualities can dwell in things, if they are conditioned by the comprehension of the knowing subject. This was a difficult test for the realism of the system. Because one wished to assert that something objective in the present depends on the knowing subject.

Here is seen again the rigorous logical consistency of the Indian philosophy of the classical time which fought shy of no inferences where they were valid, to carry through consistently to the end the basic views of the system. In the present case, man held fast to the view, as was demanded by the realism of the Vaiśeṣika, that in distantness and nearness the objective qualities of things were dealt with but it was also assumed that they originated under the influence of the knowledge of the subject. It was taught as follows : When seen from the point of view of the observer, it was said, two objects in any direction are found on different distances and when the observer sees the more distant one, then under the influence of this observing knowledge (*apekṣābuddhiḥ*) there originates the quality of distantness (*paratvam*) through the connection (*saṃyogaḥ*) of the object with space and it calls forth on its side a corresponding knowledge. The weakness and vulnerability of this theory are obvious. But it is not to be denied that it has been consistently thought out on the presuppositions of the system and it well represents the only possibility to rescue its basic realism in the present case. The origin of the quality of nearness (*aparatvam*) was also similarly explained. The corresponding view also held valid for the temporal distantness and nearness. For example, when the case of two men is considered, two men of whom one is older, the other younger, in the case of the older man in relation to the younger one, there arises, under the influence of this observing knowledge and through the connection with Time, a quality of distantness (*paratvam*) in the older one and in the reverse case the quality of nearness (*aparatvam*) in the younger ones.

All these qualities, as also the temporal and spatial distantness and nearness are naturally, according to this theory, not enduring. Their emergence rests on the observing knowledge (*apekṣābuddhiḥ*) of the knowing subject; they vanish also with the vanishing of this knowledge. Nothing especial remains to be said of them.

A further quality which was assumed in the group of common qualities is the number (*saṃkhyā*). The number plays no role in the Indian philosophy of the classical period. The sacrificial mystique of the Veda has no doubt played with the number and the philosophical systems of the later time work with the numerically defined enumerations.[184] But number itself does not belong to the ideas which are employed for explaining the phenomenal world. It has found access in the Vaiśeṣika, as, according to all appearances, it was sought to comprehend as completely as possible all categories and their sub-varieties in the formulation of the Doctrine of Categories.

In the case of number, it is now important that it was regarded as relative and conditioned by the knowledge of the observer. One was of the view that number one is ascribed to single things of nature. When, on the other hand, many things numerically form a group, it depends on the knowing subject who understands it as a group. The origin of number was regarded as similar to that of distantness and nearness e.g. when two things are understood as belonging together and as duality, there arises in the things under the influence of the observing knowledge (*apekṣābuddhiḥ*) the number two out of number one which naturally dwells in things, and the observer knows them as two. The same holds good for all higher numbers. Naturally these numbers are fleeting or perishable and vanish with the observing knowledge. It remains still to be marked that they belong to the qualities which, like connection and separation, inhere in many substances.

The last quality (*guṇaḥ*) which found acceptance in the described group of common qualities is the separateness (*pṛthaktvam*). This quality is again an example of the sharpness in distinguishing ideas which distinguished the Vaiśeṣika. As we have seen, 'Separation' was posited as a counterpart to connection and was defined as the non-union or disunion of things which were formerly united. But there are also the separate things which were not formerly united or connected. If, therefore, separateness of formerly united things was traced to a quality called 'separation', separateness of these things, which formerly were not united, was also bound to be derived from a quality dwelling in them. Such a quality was assumed to be separateness (*pṛthaktvam*).

In itself nothing especial about this quality would have been said, if the following thoughts had not emerged with regard to it (*pṛthaktvam*). It was said that the separate things not only appear singly but also could form groups and this group-formation was also established with the indwelling of separateness in them. The thought ran the course similar to the case of number. In the case of things, separateness as unity (*ekapṛthaktvam*) and separateness as duality (*dvipṛthaktvam*) etc. were distinguished. Of these, the first dwells in all separate things naturally while the other remaining ones are called forth by the observing knowledge of an observer. The process is the same as in the case of number. They vanish with the vanishing of observing knowledge and dwell in more than one substances just like the corresponding number.

With the separateness (*pṛthaktvam*), the qualities which come to be considered as a group of common qualities, in the strict sense, are exhausted and the group was closed. This group embraces the seven qualities which are enumerated in the classical system in the following order : number, extension, separateness, connection, separation, distantness and nearness. Simultaneously ended therewith the new most important creation which was inaugurated in the sphere of the category of qualities in the formulation of the Doctrine of Categories. Everything remaining which remained to be done was, on the other hand, simple.

First, beside the groups of the qualities of the Elements and of common qualities, a third group of the qualities of the soul was formulated. We have heard[185] that the old nature-philosophy regarded the soul as knowing and active and also ascribed to it different processes and conditions. We have also further heard how these different conditions were sifted and arranged until one arrived finally at a clear and well-arranged division which differentiated, besides knowledge, pleasure and sorrow, desire and aversion—to which series later in the course of further development was added 'effort' which embodied the activity of the soul. As to the question which arose as to under which category in the Doctrine of Categories, these conditions of the soul should be arranged, it appeared best to count and arrange them under qualities. They could not be considered as movement, as movement for the Vaiśeṣika implies exclusively a change of place and such a change of place is unthinkable in the case of the infinitely big souls. There was no further possibility of arrangement. It was, therefore, decided to enroll the named conditions of the soul as the qualities of soul in the category of qualities.

These new qualities represented an independent group by

itself on different grounds. On the one hand, they are the characteristic qualities which only occur to the soul and are, therefore, to be separated from the common qualities. On the other hand, they are also distinguished from the characteristic qualities of the Elements in important features. In contrast to the qualities of the soul, the qualities of the elements are by nature perishable and extend only on a part of their bearer. And also otherwise, they assume a special place for themselves according to the way of thought of the system e.g. they fall out of the usual frame of the doctrine of causality, as they have nothing to do with the formation of an aggregate. It was, therefore, justified to group them as an independent group. Thus there arose the third group of qualities—the qualities of the soul : knowledge (*buddhiḥ*), pleasure (*sukham*), sorrow (*duḥkham*), desire (*icchā*), aversion (*dveṣaḥ*) and effort (*prayatnaḥ*).

With these three groups—the qualities of the Elements, the common qualities and the qualities of the soul, the main mass of qualities was comprehended. What remained to be added were mere supplements. Among them first came into consideration the three qualities of the elements which were left out during the grouping of the characteristic qualities of the Elements. They were moisture or humidity (*snehaḥ*), fluidity (*dravatvam*) and heaviness (*gurutvam*).

Of these moisture or stickiness was a remainder of the old series of the qualities of the Elements.[186] By itself, it was not considered difficult to arrange it. Because it appeared naturally as a quality of water and was not different from the remaining characteristic qualities of the element. But the attempt towards extreme systematization and symmetry, which played not an under-estimable role in Indian philosophy, did not allow its arrangement in the proper group of the characteristic qualities of the elements, as it would have disturbed their regular construction. So it became, in a certain measure, enrolled as an appendix in a supplement. Just as with humidity, similar was the case originally with fluidity. But some difficulties arose about it. Different facts, which made its arrangement into the scheme difficult, had to be taken into account. First of all, fluidity does not only occur in the case of water but also in the case of things like fat or lac or lacquer which is considered under the element of Earth, or in the case of different metals which were considered as the appearances of the element Fire but which could appear in a fluid, flowing form. Further it was observed that water can assume solid form in snow or hail while reversely fat and lacquer become liquid under the influence of heat. These observations could have led to kinds of further knowledges. But the doctrine of categories with its predilection for external classification was not favourable to such new knowledge. So instead of recognizing fluidity or stickiness as a condition of the aggregate, it was, on the contrary, ascribed as the quality to the atoms of the substance concerned. Only one distinction was made : in water fluidity was explained as natural (*sāṃsiddhikaḥ*) and among other elements, on the other hand, as artificial (*naimittikaḥ*). Thereby the natural fluidity, because it occurs only in the case of water, was defined as a special quality, while the artificial fluidity was defined as a common quality because it appears in Earth as well as Fire. On account of this, fluidity fell out of the frame of the characteristic qualities of the Elements and it had to find a place likewise under the supplementary qualities.

Things were represented again differently with regard to the third of the named qualities 'heaviness'. In the old nature-doctrine, it had been a sub-variety of touch. Now it was to be differently arranged or classified. First in its case it was of importance that it belonged to more than one elements, to Earth and Water, according to the simple observation which were worked out in those times. But it was still more important that in the course of development, it got into quite a different circle of ideas and appeared in a different light. The heaviness, as we know, played an important role as a chief cause of movement in the mechanics of the old Vaiśeṣika and as such was considered from a different view-point than in the old Nature-doctrine. Accordingly, it was defined as a common quality which is invisible and is only inferred as a cause of the falling. It has its place in the play of forces of the mechanics where the resistance of impenetrable objects, a conscious effort, or the swing of a moved thing work against it and neutralize it. It is understandable that in this entirely different character, heaviness was not placed beside the characteristic qualities of the Elements but was accommodated in the supplement.

A further quality which arose out of the circle of the ideas of the mechanics and found its place here is the swing or force (*vegaḥ*) which keeps the moved things in motion. It was something different from the old qualities. It is a common quality because it occurs to all moving things—to all the four elements and also to the psychical organs. Therefore, it naturally belongs to the supplementary qualities. In its arrangement or classification, it was mixed with a further idea. We have seen that the Vaiśeṣika, with all their externality of systematization, show also a remarkable sharpness in the formulation of ideas and comprehended clearly every idea in its speciality and elaborated it. It held good in the case of force. It was believed and recognized that force is essentially different from the remaining hitherto accepted qualities. Its decisive feature was seen in the fact that it displaces its bearer temporarily into a condition which may cause the release of a particular operation or effect and then vanish. Something similar was also believed to have been in other cases ; for instance, Elasticity (*sthitisthāpakaḥ*) which was also included in the sphere of consideration about this period. Because when a man stretches a bow, elasticity makes it possible to assume its earlier form. Finally a similar related phenomenon was observed in the working of the memory-impressions (*bhāvanāḥ*) in the soul. Through them, the soul is displaced into a condition which releases a particular effect and endures until the effect or working takes place. In order to validate the special character of these named qualities, it was resolved to do as follows : They were not posited as three different qualities, but it was taught that there was a quality called Disposition or preparedness (*saṃskāraḥ*) which represents an arrangement for the release of a particular effect or operation. It was said that force, elasticity and memory-impressions are the three different sub-varieties of this quality named Disposition (*saṃskāraḥ*)

Thus were comprehended and classified the total qualities of the Elements which were known to old nature-philosophy and with the memory-impressions, an important supplement was added to the qualities of the soul. Still there remained, hitherto unconsidered, merit (*dharmaḥ*) and guilt (*adharmaḥ*) which were already summed up under the name of the Invisible (*adṛṣṭam*).

We have already spoken during the further development of the old nature-philosophy about the emergence of the idea of the Invisible force which is called forth by the actions of men and leads to retribution.[187] There we have also mentioned the ideas which were formulated as the constituents of this Invisible Force ; it was partially comprehended as an independent entity and partly a bearer was assumed for it. We have also said that the Vaiśeṣika decided to set it in connection with the soul. The result naturally was that in the formulation of the doctrine of categories, merit and guilt were explained as the qualities of the soul. They were placed on a par with the remaining qualities of the soul. They were adjusted in such a way that it was taught that they as well as the rest of the qualities were called forth through the connection of the psychical organ with the soul.

With merit and guilt, the summing up of the total qualities is finally completed and a number of the total twenty-four total qualities is reached. The classical Vaiśeṣika represented this number and the related systems showed no great variations. Kumārila, who regarded sound of speech (*śabdaḥ*) as a substance, enumerated in its place vibrating sound (*dhvaniḥ*) among the qualities.[188] Prabhākara explained the number as a separate category and went his own independent way on many points. But seen broadly or by large, the variations are unimportant and the dependence on the Vaiśeṣika is palpable.

In conclusion, if we cast a glance on the total category of qualities, we must say that its compilation must have involved fairly great pains. Not only a rich traditional material had to be sifted and classified but also the transmitted views had to be changed in many ways. And new thought-processes led to the formulation of new qualities.

The Category of Movement—Things were quite different with regard to the category of Movement (*karma*). The tradition offered in this respect only little. Because what was taught by the mechanics of the old nature-philosophy was the idea of movement but nothing more. A distinction of the sub-varieties of movement was lacking. But one would not be satisfied with that. When already different substances and qualities were formulated and enumerated, one wished also to put against them a corresponding series of movements. Though tradition did not offer much, one compiled, as well as it could go, one such series. Thereby raising (*utkṣepaṇam*), letting down (*avakṣepaṇam*), bending (*ākuñcanam*), stretching (*prasāraṇam*) and going (*gamanam*) were distinguished. About the superficiality and vulnerability of this classification, we need not speak. Simply different sorts of movements of the human body were compiled. The differentiation of these kinds of movement gained no further importance for the system. They were once enumerated and then there is no more talk about them. But enough was done to fulfill the necessity to juxtapose a number of the sub-varieties of movements, corresponding to different sub-varieties of substances and qualities.

There were found opponents who contested this classification of movement[189] and the Vaiśeṣika held fast, with the tenacity customary to the finished system, to the once formulated assertions. When the opponent said that the distinction of different kinds of movement lacked justification, as all movements are a change of place and a going, the representatives of the Vaiśeṣika replied that a particular group of activities called forth an entirely fixed idea different from other ideas and that corresponding sub-varieties of movement must, therefore, be accepted. Again the opponent observed that it also proved true in other cases and that one, therefore, must posit other special cases of movement like entering and going out as its sub-varieties. Thereupon, the representatives of the Vaiśeṣika retorted that in such cases no definite sub-varieties could be had, because it depends on the stand-point of the observer whether one understands it as going in or going out. But philosophically, these discussions are unimportant. They lead to no result, as it always happens, when of the two opponents one is bound by a preconceived opinion and does not wish to be persuaded or to take advice. It is, therefore, unnecessary to enter further into such discussions.

With this, we have finished the first stage in the development of the doctrine of categories. We have seen how one filled the given frame through the formulation of the first three categories. It was a very important step. With it, one had begun to build the simple basic ideas of the doctrine of categories further into a system and the basic lines of the system began already to stand out. Still it was only the first step. A further way was to be covered until the full completion of the classical system. Towards this end the development ran in two directions. On the one hand, the frame of the doctrine of categories was widened through the addition of newer categories. On the other hand, one sought to employ the stuff offered by the doctrine of categories, because it remodelled the world-picture given by the old nature-philosophy in the light of the doctrine of categories.

The Category of Commonness—The first, that occurred, was the formulation of a new category of Commonness (*sāmānyam*). It falls before the period to which our sources reach back and we can only conjecture as to which thought-processes led to it. But we know at least a doctrine with which the Vaiśeṣika could come in contact and with which probably it did. The doctrine is connected with a problem in the orbit of the philosophy of language—the question of the subject or the object of the word.[190]

To the greatest scientific performances of the Indians belongs, as is well known, what they have attained in the sphere of the linguistic science. They had already created, in the pre-Christian period, a Grammar of their classical language Sanskrit which not only deals with phonetics and accidence with unusual precision but has also considered word-formation and syntax and, even beyond that, has summed up the total language-material in a sort of a dictionary of roots. The whole represents a performance which, through its deep penetration into the structure of language and through its systematization and completeness, has remained unrivalled until in the newest times. Besides Grammar, they also occupied themselves early with the problems of linguistic philosophy. They inquired into the nature of the word and the sentence and into their subjects. In conjunction with it, the problems of epistemology were also thoroughly discussed. Their inquiry could go so far that a famous grammarian Bhartṛhari (about 460-520 A.D.) formulated a very well-known doctrine according to which the word is the 'ur-ground' (the first cause) of things. In the course of our presentation we shall repeatedly be compelled to come back to the Indian science of language and its views.

In the present case, what to us is of importance concerns the views of the Grammarian about the subject of the word.[191]

In the oldest period, when man dealt with the question as to what was the subject of the word, the natural reply was that this subject was seen in something (*dravyam*) of the external world. But soon one became conscious that one and the same word can denote a large number of individual things; then the question confronted itself as to how it was possible and to what subject the word properly clings. The reply given thereto was that it is the form (*ākṛtiḥ*) which is common to all individual things and which is, therefore, the cause why the same word is used for all. Thus there were two opinions of which one assumed that the individual thing was the subject of the word while the other believed to find the subject of the word in the form (*ākṛtiḥ*) of the thing.[192] Finally, an attempt was made to unite both these views with one another; it was explained that both an individual thing and form were expressed by the word, but then now only the one, now the other stands in the forefront.

In this doctrine of the Grammarian it is important that they distinguished between an individual thing and a homogeneous constituent which is common to many several things. The Vaiśeṣika joined in that view and it depended, above all, on fathoming the nature of the homogeneous constituent. It is characteristic of the system, how it goes far deep beyond the start offered or made by the Grammarian.

The form (*ākṛtiḥ*) assumed by the Grammarian turned out for the Vaiśeṣika as unusable or inapplicable. Form had been discussed in the formulation of the category of quality.[193] Thereby, a quality named extension (*parimāṇam*) had been accepted. In the remaining, form was known only as an arrangement of parts of which a thing is composed (*saṃsthānam*). Of them, extension could not be independently considered as the subject of the word. One would not decide in favour of the arrangement of parts. According to the spirit of Realism which rules the Vaiśeṣika, they naturally traced the commonness in the individual things back to an independent entity. In that, it was still considered that, from the stand-point of the doctrine of categories, commonness was believed to be recognized not only in substances but also in qualities and movements. Thus it was resolved to trace the commonness in all things, in substances, qualities and movements back to an independent category which could also be simultaneously regarded as the subject of the word. It was, therefore, assumed that there is a category called commonness which, as an independent entity, indwells all homogeneous things and lends them the homogeneous character. Thus it was thought, for example, that the commonness 'cowness' (*gotvam*) dwells in all cows and operates in such a way that we know and characterize them as cows.

Thus, a question of commonness in individual things was, no doubt, answered but there arose a series of new questions Above all, the following question urgently came forward: What man usually comprehends as commonness is, in no way, mere commonness. The cowness, for example, is common to all cows and allows them to appear as homogeneous or of the same kind. But at the same time it distinguishes them from the things of other kinds, for example, from the horses; in this view, it is not commonness but Peculiarity or Particularity (*viśeṣaḥ*). Thus one came to the conclusion that the so-called commonnesses have a double character—partly as commonness, partly as peculiarity. It was said : 'commonness or peculiarity depends on comprehension'.[194] A second thing came out of it. It was recognized that the sphere of different commonnesses is greatly different and it was observed that the commonnesses with larger spheres appear as commonnesses against those with narrower spheres, while the commonnesses with narrower spheres present themselves as peculiarities against the commonnesses with larger spheres. So one was confronted with the question, how these phenomena are to be assessed.

On a more precise reflection, one came to the following views : It was said that the entities, which lend the things their general character and which are predominantly considered as commonnesses, form a ladder of steps from those with the widest sphere to those with the narrowest. Of them only the borderline cases are exclusively constituted by commonness or peculiarity. Existence (*bhāvaḥ* or *sattā*) has the widest sphere. It occurs in all substances, qualities and movements and is exclusively a commonness. The entities form the contrasting border-line cases which occur in individual permanent substances and distinguish them from all homogeneous or heterogeneous things. They are exclusively a peculiarity (*viśeṣaḥ*). Everything that lies in between is partly commonness, partly peculiarity; it appears as peculiarity as against higher commonnesses and as commonness against the lower. Substanceness (*dravyatvam*) represents itself as peculiarity against existence, as it is a form of existence which distinguishes the substances from other remaining forms, from the qualities and movements. It (substanceness) appears, however, as commonness against earthness (*pṛthvītvam*), as it binds together its bearer the earth with water, fire, etc. as homogeneous. These commonnesses are, therefore, called with a double name : commonness-peculiarity (*sāmānyaviśeṣaḥ*). In later times, the term genus (*jātiḥ*) served as an expression for it.

With a view to judging all these entities and their organization in the doctrine of categories, the following formulation was made regarding them : First of all for the last peculiarity, which could no more be considered as commonness, a further category of peculiarity was posited. For the rest it was clear that the existence (*sattā*) as the highest commonness represented the category of commonness (*sāmānyam*). With regard to the lower commonnesses, there was vacillation at first. In this respect, partly an independent category of commonness-peculiarity (*sāmānyaviśeṣaḥ*) was posited.[195] Finally, the orthodox system decided to explain them as commonness, because it was said that they are basically considered commonnesses and are designated as peculiarities only in a metaphorical sense.

In this way, a clarity was attained, regarding the positing of categories and their kinds. The next question concerned the relation of these new categories to the old. In this respect, the following view was decided upon : Like all categories except substances, commonness and peculiarity cannot stand independently but require a bearer. But whereas the qualities and movements and, as man assumed, also the last peculiarities can only cling to a substance, the commonness can also dwell in the qualities and, movements. No further commonness can dwell in the commonness, just as the qualities and movements cannot dwell further in qualities and movements.

These are simple assumptions and are explicable from the point of their attempt to create the ideas as simple and as clear as possible about the relation of categories with one another. Essentially more difficult was the answer to the question as to how the working of the commonness in individual cases has been introduced. Finally, the following rule was formulated for it. There is, it was said, for every kind of homogeneous things, one and only one commonness which lends them their homogeneous character. This commonness is permanent and exists everywhere in all its bearers. The one commonness indwells undivided and entire in its every bearer.

It is a remarkable doctrine which actually challenged contradiction. It was sought to establish it in all its points in this or that way. For example, it was said that there is respectively only one commonness because the characteristic, in which we recognize it, is the same everywhere and we have no occasion to assume several commonnesses. Or it was said that commonnesses are permanent because they are different from their bearers and do not originate or disappear with them. But these reasons do not satisfy. As a matter of fact, they are not the essential ones. In reality, the cited doctrine was formulated in spite of its difficulties in order to escape still greater difficulties.[196] Naturally, under such circumstances this doctrine was the target for the attacks of the most different opponents. It was connected with detailed discussions which dragged on through many centuries in connection with the discussion of the question of epistemology. On that account we shall have to return to it in details later on. Here what has been said may suffice provisionally.

The Category of Inherence—The positing of the categories of commonness and peculiarity was the most important expansion which the doctrine of categories underwent beyond the old three categories. The classical system later added only one more category—the Inherence (*samavāyaḥ*). This category is again an example of the acuteness and clarity of the building up of ideas which distinguishes the Vaiśeṣika system of the classical time. As one learnt, through the doctrine of categories, to see things as a conglomeration of various categories, the question arose as to what holds these categories together and connects them into a unity.[197] It was seen that the quality of connection did not come into consideration in this respect. In the working out of the Category of this quality it had been defined as a union of things not formerly united.[198] It had been recognized that it originates only through a movement of things which connect themselves with one another and it is abrogated again through the separation of things. But that does not hold true in the case of Categories. There is, therefore, no union of earlier separated things. Because they only occur together. Again the things, which are united through a connection, could stand independently by themselves. It is not the case with regard to categories. On the contrary, in the case of the two categories which are connected with one another, there is one which is always the bearer, while the second always clings to this bearer and is likewise borne by it. A union of several categories is, therefore, something quite different from two things being connected by connection. It was taught, therefore, that in this case there is no connection (*saṃyogaḥ*) but an indwelling inherence (*samavāyaḥ*).

This inherence cannot be a quality. It had been assumed that the quality of connection indwells the substances which it unites. The inherence, which connects the different categories with one another, must accordingly indwell not only substances but also qualities and all other categories. But that is not possible in the case of a quality because qualities can indwell only the substances. So one was compelled to explain inherence as an independent category.

It was, therefore, assumed that the connection of different categories with one another ensues through a further category of inherence which is defined as the connection of things occurring not separated (*ayutasiddhaḥ*) which stand in relation of the bearer and the borne with each other (*ādhāryādhārabhūtaḥ*).

This definition of inherence stood the test and was, therefore, held to firmly in future. Only on one point, it, still required clarification. It turned out to be necessary to fix more exactly, what is to be understood under separate occurrences. On a reflection of all cases coming under consideration it was seen that there is a case in which no inherence but a connection (*saṃyogaḥ*) was present in which, however, the things concerned occur, in spite of everything, not separated. Above all, there was the case in which the infinitely big substances are concerned. Between the atoms of the four elements and the space, for example, there exists no inherence but only a connection. Still, the atoms and space occur not separated, as the atoms outside space cannot be thought of. Similar is the case with the psychical organs and the souls, as soon as the souls were regarded, as was done by the classical Vaiśeṣika, as infinitely great. [In order to avoid this difficulty, the separate occurrences were defined as the possibility to move, by oneself, separated (*pṛthag-gatimattvam*). This is granted in the case of atoms vis-a-vis space, as well as in the case of psychical organs vis-a-vis the souls. Thus the connection between atoms and space, as well as that between the psychical organs and souls does not fall under the definition of Inherence but can be regarded as connection without much ado. This solution was helpful where the connection between infinitely great substances and limited substnces was dealt with. It failed when one came to define the relation of infinitely great substances with one another. Because infinitely great substances, according to the Vaiśeṣika doctrine, cannot move, movement being a change of place. There was, therefore, nothing left but to infer that the infinitely great substances could not be connected with one another through connection. As no inherence was considered possible, one was, therefore, constrained to assume that between two such substances, there can be no connection. In fact, this view also was represented and one did not fight shy of the inference that under these circumstances, the souls stand in no relation to space and time.

A second case of things which do not occur separated but between which, still, only the connection and no inherence exists is, for example, that of the body and the skin called the sense-organ of touch. Both occur not separated, still there stands between them no inherence. Here one helped himself with the explanation that there is a separate occurrence also when two things inhere in separate bearers (*yukteṣv āśrayeṣu samavāyaḥ*). It is the case of the body and the skin. Therefore, they are to be considered as separately occurring and what holds them together is the quality of connection. With this solution, one did not hit the core of the matter but it helped to explain away the shocking difficulties and one rested content therewith.

Regarding what remains regarding the exact constituent

of the Category of Inherence and its operation, the following doctrine was formulated. There is only one single permanent Inherence. This stays in all things which inhere in one another and produces the connection between them. Its own existence in the things is, on the other hand, not caused by any further inherence, but is conditioned by its own nature. This doctrine, just like the corresponding doctrine with regard to the category of commonness, arose as the necessary inference in the sense of the system. And one firmly defied all the antagonist's objections.

With the category of Inherence, a number of six categories was reached and with it the circle of the categories which found acceptance in the classical Vaiṣesika system was closed. Not that there were wanting further attempts to posit further categories. But these attempts did not prevail. Already there were not lacking differences of opinion regarding the last described categories. It is evinced especially distinctly by the doctrines of related Schools. All the stronger was, therefore, naturally the opposition against the recognition of newer categories.

The Controversial Categories—Regarding the already described categories, e.g, the famous Mīmāṃsā teacher Kumārila asserted against the Vaiśeṣika doctrine of the two categories of commonness and peculiarity that there is only one category commonness, but that this commonness is no separate entity by itself but is inseparably bound up with the separate nature of individual things. There is, on the other hand, no independent category of peculiarity nor of inherence. This doctrine, according to which, there is found united a double nature in things, which allows itself to partly appear in this, partly in that, was named as the doctrine of relativity (*syādvādaḥ*) and is found also in the Sāṃkhya system[199] and in the system of the Jaina. [200] Also the second great Mīmāṃsā teacher Prabhākara, the opponent of Kumārila, differed in this regard from the named categories of the Vaiśeṣika doctrine, though to a small extent. For him, the category of commonness is a separate entity by itself and he also holds the category of inherence as valid. But he denied the category of peculiarity and asserted that the peculiarity of things is not different from the quality of separateness which dwells in the individual permanent substances.[201]

But in the case of Prabhākara, we also find the attempt to posit further categories beyond those of the Vaiśesika. Thus we have already heard that he regarded the number not as a quality, like the Vaiśesika, but considered it as a separate category.[202] Further, he assumed, besides the category of commonness, an independent category of similarity (*sādṛśyam*) which is the cause that things appear to us as similar and we compare them with one another.[203] Both these did not win any attention among the adherents of the Vaiśeṣika and gained no further importance, otherwise. Important, on the other hand, in his attempt to formulate an independent category of force or capacity (*śaktiḥ*). With that he touched a problem which was especially of interest for the Buddhist Schools.[204] In this he does not also stand alone. Because as the acceptance of category of force in Candramati's text-book of 'ten categories' testifies, the Vaiśeṣika also occupied themselves with the problem. Candramati, indeed, in accordance with the succinctness of his work, teaches that there is a category of force or capacity which inheres in substances, qualities and movements and it is a necessary presupposition that they bring forth their effect together or in isolation and this category is placed against a second category of incapacity.[205] We seek, in vain, in it, a discussion of the questions connected therewith and of a detailed proof for positing this category. In the School of Prabhākara, on the other hand, we find an attempt to establish the assumption of the category of force or capacity.[206] In general, it was said, we could infer from every effect a force or capacity in its cause by which it was brought forth. But the fact that this force or capacity (*śaktiḥ*) is an independent one, different from the cause itself, can be deduced from the following : When a conjuror through his magical word abrogates the effect of poison or of fire, the poison or fire still continues to remain afterwards as before. The activity of the conjuror, therefore, eliminates something which releases the effects or the working but which is different from the cause itself. It can only be a force or capacity which indwells the cause. This positing of proof, however, is not considered valid by the orthodox school of the Vaiśeṣika, as it denies this category in general.[207] It was said that when following the activity of the conjuror, the effect of poison or fire stays away, it depends not on the extinction of the power or the capacity which otherwise indwells the poison or fire but on the fact that it depends on the totality of causes (*kāraṇasāmagrī*) which releases the effect and belongs to the poison or fire, and that then only a change comes in. That this totality of causes brings forth their effect, presupposes that a hindrance which would hinder their working, does not exist (*pratibandhakābhāvaḥ*). When, therefore, a conjuror interferes, this presupposition is not fulfilled, the totality of the causes is not the same and consequently, its effect cannot take place.

A further idea with which man occupied himself about the same period in a lively manner and which also led to the attempt to formulate a new category is non-existence (*abhāvaḥ*). The impulse to it was given by the theory of knowledge and formed the starting point of the question viz. how it is possible to know a non-existing thing. The view was put forward that every knowledge is caused by its object and now it was asked how non-existence can be operative as a cause. In order to answer this question, it was taught that every non-existence is only another aspect of existence. The non-existence of a pot, for example, consists in the fact that the pot is not available in that place of the ground, in which one expects to find it. Its non-existence is, therefore, to a certain extent embodied by this place of the ground, in so far as the pot is not found in it. In the same way one cannot find the non-existence of an effect in a cause, in so far as it does not contain it. In a similar way, all other cases can be interpreted on the basis of these views. Candramati, the Vaiśeṣika author, made a statement that there is a category of non-existence. He distinguished five kinds of non-existence—the earlier or former non-existence (*prāgabhāvaḥ*), non-existence through vanishing (*pradhvaṃsābhāvaḥ*), reciprocal non-existence (*anyonyābhāvaḥ*), non-existence with regard to a connection (*saṃsargābhāvaḥ*), and the complete non-existence (*atyantābhāvaḥ*).[208] Of these, the earlier or former non-existence is the non-existence of effect in the cause, the non-existence through vanishing is the non-existence of the cause in the effect. Under reciprocal non-existence is to be understood the non-existence of a horse in a cow and of a cow in a horse. Non-existence with regard to a connection is the non-existence of anything in others, so far as they are neither connected with them nor inhere in them; finally complete non-existence deals with the non-existence of horns on the head of a hare.[209]

Almost the same kinds of non-existence were recognized by the remaining representatives of the Vaiśeṣika and in the different schools of the Mīmāṃsā. But in respect of the assumption of an independent category, Candramati's view did not prevail at least in the Vaiśeṣika. We, therefore, find in the concluding presentation of the classical Vaiśeṣika system—in the *Padārtha-dharmasaṃgrahaḥ* of Praśastapāda, the category of non-existence not cited. But the question was, in no way, settled. The discussions were continued further and led to a change of views on certain points. Finally non-existence came to be enrolled as the seventh category in addition to the six categories of the classical system. But it is a development which already exceeds far beyond the period with which we are here occupied and in which later influences have cooperated. We shall, therefore, not enter into it further at this place and shall return to our proper subject viz. the origin and formulation of the doctrine of categories in the Vaiśeṣika system of the classical period.

We have already, hitherto, described how the doctrine of categories originated, i.e. how one came to distinguish categories as different forms of existence and how one gradually formulated different categories, determined their nature and delimited their spheres. The development, however, did not end therewith for a long time. As we have already pointed out during the origin of the doctrine of categories,[210] the doctrine of categories in India reached such importance, because one, with the genuine Indian profundity, thought out to the last their implications and exhausted all the possibilities of application implicit in them. It occurred in the following manner:

With the hitherto existing thoughts, the basic ideas of the doctrine of categories were already there. But one was not satisfied with that. On the other hand, a further step was taken to employ these basic ideas i.e. an attempt was made to think out through and through the old nature-philosophy and to clothe it in the form of the Categories. Thus an effort was made to create a complete system which rested on the scaffolding of the categories.

We shall now try to get acquainted with and understand that system. Because its importance is not small. It represents, in a certain measure, the test of the doctrine of categories on its possibility of application and its worth. But above all, its manner of looking at things has become standard or authoritative for a wide sphere of Indian philosophy and has remained valid up to the latest period so that we shall have also to reckon with it in our later presentation. While we recognize its historical importance from the beginning, we shall not overlook the serious disadvantage in which this development resulted. The fault lies mainly, in the fact that the Vaiśeṣika gradually got lost in an unfruitful scholasticism. We had hitherto many occasions in the course of presentation to point out this disadvantage. But at this point of development, however, it stood out prominent in all its full extent. Here, therefore, it would not be out of place to speak a few words about it and about the Indian Scholasticism in general.

The Emergence of Scholasticism—With the name Scholasticism, I characterize a form of philosophizing in Indian philosophy which does not start from a living view of things but which rests on a data, once given, of ideas and develops a system out of them. This is the essential thing. These ideas need not be given through revelation and, in their demonstration, need in no way an appeal to authority in place of logical reasoning, as it was often emphasized in European Scholasticism. Therefore, it is possible, as we shall see, for example, in the Vaiśeṣika that in India a nature-philosophy also falls into a Scholasticism.

The way it occurs is, as a rule, as follows : One seeks to employ the given ideas in a practical way, as he attempts to explain with their help the things, for the interpretation of which he is endeavouring. Thereby, different assumptions turn out as necessary. On the basis of these assumptions, an edifice of hypothesis is built up. When difficulties come up, new assumptions are seized upon. Thus arises an airy, fanciful complicated edifice of thought which, finally, has scarcely to do anything with real things. Because one seeks the confirmation of the assumption made, not through observation and experience, but on the other hand, is satisfied, if with their help, the erected hypothesis-edifice suffers no jolts or knocks and exhibits no contradictions.

I will elucidate it from some examples of the Vaiśeṣika. According to the old Nature-doctrine of the Vaiśeṣika, things are formed out of the Elements. These are characterized by qualities and their movement causes every rise and disappearance. Thereby, there appear, in abundance, many phenomena which are homogeneous with each other and also different from the heterogeneous ones. Everything is translated into the idea of the doctrine of categories. The things are built out of substances in which qualities and movements inhere and which are, besides, characterized by different commonnesses. In order to carry out these ideas lucidly or graphically the following assumptions were seized upon. The bearers of different categories, out of which things are composed are the substances. Qualities and movements inhere in them. In them no further qualities and movements could inhere. Because the inherence of qualities and movements is the essential sign of substances. Moreover, otherwise the inherence of further qualities and movements would continue endlessly. Similarly, commonnesses inhere in the substances, qualities and movements. On the other hand, no further commonnesses inhere in the commonnesses. The inherence finally is the cause by which the rest of the categories inhere in one another. But they cannot cause their own inherence.

These fundamentals were used in all individual cases and one did not hesitate from the conclusion where it seemed necessary, with a regardless or ruthless consistency, peculiar to classical Indian philosophy. We shall take, as an example, the doctrine of sound. The old nature-doctrine had assumed that the sound moves towards the ear from the place of its origin. But now that confronted difficulties. Because, it was already formulated as a basic tenet that the qualities cannot inhere in any movement i.e. they, therefore, cannot move. But according to the doctrine of the school, sound is a quality, namely, of Ether and cannot, therefore, move. How then does it reach the ear? In order to remove the difficulty the following assumption was made : The sound, it was said, disappears immediately after its rise. But simultaneously, it calls forth a new sound which again calls a new one and this propagates itself like a wave until it reaches the ear of the hearer. This theory reminds us, at the first glance of the modern idea of propagation of sound-waves. In reality, it has naturally the least to do with it. So, as it was originally meant, this idea of a series of continually originating new qualities is rather remarkable.

A similarly strange doctrine, which one comes across, is the theory of movement, though in a different way. When we assume that a body is put in motion by an impulse or a stroke and moves as long as it hits another body and comes to rest, it presents itself according to the doctrine of categories in the following way : The impact which brings the movement to a stand-still is a connection (*saṃyogaḥ*). The connection originates in both when the moving body comes in contact with the body in rest. It is caused by movement while the movement itself disappears when the connection arises. It was, therefore, taught that the effect of the movement i.e. connection abrogates its cause—the movement itself. But this assumption raised doubts. With the impact, the moving body moved a certain distance wide through space and therefore came into connection with different places of space. As we know, according to the Vaiśeṣika, every position in space depends, according to the Vaiśeṣika doctrine, on a connection of the object concerned with the substance named space. If one did not wish to abandon the previous assumption that the connection called forth through movement abrogates the movement itself, it must be also held good to apply to all these connections with space. As a matter of fact, one did not fight shy of such a conclusion. So one arrived at the doctrine that every movement in space consists of a series of movement-moments of which every one disappears again immediately, while the spring or force of the moved body calls forth the next.

This may provisionally suffice as an example in order to characterize the manner of thought which I name as Scholasticism and which came to prominence now in the Vaiśeṣika. In this way the doctrine of categories was applied to the old Nature-doctrine and was developed into a system. Indeed, it never attained to a complete system, although it gained validity for the whole sphere of old nature-doctrine. It is due to the fact that its application on a wider sphere did not bring in anything essentially new in the world-construction or the construction of the human organism. Therefore, one left, out of account, an exhaustive treatment of this sphere in the new way and rather restricted himself to the more exact handling of isolated important fundamental cases. We shall, therefore, in our presentation, reckon with and restrict ourselves to a few cases which gained an entirely new look in the light of the doctrine of categories and which are of general basic importance. They are the Theory of the Aggregates, the Causality-Theory, and the Theory of Perception.

The Theory of Aggregates—Regarding the Theory of the Aggregates, we shall distinguish between the coming about of the aggregates and their constituents ; we shall first of all deal with how the aggregates come into existence.

In the description of the atom-doctrine of the old Vaiśeṣika we have heard that according to this doctrine, the origin and disappearance of all things depends on the connection and the separation of Atoms. But that produced a difficulty into which every atomic theory, created out of theoretical considerations, gets entangled irretrievably—the difficulty to bridge over the chasm between the indivisible and endlessly small atom and the aggregates formed out of them. It must be said that this bridging over has not succeeded in the atom-doctrine. Here came in now the doctrine of categories. Because it enabled to let the problem appear in an entirely different light and to lead to the solution satisfactory at least from its point of view.

From the stand-point of the doctrine of categories, this problem was presented as follows : The Atoms and the aggregates, according to their size, distinguish themselves through the fact that they are the structures of the elements in which different sorts of the quality of extension (*parimāṇam*) inhere. As we have seen during the description of the quality of extension[211], besides the indivisible infinite smallness or roundness (*pārimāṇḍalyam*) of the atom, they also distinguished smallness (*aṇutvam*) and bigness (*mahattvam*). Of them, smallness is designated by the smallest extension, while everything beyond that is to be considered as bigness. Smallness (*aṇutvam*) was ascribed to the double atoms (*dyaṇukāni*) consisting of two atoms and bigness (*mahattvam*) to all further aggregates. In the formation of the aggregate, it was considered valid to explain how in the transition from the atom to the double atoms and greater structures, another sort of extension steps in, in place of one sort of extension.

Now, indeed, it was not possible to derive the one from the other without much ado. Because it belongs to the basic maxim of the system that in the formation of aggregates out of the qualities of their constituents, only homogeneous qualities can arise forth. That is to say, in application to our case, when out of big aggregates still greater ones are formed, the greatness of the one can arise from the greatness of the other; but neither out of roundness (*pārimāṇḍalya*) can arise smallness (*aṇutvam*) nor out of smallness can bigness be derived. In order to obviate this difficulty, the following way out was chosen. It was said that it is the number of atoms which bring forth the extension of the aggregate. When two atoms form together into double atoms, it is the number two inhering in both the atoms which brings forth the smallness (*aṇutvam*) of double atoms. When many atoms form a bigger aggregate, it is their plurality which causes the bigness (*mahattvam*). Thereby, originally greater aggregates are allowed to rise directly out of the atoms. Later on, it was taught that they are formed out of the double atoms.[212] Evidently, one wished to derive their bigness not directly out of the roundness of the atoms but wished this course of development to pass through an intermediate stage of smallness (*aṇutvam*).[213]

The formation of the aggregates is carried out in the following way : When atoms come to a conglomeration, first of all, two atoms form together double atoms. Thus, the number two indwelling the two individual atoms calls forth the extension of smallness (*aṇutvam*) in the double atoms. Three or more of such double atoms form, then, the greater aggregates whereby the number three or more inhering in them calls forth in these aggregates the extension, bigness (*mahattvam*). When further on, such aggregates form still greater unities, their bigness arises out of the bigness of these aggregates.

With this doctrine, there was given a satisfactory explanation of the origin of the aggregate in the sense or light of the system—indeed, in the sense or light of the system only. To us, this working with the idea of the doctrine of categories appears rather arbitrary. Above all, it shows distinctly the dangerous slipping off of the old Nature-philosophy from the graphic reality into the construction of a pure thought-world—a slipping off, which essentially contributed towards cutting off further development, as in the place of the living knowledge of nature, there finally stepped in the empty play of hollow scholasticism.

Not only the origin of the aggregate but also its constitution allowed or made the doctrine of categories itself to appear in an entirely new light. According to the doctrine of categories, all things represent a complex of different categories and, no doubt, they consist as such, if we restrict ourselves to the essentials of a substance, which is the bearer of different qualities and in which their qualities as well as a number of commonnesses inhere. It holds good naturally in the case of the aggregates as well as in the case of their constituents. Now it is clear that the qualities and commonnesses which occur in an aggregate are different from those which characterize their constituents. To give only a simple example, the extension (*parimāṇam*) of a cloth is different from that of the individual threads of which it is woven and the commonness-clothness (*paṭatvam*) inheres only in the whole cloth but not in the threads. With the force of logic, it follows from it that the aggregate must be something different from its constituents. This doctrine was therefore formulated and presented by the adherents of the Vaiśeṣika.

But how have we to think of such an aggregate? How is it related to its constituents? These questions were answered by the Vaiśeṣika in the following way: Through the connection (*saṃyogaḥ*) of parts (*avayavāḥ*) of which a thing is composed, there arises quite a new thing, a uniform whole (*avayavī*) different from its parts and which inheres in these parts. Out of the substance of the parts arises the substance of the whole, out of the qualities of the parts arise the qualities of the whole Thereby, as a rule, the qualities of the whole are of the same kind as the qualities of the parts but many are also different as, for example, their extension (*parimāṇam*). Also new qualities step in, for example, connection (*saṃyogaḥ*) which unites the parts to the whole. But, above all, there arise in the whole, when it originates, a number of commonnesses which inhere in it and lend it its peculiar character. This whole is, in contrast to the permanent atoms, perishable. As it originates through the connection of its parts, it also perishes together with the qualities, when these parts again separate from one another.

This is the doctrine of the whole, the most characteristic but also the most controversial doctrine of the Vaiśeṣika. Because this idea of a whole, indwelling the parts as a separate entity different from the parts, which might have been thought out consistently from the presuppositions of the system is highly remarkable. It challenged opposition and was the target of violent attack continually. From the side of the Vaiśeṣika it was tenaciously defended. This discussion continued through centuries, through the whole period of the second or a late flowering of the classical period of Indian philosophy, to which we shall have to return again in the presentation of that period.

The New Form of the Theory of Causality—With this doctrine of the whole, the whole world-picture of the Vaiśeṣika suffered an essential change. As we have already seen, for the older Vaiśeṣika an atomistic-mechanistic interpretation held good, according to which all origin and destruction is a play of the permanent and unchangeable atoms and we have shown how this grand view of the picture appears as a counterpart to the likewise sublime conception of the Sāṃkhya of the permanent changing Urmatter.[214] Now came into this world-picture a rift. It was no more the permanent atoms alone which ruled all origin and disappearance. Besides them, there emerged now the different perishable aggregates. And the origin and disappearance no more appeared as mere conglomeration and separation of atoms but as origination and disappearance of something quite new which did not exist before. It was an essentially different comprehension which had replaced the old world-picture. This new comprehension found its expression in a theory which represents the most characteristic maxim of the classical Vaiśeṣika and has been continually regarded as such. With respect to the great rival Sāṃkhya and in contrast to it, this doctrine was formulated and was given a corresponding form The adherents of the Sāṃkhya, in their doctrine of the incessant modification of the one permanent Urmatter, had seen the essential in the persistence of Urmatter itself. For them the decisive thing was that it was enduring in all change, that it was already present in all origination and disappearance, appearing continually in newer forms. The Sāṃkhya had, for all causal occurrences, formulated the doctrine that it is never something new which arises, but it is already present in this cause—the so-called *Satkāryavādaḥ*.[215] As against this, now, the representatives of the

Vaiśeṣika formulated, on the basis of their comprehension of the whole, the opposite doctrine. For them, every new arising is the origination of something completely new and they represented the theory that the effect is not present in the cause: the *asatkāryavādaḥ*.

It was not only the general picture of the causal occurrence which appeared in a new form. The causality-theory of the older Vaiśeṣika was also completely remodelled on the basis of the doctrine of categories. Indeed, with this remodelling, the system was not very happy and the result was a difficult and confused theory.

As we have earlier said,[216] the older Vaiśeṣika distinguished between the material cause (*kāraṇam* in the strict sense) and the occasioning cause (*nimittam*) and the interest held good, as in the Sāṃkhya, above all, in the case of the material cause. According to it, the material cause of all things was seen, according to the old Atomic doctrine, in the atoms out of which things are formed. The Atoms are, in consonance with this theory, according to the matter, of the same nature or essence with their products. This relation was represented quite differently on the basis of the doctrine of the whole. Because the whole is something new, quite different from the atoms. The causal connection between the Atoms and the whole must be established in a different manner from that through material identity and in consonance with the views of the doctrine of categories.

The following point of view was offered for consideration: From the point of view of matter, Atoms and the whole are likewise different from one another, according to the comprehension of the doctrine of categories, as the occasioning causes (*nimittakāraṇam*) and the things which they occasion. Still there exists an intimate relation between both—a relation which most closely connects them with one another. As we have heard, according to the doctrine of the classical Vaiśeṣika, the whole inheres in its parts. On this inherence was established the new definition of the causal relation.

Thereby, it indeed became necessary to consider the doctrine of categories to the fullest extent. That is to say, cause and effect required to be considered not simply as matter, but as substances in which different other categories inhere. It was, however, still not too difficult. In the classical Vaiśeṣika, it was decided that the last three categories—commonness, peculiarity and inherence do not share in the causal occurrence.[217] So one had practically to reckon, besides the substances, only with the qualities. Therefore, the things represented themselves now as follows: In the rise of the whole, the substance of the whole arises out of the substances of the parts, the qualities of the whole out of those of the parts. A close relation stands between both through the fact that the whole inheres in the parts. This relation connects the substances directly; therefore, the substance of the parts as a cause of the substance of the whole was named as an inhering cause (*samavāyikāraṇam*). Somewhat more difficult is the case with the qualities, because qualities cannot inhere in one another. The qualities of the whole, therefore, are not bound with the qualities of the parts through direct inherence but through the fact that both inhere in the two inhering substances. In order to express it, the qualities of the parts as cause of the qualities of the whole were named as non-inhering causes (*asamavāyikāraṇam*). This expression is, indeed, not very happily chosen. Because it is not supposed to be said that, in general, there is present no inherence. Then it would apply to the occasioning cause (*nimittakāraṇam*). On the contrary, it is only meant that there is no direct inherence and we need never lose sight of it.

So far the new Causality-Theory represents itself very simply. Only in place of the old material cause, corresponding to the distinction between substance and qualities, there have stepped in the substances, the inhering cause and the quality as the non-inhering one. But this seeming simplicity did not continue and was soon crowded out by supplementary distinctions. As soon as the things began to be thought out on more exact lines, it was discovered that the new definitions did not conform to the real relation. Above all, the limits between the different cases of causal occurrences threatened to disappear and there was the contingency of different phenomena threatening to coincide as homogeneous. That was sought to be prevented.

The doctrine was formulated that the substance of the parts, in which the substance of the newly originating whole inheres, is its inhering cause. But could not one equally well say of the qualities of the newly originated whole that the substance, in which they inhere, should be considered as its inhering cause? Because in a certain sense, every substance renders possible the origin of the qualities which inhere in it. It was decided, therefore, to affirm this view. But the qualities originate not only in the origination of the whole. Also the sound in the Ether and the qualities of the Soul arise and vanish again. Consistently, therefore, Ether and Soul must be considered valid as the inhering causes of sound and the soul-qualities. Thus the idea of the inhering cause extended its validity gradually far beyond its original sphere.

Similar was the case with the non-inhering cause. During the arising of the whole, a movement of the parts is the cause, so that these join themselves with one another, that is to say, the quality of connection (*saṃyogaḥ*) arises in them. Thereby the movement (*karma*) inheres in the same substance in which it calls forth the quality of connection without being directly connected with it through inherence. It is, therefore, clearly the non-inhering cause. Then the same must hold good for all mechanical processes which happen during movements (*karma*). When a motion makes an object rebound on another and causes a connection with it, it is the non-inhering cause of this connection. In the reverse, an impulse i.e. a connection which sets an object in motion is the non-inhering cause of this movement generated in it. The same holds good for the qualities of heaviness and fluidity when they call forth motion. Otherwise the qualities could be the non-inhering cause of other qualities, unless the origination of the whole is concerned. When a quality of the soul calls forth another, it is, according to the Vaiśeṣika, an occasioning cause (*nimittakāraṇam*). But with the bringing forth of the sound, it is already different. The connection of a stick with the drum is an occasioning cause for the origin of sound. Still the simultaneous connection of the drum with ether is a non-inhering cause. And the sound, which brings forth the next following sound, is finally the non-inhering cause.

This widening of the original sphere of validity of the inhering and non-inhering causes led to the result that the phenomena which appeared as completely heterogeneous, according to the old Nature-philosophy, now fall in the sphere of the same form of causal occurrences. Thus again there was an occasion to hit upon new distinctions which better corresponded with real relations. One of these distinctions was as follows : In the origination of the whole, a new substance arises and the newly brought forth qualities inhere in it. In all the rest of the cases, on the other hand, the substances in which the new qualities are brought forth, are already existent and as a rule, the cause inheres in the same substance as its effect. In consequence, one differentiated, among the non-inhering causes, such as generate an effect which inheres in their proper bearer (*svāśrayasamavetārambhakaḥ*) and such as bring forth their effect in another substance (*paratrārambhakaḥ*). This distinction is, in general, true ; still as an example, the second definition, in the case of the quality of effort (*prayatnaḥ*) could be included as an occasioning cause (*nimittakāraṇam*). According to a second distinction, there were qualities which produce a homogeneous effect (*samānajātīyārambhakaḥ*) as against others which produce unlike effect (*asamāna-jātīyārambhakaḥ*). The first proves true in the case of the qualities (*guṇah*) which originate in the formation of the whole, and the second in all other cases. Indeed there are also exceptions here. When a sound calls forth a second sound, it is a homogeneous effect, without having anything to do with the origination of a whole. A further distinction was, therefore, added. The qualities which go back to a quality in a cause (*kāraṇaguṇapūrvakaḥ*) are distinguished from those in which that is not the case (*akāraṇaguṇapūrvakaḥ*). These definitions are clearly calculated to distinguish the cases which are connected with the origination of the wholes from all other cases. Because under cause (*kāraṇam*), only the parts are meant—the parts which form the whole. But, thereby, further definitions and classifications were not superfluous.

All these definitions with their exceptions and special cases, in which different definitions intersected, produced a difficult and an exceedingly complicated Causality-Theory which is to be understood as having been formulated out of the attempt of the theory of categories at arranging and classifying ; still it contributed little to the explanation and better understanding of things in the spirit of the old nature-philosophy. So we may characterize, it on the whole, not as happy.

In this connection, the following, in short, should be marked. The Causality-Theory of the Vaiśeṣika not only included the origination but also the disappearance of things in its orbit of consideration. Here the doctrine of categories was taken into consideration. In that, there is, concerning the substances, an origination and disappearance only in the case of the wholes (*avayavinaḥ*) and in a whole, the destruction follows through a movement in its parts which abrogates their connection. The atoms of the elements as well as all the remaining substances are, on the other hand, permanent. More difficult are the relations in the case of the qualities. The qualities of the whole perish naturally with the perishing of the whole, their bearer. But there are also numerous qualities which are perishable in themselves. The case is entirely different with them. An important case may be mentioned that the Vaiśeṣika knew the qualities, which are destroyed through their effect. It holds good, above all, of the characteristic qualities of the soul. But also a sound which is brought forth by another sound annihilates the previous one during its origination. In the rest of the cases, to enter into details will be uninteresting. In conclusion, it may only be remarked that the movement by which the connection is caused by it is destroyed and that, as we have heard,[218] has only the duration of the twinkling of an eye.

With this, we have said what was the most important about the theory of causality of the classical Vaiśeṣika and can now go over to the next point which we wish to handle in this place, namely the remodelling of the doctrine of Perception under the influence of the doctrine of categories. Here we meet with especially incisive changes. Because through that, as the categories doctrine has placed, in place of the simple things with which the old nature-philosophy had reckoned, a complicated picture compounded of different categories, the views about the objects of Perception as also about the process of perception itself were bound to change from the very basis.

The Theory of Perception—The Theory of Perception had originally to do with the qualities of the elements which corresponded as objects to the different sense-organs. No doubt, it was then believed that the things were perceived with their qualities because the sense-organs came into contact (*saṃyogaḥ*) with them. Now one had learnt to distinguish between the qualities and the substances which are their bearers. It was, first of all, of importance for the assessment of connection between the sense-organs and the objects. Though in this case, the qualities of things are the object of perception, it was still clear that the connection of the sense-organs can ensue directly only with the objects. It was said, one sees, therefore, colour, when the eye enters into union with the substance in which the colour inheres (*saṃyuktasamavāyaḥ*). Besides, the old Nature-philosophy had recognized the large size of the things concerned and the clear-cutness of qualities as a pre-supposition for Perception.[219] It required now a change and the idea of largeness required a more precise definition. Because, according to the doctrine of categories, a large size was known as a special quality which only belongs to the aggregates which are formed out of at least three atoms. The bearer of the colour with which the eye enters into conjunction must, therefore, be an aggregate consisting of more substances. Only in the last definition—the clearcutness of qualities—the doctrine of categories did not make any change; one was satisfied to speak merely of a particular or special constitution of colour. Thus one came to the following formulation: "A colour is perceived, when it inheres in more substances and when the colour exhibits a special constitution."[220] Similarly it holds good for the qualities which form the objects of the rest of the sense-organs—i.e. for taste, smell and touch.[221] Only the sound assumes a special place. Because the sense-organ, which perceives it, viz. the ear is a part of Ether in which sound inheres; so its perception directly follows on the basis of this inherence.

In this way, the traditional doctrine of Perception attained an entirely new outlook. But the mentioned changes were unimportant in comparison with the new questions which were raised by the doctrine of categories. If a distinction was made between the substances and the qualities, the question, above all, was bound to be raised whether only the qualities are perceived, or not also the substances. Further, during the formulation of the doctrine of categories, one had, besides the old traditional qualities of the Elements which alone were considered till that time in the Theory of Perception, known a whole series of other qualities, especially the common qualities. Now it was bound to be asked : What happens in the case of the perception of these qualities ? What happens also in the case of other remaining categories : movements, peculiarity or particularity, inherence and above all the commonnesses ? All these questions pressed forth for answers; long effort and discussion were required until clarity could be created and a definite doctrine fixed up about them.

Regarding the question of the Perception of substances, the Vaiśeṣika taught that the substances could be perceived. During the sight of an object, it was believed that not merely a colour but a colourful substance was also seen, not merely redness but the red cloth. Thus there was the comprehension that the substances are perceived. It agreed with the traditional views. When one, in order to demonstrate the existence of the soul, had appealed to the fact that things were seen as well as felt, that it perceives through the two sense-organs and knows or recognizes still one and the same thing with it, the perception of things was presupposed besides the perception of qualities. But now one began to think out through the whole circle of questions more exactly. In that connection, above all, one question thrust itself in the foreground viz. whether the substances are perceived independent of qualities or whether their perception is necessarily bound up with the perception of qualities.

These questions were, first of all, answered in the sense that the substances are perceived with their qualities and that their perception presupposes the perception of the qualities. But one soon saw himself compelled thereby to distinguish between different qualities. One believed to have observed that only some qualities together with the substances are perceived, while on the other hand, others are not. Because, one had the impression that during the feeling of smell and taste merely the qualities i.e. the smell and taste concerned are perceived and that in the case of the perception of form and touch, besides the qualities, their bearers—the substances also are known. Therefore, it was taught : "The substances are visible and touchable."[222]

With that, one had decided for the view that the perception

of substances ensues though seeing and touching and presupposes the qualities of colour and touch. But at the same time, perceptibility was restricted to a small circle of substances—namely such as possess the named qualities. Besides, one point had still to be considered. The colour is not ascribed to air but only touch is ascribed to it. It was the old doctrine of the school that air was only felt but is not perceived ; however, it is only inferred from touch.[223] Therefore, the air stands separate. Therefore, according to the doctrine of the classical Vaiśeṣika, only earth, water and fire remain as perceptible substances.

For the rest, one thought of the perception of substances as similar to that of the qualities. The touch with the sense-organs follows in their case through simple connection (*saṃyogaḥ*). The presupposition for its Perception is its largeness. They must be aggregates which are formed out of more substances. Further they must possess the qualities, colour and touch in a pronounced form. It was therefore, taught—"a substance is perceived, if it is large, embraces more substances and exhibits colour in a clear-cut form."[224] The quality 'touch' is not named in this connection because according to the traditional accumulation theory, everywhere where colour is ascribed, touch also must exist. Simultaneously air which is not held to be perceptible, is on that account, shut out. Because it is said, "The air is not perceived because it is without colour."[225]

This doctrine of the perception of substances shows some isolated deviations in the related schools. The Mīmāṃsā school of Prabhākara represents the view that air is perceived. For that it was invoked that in the perception of touch, the substance which is the bearer of the quality of touch, is recognized through the temporary constitution of this touch—because the touch of fire is hot, of water cold and that of air, on the other hand, is neither hot nor cold.[226] Further it is to be mentioned that the question of the perceptibility of substances plays a great role in the dispute of the schools. The Buddhist Schools for instance denied the idea of substances and lively discussion developed itself when especially from the side of the Nyāya, the perceptibility of the substances is energetically defended. Thereby, one occasionally went so far as to assert that the substance can be perceived without qualities also. For example the Nyāya author Aviddhakarṇa says : "Also without the comprehension of colour, a comprehension of substance takes place. Because in a quite feeble light, without the colour etc. being grasped, a substance is recognized in an undefined form as cow or horse."[227] But we shall return to these discussions on a later occasion.

The next question worth while answering was the question of the perception of common qualities. As we have already seen during the description of the category of quality, the most important new creation in the formulation of this category was that man posited, besides the traditional group of the qualities of the Elements, a group of common qualities viz. the qualities, number, separateness, extension, connection, separation, distantness and nearness. In consonance with the fundamental realism of the system, these qualities were considered as real entities just like the qualities of the Elements ; one must, therefore, assume that they also like these are perceived. Now, since old times, the qualities of the elements held good as the objects of the sense-organs, whereby to every sense-organ, a quality corresponds as an object. In the common qualities, on the other hand, there could be no talk of any such connection with the sense-organ. So the question was bound to confront itself as to how their perception is to be conceived.

Here the following observation offered the starting-point : First of all, one believed to find that the common qualities are never perceived without the things i. e. the objects concerned. For example, it never occurs that the quality of extension is perceived by itself without its bearer. Further, the common qualities are not connected like the qualities of the elements with only a few substances, but they occur to all. Thereby, they are perceptible only in the visible substances. In the invisible substances, they are as little perceptible as those substances themselves. It, therefore, followed that the common qualities are perceived in the same way as the substances. The contact with the sense-organs follows, not through simple connection, but through the fact that they inhere in the substances which are conjoined to the senses (*saṃyuktasamavāyaḥ*). But they are perceived like substances through both the sense-organs of sight and touch. Their perception takes place under the same conditions, namely, when the substances, which are their bearer, show the necessary largeness of size and possess the qualities of colour and touch in a clear-cut form. It was, therefore, taught, as these views were sought to be expressed in the shortest form—"number, extension, separateness, connection, separation, distantness and nearness are visible when they inhere in the substances which possess the quality of colour". "In such as do not possess colour, they are not visible."[228]

These views, formulated, during the perception of the common qualities, allowed themselves to be used in other cases also. First it occurred in the case of the remaining qualities of the Elements: moistness, fluidity and swing. These could not be regarded as objects of particular sense-organs ; it was, therefore, taught that they also, like the common qualities, are perceived with the eye and the touch and under the same conditions. An exception was made in the case of the last quality of the Element—heaviness. With regard to it, the classical Vaiśeṣika taught that it is inferred from its effect, from the falling of a heavy object.

This gained knowledge was found useful not only for qualities but also for the category of movement. The Vaiśeṣika represented the view that movement is perceptible. But its perception is not bound with any particular sense-organ but presupposes the perception of the moved substance. Therefore a general rule, as in the case of the perception of common qualities, was formulated. By the way, the Mīmāṃsā School of Prabhākara again differed from the Vaiśeṣika in this case ; they held that movement is not perceived but only inferred out of the change of place of moved substances. But this view did not find a further dissemination and the Vaiśeṣika as well as later on the Nyāya held fast to their own doctrines.[229]

The doctrine of Perception with regard to the remaining three Categories viz. commonness, particularity and inherence shaped itself quite differently from that in the case of the first three categories. Regarding the particularities, they could remain unconsidered as they indwell only the invisible, permanent substances and are, therefore, inaccessible to usual perception. The inherence is considered in the Classical Vaiśeṣika as not perceptible on the following grounds : As we have heard,[230] it had been assumed that inherence, which connects all inhering things, does not itself inhere in these things and so no possibility was seen as to how a contact of the sense-organs with inherence can exist. In the case of the qualities, one had assumed that the contact is produced through the fact that they inhere in the substances with which the sense-organs enter into contact. In the case of inherence, on the other hand, this possibility of explanation had been cut off. So it was taught that inherence is not perceivable but is only inferred from the presence of inhering things in their bearers. Later it was assumed for inherence as well as for non-existence (*abhāvaḥ*) that there is a peculiar sort of connection (*saṃyogaḥ*). It was stated that it stands to its bearer in the relation of the defining and the defined (*viśeṣaṇaviśeṣyabhāvaḥ*) and it was taught that it becomes perceivable on the ground of this connection. But this doctrine did not win great importance.

The more important was the question of the perception of commonness. Here the things were similar as in the case of common qualities, because the view was unanimous that the commonnesses are perceptible and that their perception is conditioned by the perception of their bearer. Still some differences showed themselves. First of all, the commonnesses inhere not only in substances but also in qualities and movements. Out of that is produced a different sort of contact with the sense-organs. This depends, in such cases, on the inherence in things which, on their part, inhere in the substances which are connected with the sense-organs (*saṃyuktasamavetasamavāyaḥ*). But before all, the commonnesses are perceivable through all senses. Because they not only inhere in the substances and the qualities which are perceived through the eye and the sense of touch but also in such qualities as are the objects of smell, taste and sound ; they are also perceived through these senses.

With the perception of commonness was connected still an important question. When we consider homogeneous things, we perceive, not so much separated, the homogeneous character embodied in the commonnesses, but we recognize before all the things themselves as homogeneous. The knowledge of things is, therefore, influenced and defined by the knowledge of commonnesses. That is how the question arises.

The Vaiśeṣika answered the question as follows : The knowledge of commonnesses, which defines the character of its bearer (*viśeṣaṇam*), arises out of the knowledge of the bearer which is defined by it (*viśeṣyam*) and influences it. First the commonness is recognized and then under the influence of the commonness, one knows the bearer as homogeneous. The same holds good everywhere where it deals with a similar relation; it may be that a substance is precisely defined or delimited by another substance, by a quality or by a movement. For example, in the case of a white object, it was said—"Through the inhering whiteness and the knowledge of whiteness, arises the knowledge of whiteness. These both (knowledges) are cause and effect."[231] This doctrine was further built and formulated in particulars. That the substances appear as homogeneous is conditioned by the commonnesses which inhere in them. In the case of the commonnesses themselves, it is not possible because no further commonness could inhere in the commonnesses. It was said therefore, : "Because in the commonnesses there is no commonness present, the homogeneous knowledge arises through it alone." "In the case of substances, qualities, movements, on the other hand, it is conditioned through the commonness."[232] Similar is the case when substances are defined more precisely through substances, qualities and movements. In this case, the qualities and movements could well define or particularize the substances but they themselves can be particularized by no other qualities or movements. So it was stated : "In a substance, such a knowledge is conditioned by substances, qualities and movements." "In the case of qualities and movements, on the other hand, there is no such knowledge which would be conditioned by qualities and movements, because qualities and movements are not present in them."[233]

All these rules are thought out consistently in the spirit of the Vaiśeṣika and could appear clear and intelligible. But still there were lively discussions with regard to them. The Buddhistic opponents of the Vaiśeṣika and of their extreme realism raised the question, namely, as to how many of such perceptions arose as a matter of fact from the external world and presented, thereby, the origin and constitution of this process of knowledge in a completely new light. Thus the representatives of the Vaiśeṣika were compelled to take a new attitude to this problem and though they did not intend to abrogate their doctrine, still they wished to formulate it in accordance, at least, with the requirements of the times. The opposing objections rose predominantly from the logical schools of Buddhism. The defence of the Vaiśeṣika doctrine was for the most part led by the representatives of the Nyāya. The discussions took place in the frame of the general epistemological disputations which filled the last period of the classical time of Indian Philosophy. We shall do better, therefore, to break off here in order to return to them again in our presentation of the Epistemological Theories on the subject.

Similar is the case with the last problem of the Theory of Perception with which we have still to occupy ourselves, viz. with the perception of the Soul and its qualities. The old Nature-philosophy had scarcely occupied itself with this problem. Because, in accordance with its interest predominantly directed towards the external world, it had merely inquired into the sense-perceptions and their objects. Regarding the soul, one had merely endeavoured to prove its existence and presented the view that it is not perceptible but must only be inferred. One saw himself induced towards an exhaustive preoccupation with the inquiry into the perceivability of the soul and its qualities when he was compelled to do it by the doctrine of categories to posit the question of the perceptibility of the objects. One held fast to the view that as far as the soul is concerned, it is unperceivable. Regarding its qualities, their perceptibility was not, indeed, to be doubted. Now the question was, how this perception took place. As an answer to this question, one held now to the prototype of the remaining perceptions. In them it was assumed, according to the mechanistic basic views of the system, that perception follows through contact with the objects and with the help of the psychical organ. The psychical organ, therefore, plays, in this case, the same role as the sense-organs in external perception. It was placed, from this point of view, on the same level as the remaining sense-organs and it was expressly counted occasionally as the sixth organ. In the rest, it was assumed that the soul knows its own qualities through the contact of the psychical organ with it. It sounds, indeed, remarkable and may appear also unsatisfactory. But with the ideas developed by the doctrine of categories, any other solution was hardly possible. So one held fast to these views in the Vaiśeṣika as also in the related systems.

Though one could not decide, with respect to the qualities of the soul, to accept change of view in the doctrine of perception, it was a different case in the case of the soul itself. Not only that, even some representatives of the Vaiśeṣika and Nyāya passed over[234] the teaching of the perception of the soul. Before all, the adherents of the Mīmāṃsā represented from old times this view and showed themselves ready to build the doctrine further in accordance with the requirements of the times. The Mīmāṃsā was, from old times, closely connected with the Vedānta. Many teachers wrote works on both the systems. It can be no wonder, therefore, that the doctrine of the perception of the soul which held good in the Vedānta,[235] was also taken over by the Mīmāṃsā. It was taught that in every knowledge, the knowing subject becomes conscious of itself because one thinks 'I know'. Also the remembrance of earlier knowledge presupposes that one was conscious as the knowing subject. And through this consciousness, the soul is perceived as the knowing subject. This doctrine was further formulated in the Mīmāṃsā School of Prabhākara as follows: The logical school of the Buddhists had put forward the formulation that every knowledge follows in this way : the knowledge (*vijñānam*) which according to the Buddhistic views is the proper bearer of psychic occurrence reflects simultaneously the subject and the object and becomes conscious of itself. This idea was taken over by the School of Prabhākara and was carried over to the soul and it was taught that through becoming conscious of the subject-part of the knowledge, the soul becomes perceived.[236] In this way one had gained a finer and elaborate idea of the nature of the knowledge-process and at the same time the possibility of the perception of the soul was derived from it. However, in so doing, one leant on or took the support of the prototype of the logical school of Buddhism. With that again, the point is reached where the doctrine of knowledge of the Vaiśeṣika and related schools, so far as they attempted to adjust themselves to the process of development, fell in with the general stream of development of the knowledge-theory which filled the last period of the Indian philosophy of the classical period. We shall reserve the further treatment of this question until the presentation of that period.

With this we have finished what we had to say about the transformation of the old nature-philosophy in the sense of the doctrine of the categories and also ended our description of the rise and general development of the classical Vaiśeṣika system. We have got introduced to the old Nature-philosophy and have seen how there developed in it the doctrine of categories which made up the chief contents of the classical system. We shall, now, go over to represent this system in its final form, in which it was finally confirmed in writing.

The Final Formulation of the Vaiśeṣika—The development of the Vaiśeṣika, as we have described it, embraces a great period. Its beginnings fall far back in the pre-Christian times, while the last described position is supposed to have been reached about the beginning of the fifth century A.D. The development also found its literary expression during this period. As it was customary in the older times,[237] the doctrines of the School were early put down in a collection of aphorisms which stamped the memory and were continued orally with explanations and elucidations from generation to generation. The aphorisms took part in the changes of the doctrine. As the further formulation of the doctrine required, they were remodelled and supplemented by supplements. Thus they gradually gained a very variegated look. The old stood beside the new and as the arrangement of the new often created difficulties, its construction became continually badly arranged. The result of all these changes was finally unsatisfactory. Through the introduction of the doctrine of categories, the system had undergone a transformation which gave it another form basically. In order to justify it, the remodelling of old aphorisms was not enough. The new wine could not be filled in old hoses. Thus finally there came a moment in which it broke them. That occurred about the turn of the fifth to the sixth century.

The man who took the decisive step and, as the first one, carried out the changes, which had become necessary, unhesitatingly and consistently was Candramati (between 450 and 550 A D.). The doctrine of categories had gradually become the essential contents of the system. He made it, therefore, the exclusive subject of his treatise. Already he brought it to expression in the name of his work, because he named it "a text-book of ten categories" (*Daśapadārthaśāstram*). In particular he placed, at the head of his work, the enumeration of categories. He, then, gave a short explanation and joined it with a somewhat detailed treatment of their constituents and their qualities.

This procedure of Candramati corresponded to the condition of development and to the requirements of the period so that it was bound to have a necessary result. Still many doubts soon arose. Candramati had been too gruff and had, in a certain measure, thrown out the baby with the bath. In order to help the doctrine of categories towards its rightful position, he had thrown everything else overboard. He had abandoned the whole old inheritance of nature-philosophy. It occurred thus: It is only natural that a bold innovator who shapes newly the whole structure of a system from the bottom, does not shrink from changes. That was the case, in fact, with Candramati. He not only changed the form but also the content of the system. He received new categories into the system and added four more to the old six. That was bound to arouse opposition in orthodox circles of the School and therefore a setback did not fail to appear. Thus it transpired that it was not Candramati who gave the final form to the classical Vaiśeṣika system but another, Praśastapāda (presumably second half of the sixth century A.D.).

The Work of Praśastapāda: The performance of Praśastapāda may be characterized, in its essentials, as follows: He has taken over the decisive innovation of Candramati because he had made the doctrine of categories as the basis of his treatise and he expresses it in the title of his work which is named as the summarization of the qualities of Categories (*Padārthadharmasaṃgrahaḥ*). But as against Candramati, he has reiterated the orthodox doctrines of the School. He has received in his work everything which appeared worth preserving from the old tradition and which could be inserted in the frame of the doctrine of categories. His treatise restricts itself, therefore, to the old traditional six categories. But in this frame, he has inserted all essentials from the old nature-philosophy. He, thereby, continually emphasises the orthodox character of his treatise, as he demonstrates his agreement with the old tradition, with continual cross-references to the old aphorisms (*sūtrāṇi*).

The work of Praśastapāda is one of the entirely great

performances of the Indian philosophical systematics. The whole content of a great philosophical system is summarized in it with very great clarity and in a very concise form. In spite of it, it does not show the perfection which characterizes, for instance, the Sāṃkhyakārikā of Īśvarakṛṣṇa.[238] It is partially due to the fact that the whole stuff is arranged under the ideas of the doctrine of categories and is executed in the frame of ontology. In this way, we get, in a certain measure, the building-stone of the system but not the erected edifice of doctrine erected out of that. The polemic attitude is found in Praśastapāda from the beginning as a reaction against Candramati. It follows from it that some difficult or controversial points are handled with annoying prolixity. But the work is mostly damaged by the fact that in it the Scholastics begin already to degenerate. And as the constitution of the work and its impression on the reader is determined essentially by these things, it would be advisable to go into it more closely.

The degeneration of the Scholastics—In a previous section of our treatise, we have already described how Scholasticism came into the Vaiśeṣika and how that manner of thought gradually penetrated the whole system. Thereby we have seen its character in the fact that an edifice of hypothesis was erected under the presuppositions of definite assumptions and on the basis of given ideas without living contact with the phenomenal world. A characteristic feature of the Indian Scholasticism consists (as we have already seen) in the fact that a test for the rightness of a made assumption holds good when with its help an erected edifice of hypothesis exhibits no contradiction and if it makes possible the clarification of any isolated or individual case. With it was the door opened to degeneration. The opponent tried with all zest to discover cases in which the formulated hypothesis confronted difficulties, while one himself got more and more involved in puzzling out special cases in order to triumphantly show how his own theory was preserved in spite of difficulties. Thus one lost himself continually more and more in subtle sophistry and hair-splitting which have hardly anything to do with genuine philosophy and an honest attempt for understanding the world of phenomena. Finally, in the case of unfamiliar objects, this whole drive found entrance in the superficial systematics so popular in India, which concerns itself with purely mechanical view-points of classification and distinguishes sub-varieties in which the nature of the phenomena is not, in the least, touched.

I shall elucidate this kind of Scholasticism as it occurs in Praśastapāda, in short, through some examples. As we have seen in the course of our presentation, the Vaiśeṣika, in the process of development, had come to assume in the case of different things that they only last for a moment ; e.g. the different knowledge-processes or the category of movement. That was bound to be considered, when it came to explaining an occurrence in its causal connections. Now thereby, there arose many difficulties. It turned out that, in many cases in the assumed momentariness, some factors of some single cause must have already vanished before even its effect turned up. It was, therefore, necessary to find a way out of this difficulty. One of such cases concerns the quality, 'number'. We shall take as an example the number two or twoness (*dvitvam*).[239] As we have already heard,[240] when two things are recognized as duality under the influence of the observing knowledge (*apekṣābuddhiḥ*) of an observer who observes both things, the number two, according to the Vaiśeṣika doctrine, arises out the number one inhering in them, whereupon he knows them as two. With the vanishing of the observing knowledge, the number two also vanishes again. But the observing knowledge vanishes already with the emergence of the knowledge of duality, as according to the theory of the school, two knowledges can never stand beside one another, but every new knowledge crowds out the earlier one. The duality, therefore, lasts only for quite a short time.

Now the following is to be further considered. In the doctrine of the perception of categories, we have heard[241] that the knowledge of a substance characterized by a quality requires that one knows this quality beforehand and as this gains its character through the commonness indwelling in it, one must first know the commonness before the quality. For the described knowledge of duality, the following is the knowledge-sequence. The observer first knows, in the two objects which he observes, the commonness number one, then he knows the quality of number one and finally he knows the objects themselves as each one. Thereupon arises on the basis of this observing knowledge, in both the objects, the quality of duality in which naturally the commonness of twoness inheres. And now he again knows first the commonness of twoness, then the quality of duality and finally he knows both the objects themselves as two. But as every one of these knowledges destroys the foregoing, naturally in the last moment, in which one knows both objects as two, the observing knowledge and with it the quality of duality has already vanished since long; that is to say, that one knows the objects as two in a moment in which the duality is no more in them.

In order to avoid this attack the following theory was formulated. It was said, between two moments of knowledge, there is an antithesis (*virodhaḥ*) on account of which they crowd out each other. This antithesis, however, is not of that kind that it cannot stand near each other (*sahānavasthānavirodhaḥ*), so that one knowledge perishes and another steps in its place. On the other hand, it consists therein that one knowledge destroys the other (*vadhyaghātakavirodhaḥ*). That is to say, when a new knowledge arises, it does not enter simply in the place of the previous one but it first steps beside it, whereby destroying it, influences it. Only in the next moment is the older knowledge destroyed and the new one steps in its place. Thus in the case of knowledge-processes and of quickly vanishing things, many moments of existence were distinguished. They were three: The first is the moment of origination (*utpadyamānatā*), the second the moment of the originated or the existent (*utpādaḥ*) and the third the moment of destruction (*vinaśyatā*) on which only the full destruction (*vināśaḥ*) follows. In the knowledges following one another, the moments follow one another thus: The moment of the origination of one knowledge comes in during the existence of the previous knowledge. The moment of its existence occurs together with the moment of the disappearance of the previous one and with the moment of the origin of the following knowledge. In the moment of its disappearance, finally, the following knowledge is already existent and the next following in origination, whereas the previous one now finally perishes and is destroyed.

This theory makes it possible to solve the above-mentioned difficulty with regard to thek nowledge of duality thus : On the origination of duality, there follows the knowledge of commonness of dualness. With it the previous observing knowledge enters into the condition of disappearance, and also the following knowledge of the quality of duality is originated and the knowledge of the commonness of twoness enters into the condition of disappearance. In the same moment, the observing knowledge disappears and the duality called forth through it begins to distherefrom disappear. But simultaneously also the knowledge of two objects is already in origination. And when, therefore, also in the next moment, in which this knowledge enters into existence fully, the duality itself has gone into the past, the processes are so connected with one another that the causal connection is preserved.

This Theory shows well enough how artificially Praśastapāda erected the edifice of his hypothesis. In the present case, it can be said that it deals with an important phenomenon in the succession and causal interlacing of knowledge-processes which had to be explained and the theory presented offered an artificial but an intelligible and satisfactory explanation. This manner of explaining the knowledge-processes is found not only in Praśastapāda but also was seized upon and employed otherwise and we shall again meet with it later in the presentation of Epistemology and Logic.[242] On the other hand, a pure play with airy hypothesis occurs in the following case :

For the large number of qualities which dwell in substances, the general rule holds good that those in eternal substances are eternal and those in aggregates are transient and that they vanish with the disintegration of the aggregate. Besides there are a few qualities (*guṇāḥ*) which are themselves transient.

In the more precise thinking out of all possibilities, it was discovered that these also, when they stick to aggregates, can become destroyed by the dissolution of the aggregate and it is the case when the dissolution of the aggregate sets in, before the causes, which usually cause destruction, can become operative. Naturally these deal with some sporadic special cases which are practically of no importance. But Praśastapāda goes into them precisely and discusses every quality coming into consideration as to how it occurs.

Let us take the example, again, of the case of number.[243] The disintegration of the aggregate follows, according to the doctrine of the categories of the Vaiśeṣika, as follows : First a movement originates in the parts of the aggregate. This movement calls forth the quality of separation. The separation abrogates as its opposite the quality of connection which has united the parts into an aggregate. With the vanishing of connection, the aggregate falls to pieces. For the case of the destruction of duality Praśastapāda puts forth the following consideration : When in the moment in which one knows the number one in both the observed things, a movement sets in their parts, which is suitable to call forth the disintegration of things; simultaneously arises, with the observing knowledge, a quality of separation in them. Simultaneously with the rise of duality, there follows the abrogation of the quality of connection. And in the same moment in which the knowledge of duality arises, abrogating the observing knowledge and thus leading, in the usual course of things, to the disappearance of duality, both the things already dissolve themselves and with them vanishes the quality of duality dwelling in them. And this occurs, before the destruction of the observing knowledge can be operative.

Praśastapāda puts forth a whole series of possibilities in the case of the qualities of distantness and nearness.[244] These originate through the connection of things with the substances—space and time and through the observing knowledge of an observer. Their destruction can ensue as well through the disappearance of the observing knowledge as also through the abrogation of connection, to which as a third factor there also is the disintegration of things themselves. Praśastapāda reckons quite exactly in which cases their destruction results, through one, two, or finally through all the three causes together and puts forth in all seven cases which he describes in details.

That is enough to give a sufficient picture of the luxuriance of Scholasticism in Praśastapāda and we shall let the matter rest there. But it is now clear that the handling of all these special cases with the prolixity corresponding to their complicatedness disturbs the symmetry of the presentation in the work and the clear, concise recital of the system is disturbingly interrupted. Through these subtle discussions and the occasionally casually mentioned polemic, an imbalance is created. Thus it is partly a clear and concise handbook of the Vaiśeṣika and partly a collection of the discussion of difficult special cases.

In spite of all this, the greatness of the performance need

not be overlooked. The work of Praśastapāda is still the concluding presentation of the classical Vaiśeṣika which summarizes all things hitherto contained in it with unusual completeness and clarity. From the point of content, it adds little new.[245] It is well ascribed to him that he has given the system, at least outwardly, the form of a doctrine of Deliverance. Still it is only an external addition and does not go deeper. Further, it is characteristic of him to draw in occasionally the god-idea. But it also restricts itself to unimportant particulars. Both things do not represent a special advance of Praśastapāda but they are striking as features in the course of general development. His importance depends not on the creation of new path-breaking thoughts but on his surpassing performance as a systematizer.

The validity of his work in the after-times corresponds to the greatness of his performance. His *Padārthadharmasaṃgrahaḥ* has always remained the authoritative representation of the classical Vaiśeṣika system and the whole later development is grounded on it. The old *sūtras* have been besides preserved. That bestowed the reverence on the texts which were considered as the revelation of a holy seer. Later, they have been preferred in a renewed way and commented on. But practically now, as before, Praśastapāda has remained the basis.

Under these circumstances, it is self-evident that the short summary which we shall present of the classical Vaiśeṣika must be based on the work of Praśastapāda. I betake myself to this procedure more closely than in other cases, on account of the following reasons: His presentation offers, as I have already said, only the building-stone of the system, not the fully executed edifice of the system. But it is this form in which it stands before our eyes in later times. Whenever, in the course of our narration, we have to refer to the classical Vaiśeṣika for the comprehension of later development, we must presuppose this form. Therefore we are entitled—and rightly—to state it in this form. In particular, I would like to observe that I only recite the comprehensive systematic presentation of Praśastapāda. For the special cases, which have been described above sufficiently and are philosophically of no great interest, I satisfy myself with a short narration.

With this, everything which is necessary has been said

about Praśastapāda and his work and we can now pass on to the presentation of the classical Vaiśeṣika system in the form created by him.[246]

The Six Categories—The orthodox Vaiśeṣika system as represented by Praśastapāda knows six categories (*padārthāḥ*) : substance, quality, movement, commonness, particularity and inherence.[247] To all these categories three characteristics are common—the existence (*astitvam*), knowability (*jñeyatvam*) and nameability (*abhidheyatvam*).[248]

The essential thing about the categories lies in the fact that they do not deal with independent entities but with different forms of existence which are only possible in connection with one another and which form in their union the things of the phenomenal world. Thus substances represent the bearer (*āśrayaḥ*). The remaining categories cling to the substances (*āśritatvam*). This clinging has the form of Inherence (*samavāyitvam*), taken as a category of inherence itself which binds the remaining categories with one another but not itself. For the rest the following rules hold good for the union of the categories in the things. Qualities and movements inhere in substances but neither in themselves i.e. in other qualities and movements, nor in the remaining categories. In a similar way, commonnesses inhere in the substances, qualities and movements but neither in themselves nor in particularities and inherence. Therefore the existence of these last three categories depends, not as in the case of the first three categories, on the connection with the commonness of existence (*sattāsambandhaḥ*) but merely on the existence of its essence (*svātmasattvam*). So also they are not characterized by an inhering commonness but only by the knowledge which they call forth (*buddhilakṣaṇatvam*).

It is further important that every causal occurrence restricts itself to the first three categories—also the moral action which determines the course of the cycle of births. Thus all the three with the exception of some qualities (*guṇāḥ*) are the cause (*kāraṇatvam*). The substances as aggregate, the large part of the qualities and movements are, besides, the effect (*kāryatvam*) and as such impermanent (*anityatvam*). The last three categories are neither cause nor effect and are, therefore, permanent.

As regards the individual categories[249], there are nine substances : earth, water, fire, air, ether, time, space, soul, and the psychical organ. They are all characterized by the genus of substances (*dravyatvam*) which occurs to them all. For their essence as substances, the decisive thing is that they are the bearers of the remaining categories, which inhere in them. There are seen in individual cases, indeed, many differences due to different causes. First of all, the entities out of which the old Nature-philosophy built its world-picture take a special place viz. the Elements and the Souls; among them again, the elements form a close group. Then the constitution of the several substances makes itself valid. It is suggestive of the difference whether a substance is represented by only one entity like ether, space and time or by many (a multiplicity). Further it is important whether substances are limited (*mūrtaḥ*) or unlimited (*amūrtaḥ*). The first holds good for the four traditional Elements and the psychical organ which have the atom-form and are infinitely small. The second holds good for ether, space, time and the souls which are infinitely great (*paramamahattvam*). The infinitely great is to be understood in the sense that they are all-penetrating (*sarvagatatvam*), or as it was more exactly determined by way of supplement that they assume the same place with all things with which they come into contact. (*sarvasaṃyogisamānadeśitvam*) Among the substances the aggregates take a special place ; they are distinguished from the simple substances by the fact that they inhere in other substances—their causes and that they are impermanent.

The different classification of the categories which inhere in the individual substances corresponds to this different constitution. Qualities inhere in all substances. But the substances which are taken over from the old Nature-philosophy possess special qualities which only occur in them (*vaiśeṣikaguṇāḥ*), while, above all, time and space possess only common qualities. In particular it may be marked that a particular situation in place and time i.e. the qualities of distantness and nearness are possible only in limited substances, so also the swing (*vegaḥ*) which is compulsorily connected with movement. Movements can also inhere in limited substances only. Because, according to the Vaiśeṣika doctrine, the infinitely great substances are partless and offer no resistance to other things. Therefore they are incapable of movement. Further, concerning the commonnesses, it is to be noticed that a genus which determines the entity can inhere only in such substances as are represented by a multiplicity. Because it is the nature of commonness that it must be common to more things. The last particularities finally inhere in all substances with the exception of the aggregate.

The causality of the substances embraces the bringing forth of substances and of qualities and movements. The first case deals with the rise of the aggregates out of the atoms of the four traditional Elements. The second case deals with the rise of the qualities and movements in any substances. In both cases, the substances are the inhering cause and bring forth the effect by themselves (*svātmani ārambhakatvam*). A further thing is to be mentioned. In the causality of qualities and movements, there is often an opposition between cause and effect so that the effect abrogates and annihilates the cause ; sporadically the cause also abrogates and annihilates the effect. Among the substances there is no such opposition between cause and effect (*kāryakāraṇavirodhitvam*). An annihilation of the cause through the effect does not occur in them.

Regarding the individual substances, the earth is characterized by the fact that the genus 'earthness' (*pṛthivitvam*) inheres in it.[250] It possesses the following qualities : the four qualities of the old Elements: form, taste, smell and touch. Further, there are the seven common qualities : number, extension, separateness, connection, separation, distantness and nearness. Besides, there are also heaviness, fluidity and preparedness or disposition (*saṃskāraḥ*) under which swing (*vegaḥ*) and elasticity are to be understood. Of the four old traditional qualities the smell is exclusively peculiar to the earth. As regards the sub-varieties of these qualities, as far as the earth is concerned the form embraces all sorts of colour—white etc. The taste is represented by all six kinds. The smell appears in both forms : sweet-smelling and obnoxious. Finally, the touch is, by nature, neither hot nor cold but can be changed by heat.

The earth has two phenomenal forms.[251] It is permanent and impermanent. It is permanent in the form of atoms. It is impermanent as effect, that is, as an aggregate.

As aggregate, it is divided three-fold in the construction of the world of phenomena : the bodies of creatures, the sense-organs and the objects. The bodies of creatures are of two sorts : born out of the mother's womb and not so born. Among the latter are the bodies of gods and of many holy seers of ancient times who are born directly out of the Earth-atoms on the ground of their special merit (*dharmaḥ*). Also the bodies of the smallest living creatures, which expiate their special guilt (*adharmaḥ*) in this existence, are also formed directly out of the Earth-atoms. The bodies which are formed from the mother's womb originate from the union of the father's semen and the mother's menstrual blood.They can be born out of foetus (*jarāyu*). Out of foetus are born men and domestic and wild animals. Out of egg are born birds and reptiles. In the formation of the sense-organ, the earth has its share in that the sense of smell is formed out of it. This organ, which exists in all creatures and renders possible the perception of smell, preponderatingly consists of the earth-particles with which in a small measure other elements are also mixed. As objects, the earth embraces, in three ways, the earth in its strict sense, the stones and the plant-world. The earth in the strict sense includes all that is born of clay—walls, tiles, etc. Among the stones are rocks, precious stones, diamonds, etc. In the plant-world are counted grass, herbs, trees and creepers, tendrils, etc.

The water (*āpaḥ*) is characterized by the genus 'waterness' (*aptvam*).[252] It possesses the following qualities—the old qualities of the elements: form, taste and touch to which fluidity and moistness are added. The seven common qualities : number, extension, separateness, connection, separation, distantness and nearness ; further there are also heaviness and preparedness or disposition (*saṃskāraḥ*). Regarding the sub-varieties of the qualities of this Element, the colour of water is white, the taste is sweet and the touch is cold. Moistness and natural(*sāṃsiddhikaḥ*) fluidity are a special peculiarity of the water.

The water has two phenomenal forms, so far as it is permanent and impermanent, permanent in atoms and impermanent in aggregates. As aggregate, it appears in bodies, sense-organs and objects. Bodies which are formed of water are in the world of the water-God Varuṇa; these are born not out of the mother's womb and are strengthened by earth-particles which make it capable of life. The sense-organ formed out of water is the taste.

It occurs in all living creatures, renders possible the perception of taste and contains parts of the other elements mixed in a small measure. As object, the water appears in rivers, oceans, snow hail, etc.

The fire (*tejaḥ*)[253] is characterized by the genus fireness. It has the following qualities : the old elementary qualities of form and touch, also the seven common qualities : number, extension, separateness, connection, separation, distantness and nearness; besides there are fluidity and preparedness or disposition (*saṃskāraḥ*). Its colour is white and bright and the touch is hot.

Also in fire, there are to be distinguished two forms of appearance; permanent as it appears in atoms and impermanent as it appears in aggregates. As aggregates it appears in bodies, sense-organs and objects. The bodies formed out of fire are in the world of the Sun. They are not produced from the mother's womb; they are capable of life through the mixing of earth-particles. The sense-organ formed out of fire is the eye. It occurs in all creatures and makes possible the perception of form and contains, in a small measure, a mixture of the remaining elements. As objects the fire appears in four forms. The earthly fire, which is contained in the fuel, flames upwards and brings about cooking, burning, perspiring and the like. As heavenly fire to which water serves as fuel, it is in the sun and lightening and similar things. As fire in the abdomen, it digests the eaten nutrition and changes it in the sap of nutrition. Finally as fire, which is found in the mines, by which are to be understood metals such as gold.

The air (*vāyuḥ*)[254] is characterized by the genus airness. To it belongs the old elemental quality touch. Further it possesses the seven common qualities : number, extension, separateness, connection, separation, distantness and nearness and, besides them, preparedness(*saṃskāraḥ*). The touch of air is neither warm nor cold and is not changed by fire.

Air appears like the other elements in two forms: parmanent in atoms and impermanent in aggregates. As aggregates it appears in sense-organs, objects and, besides, in breath; bodies in the world of wind (*vāyuḥ*) are not formed from the mother's womb. It also holds good in their case that they are not born from the mother's womb and they are capable of living through the mixture of earth-particles. The sense-organ made out of air is the organ of touch, namely skin. It occurs in all living creatures, makes possible the perception of touch, contains a mixture of other elements and extends itself over the whole body. As object, air is the bearer of touch which is perceived. It itself is not perceptible but is inferred from the touch and from the sounds which it causes such as the rustling of the leaves and from the fact that it carries or moves the objects. It moves naturally horizontally and is able to drive and carry the clouds. The multiplicity of air, though it is not perceptible, can be inferred out of the mixture of different air-currents. When two opposite air-currents, which have the same velocity, meet and hit each other, they meet and move themselves now upwards, as can be known from the movement of the blades of grass etc. Finally as Breath, the Air in the body causes the movement of basic elements (*dhātavaḥ*) of the food juice and of urine and excreta. The Breath is according to its nature a unity but is named by different names on the basis of its different functions.

Out of the four Elements which all consist of atoms, the world is built; the permanent atoms, during world creation, bind themselves to form worlds and creatures; during the world-destructions, on the other hand, they separate. The process happens thus:[255] When the world has continued for a hundred years of Brahmā and a moment has arrived for the dissolution of the present Brahmā, the highest God (*Maheśvaraḥ*) resolves to destroy the world in order to give a pause of rest to the creatures which are exhausted through the long wandering in metempsychosis. Therefore, the Invisible(*adṛṣṭam*) which clings to the souls and represents the driving power of world-recurrence, suspends its work. Now there originates, according to the will of the highest God, a movement (*karma*) in the atoms through the connection of the souls with the atoms, which form the body and the sense-organs; out of the movement arises separation (*vibhāgaḥ*), and the separation abrogates the connection (*saṃyogaḥ*) between them: Through that the bodies and the sense-organs disintegrate and dissolve themselves in the atoms. In a similar way, the Elements also disintegrate. First, the earth, then water, then fire and finally the air, until finally the whole world is dissolved in isolated atoms. This condition lasts for a hundred years of Brahmā. Then the highest God resolves upon a new creation. The 'invisible', which clings to the soul, begins to operate anew. Under its influence through the connection of the souls with the atoms, there, first of all, originates a movement in the atoms of air. They join to form aggregates and create the air which, roaring, fills the space. Next originates, in the same way, water which heaves as a mighty ocean. In it, the earth conglomerates itself. Last of all, there arises, from the ocean, fire as a mighty mass of heat. Now again once more the highest God intervenes. Out of his mere will, the world-egg (*brahmāṇḍam*) forms itself out of the atoms of fire and earth. In it, he creates the first Father of the whole world—the four-headed God Brahmā, together with all the worlds and charges him with the creation of beings. This Brahmā possesses, in the highest measure, knowledge, passionlessness and creative power and knows exactly the merit and guilt of all creatures. He begets, first of all, his spiritual sons—the Prajāpatis—the lords of the created beings. Then he allows out of his mouth, arms, thighs and feet the rise of four castes or classes and finally creates the rest of the creation according to their actions.

On the rise of the four elements, follow next the substances.—Ether, Time and Space.[256] They all occur each as one. Therefore, there is no genus which inheres in them and would characterize them. The names, which man gives them, depend not, as is the general rule, on an inhering commonness but are purely conventional (*pāribhāṣikaḥ*).

Concerning, first of all, the ether[257], a substance of this name is not perceived. It is inferred, on the contrary, only as a bearer of sound, which as quality needs necessarily a substance as bearer. The sound is perceptible like the qualities of the old elements—like form, taste, smell and touch but is different from them in other essential features. The qualities of the old Elements are perceivable only in Aggregates in which they arise out of the qualities of their parts; they last as long as their bearers and are perceived in their bearers. All this does not apply to sound. It cannot, therefore, be like any one quality of the four Elements. It can as little or not be a quality of the soul, as in contrast to the qualities of the soul, it is perceived by an external organ ; it is perceived not only by one's own but also by other souls ; it does not inhere in the soul and is besides comprehended as different from the 'I' consciousness, as something different from the soul. Finally it cannot be a quality of Time, Space or the psychical organ, as it is perceived through the ear, and is a special quality, that is to say, characteristic of that one substance (*vaiśeṣikaguṇah*), whereas, only general qualities occur in time, space and the psychical organ. Nothing, therefore, remains but to assume a peculiar substance of the kind of ether as its bearer and this substance is the ether.

This proof for the existence of ether shows its peculiar intermediate place between the four Elements and the remaining substances. The qualities, which occur in it, show the same. Besides the sound, the five general qualities are ascribed to it : number, extension, separateness, connection and separation. Distantness and nearness are missing, as it is infinitely big and is permanent; a position in Space and Time is not considered, Of these qualities, number occurs in the ether as one (*ekatvam*) and correspondingly, as, in contrast to the numberless atoms, of which the four Elements consist, it is one unity',[258] a separateness, an individual unity (*ekapṛthaktvam*). As regards extension, it is, as compared to the other elements, infinitely large because sound can be perceived everywhere. Also connection and separation in ether are somewhat different from those in the atoms of the four Elements. They are ascribed to it only because, according to the logic of the system, the connection or separation of things which beget the sound must be accompanied by the connection with or separation from the ether; because only then a quality in the ether can be called forth.

In contrast to the four Elements, ether has further only one form of appearance. It is exclusively permanent. Because, it is infinitely large and does not consist of atoms, it can form no aggregate. On the same ground, there are no bodies formed out of ether. Only one sense-organ consists of ether and it is the Ear. But this is only a part of the infinite Ether enclosed by the ear-passage. It occurs in all living creatures and renders possible the perception of sound. That a part of Ether enclosed by the ear-passage is capable of perception depends on the influence of the 'invisible' (*adṛṣṭam*) on merit and guilt. A denial of the organ in the condition of deafness cannot be caused by a damage to the same which is impossible in the case of the permanent ether but has its cause in the absence of the influence of the Invisible.

The time (*kālaḥ*) [259] is inferred out of the ideas of temporal distantness, nearness, the simultaneousness and the non-simultaneousness, slowness and quickness. When these ideas arise in connection with objects which were earlier known without them, there must be a further cause joining with it, which does not lie in the essence of the object concerned; this cause is time. The time is further the cause of origination, duration and destruction of all causally originated things. It is due to the fact that they are brought into connection with time because one speaks of the origination, duration and destruction. Besides, on it depends the assumption of different time-units from a moment to the longest world-period.

As qualities (*guṇāḥ*), five common qualities occur to time: number, extension, separateness, connection and separation. The number which inheres in it is the number one—the signs from which time is inferred are always the same and, therefore, the same can be inferred. Accordingly, separateness also occurs in time as a single thing. It is infinitely great because the signs of time are perceived everywhere. Connection and separation occur in it, because through the connection with time in the things, the qualities of distantness and nearness arise.

The time is permanent, because it has not arisen out of any cause. In spite of the fact that there is only one time, one speaks of a time of beginning, of action, of origin, of continuing, of disappearance, as if one dealt with a plurality of time. But this impression is caused on account of the connection with the additional particulars just as a crystal, according to the things which lie near it, appears now blue, now red, now green, or as a man according to his activity is called now as a cook, now as a reader, as if different persons were dealt with.

The space (*dik*)[260] is similarly explained as Time. It is inferred out of the ideas of Eastern, Western, etc. When in connection with a limited object confronting another limited object, the ideas arise: "That is, seen from that point, eastern, southern, western, northern, south-eastern, south-western, north-western, north-eastern, below and above," these ten ideas must have a special cause because the causes which otherwise cause the ideas of the objects concerned are not sufficient for their clarification. Thus the special cause is the space.

The space possesses the five common qualities: number, extension, separateness, connection and separation. The number is one, the extension is infinite bigness and separateness is the separateness as a solitary thing. The reasons for these correspond to those proofs of the qualities in the case of time. Concerning the connection and separation, these are ascribed to space because the spatial layout of things, that is to say, the qualities distantness and nearness. indwelling in them, are conditioned by the connection with space.

In reality space is a unity or one. Still, the holy seers of antiquity, when they firmly formulated the usual linguistic usage, have created from practical grounds the names south, etc. for the regions of space with which the sun, in its cyclic round around the divine mountain Meru, serially enters into conjunction and which are protected by different godheads as the guardians of the world. Therefore one speaks metaphorically of ten spaces or quarters (*diśaḥ*).[261] These quarters according to their guardian deities are called the quarters of Indra, Vaiśvānara, Yama, Nirṛti, Varuṇa, Vāyu, Kubera, Īśāna, Brahmā and of the serpent-gods—the Nāgas.

The soul[262] is characterized by the genus soulness (*ātmatvam*). According to the Vaiśeṣika doctrine, it is not perceivable on account of its subtleness (*saukṣmyam*) but must be inferred. For its existence, numerous proofs are brought forth. Partially they are the old proofs of the Nature-philosophical schools with which we have been already acquainted.[263] The soul was inferred as the cause of various life-forces, as the director of the body, and as the doer who uses the sense-organs as instruments. But partially also, the ideas of the doctrine of categoies were also used because the soul was inferred as the bearer of its qualities. Above all, one got the support from the spirituality of the soul, that is, from the quality of knowledge (*buddhiḥ*). It was said that this intelligence or spirituality cannot cling to the body, because, like a pot, it is only a product of the unspiritual or unintelligent elements and because in the dead body, the intelligence or spirit is missing. It cannot occur in the sense-organs, because they are mere instruments and because one, during injury to these organs and during the absence of an object, still observes that remembrances occur and therefore, spirituality or intelligence further continues. To the psychical organ also the spirituality or intelligence cannot be attributed because the psychical organ (*manaḥ*) is inferred from the fact that it is a mediating organ,. that, on account of it, the knowledge-processes cannot emerge at the same time.[264] If the psychical organ were to be itself a bearer of knowledge or spirituality, its mediating role would fall away and the result would be the simultaneity of knowledge-processes. Besides, the psychical organ as organ is only an instrument. Under the same circumstances, there is no other go but to assume an independent substance as the bearer of knowledge or spirituality and this substance is the soul. In a similar way, the existence of the soul was inferred from its remaining qualities, pleasure, pain, desire, aversion and effort. These could neither be the qualities of the body nor of the sense-organs, because they cannot be referred to the 'I'. Besides, the body and the sense-organs are formed out of the Elements. The qualities of the Elements extend over their whole bearer, continue as long as the bearer continues and are perceived through the external sense-organs. All these do not apply to the qualities of the soul, named above. They must, therefore, have another substance as the bearer, and that is the soul.

Regarding the constitution of the soul, it possesses the following qualities : The qualities, characteristic of it, are knowledge, pleasure, pain, desire, aversion and effort where-to also are added merit and guilt and memory-impressions. Further it also has the general qualities of number, extension, separateness, connection and separation. Its number is a multiplicity. The corresponding multiplicity holds good for separateness. Its extension is infinite greatness. Connection and separation occur to it so far as it enters into contact or connection with the psychical organ during the origination of different psychical processes.

The last substance is the psychical organ (*manaḥ*)[265] which is characterized by psychical organness (*manstvam*). Its existence is inferred on the following grounds : We observe that knowledge and other psychical processes which did not exist before, in spite of the preparedness or disposition (*saṃskāraḥ*) of the soul and the sense-organs, appear later on and could only be inferred from the existence of a further organ. Again we observe that recollections come into existence without the activity of the sense-organs and we see that there are objects of perception such as pleasure, pain, etc. which are not perceived by the external sense-organs but which are still perceivable and that leads likewise to the assumption of a further organ—an inner organ. That is precisely the psychical organ (*manaḥ*).

As qualities, the psychical organ possesses the seven common qualities : number, extension, separateness, connection, separation, distantness, nearness; further it possesses the preparedness or disposition (*saṃskāraḥ*) of swing or motion ; and as bearer of these qualities it is to be naturally considered as a substance. There are numerous psychical organs ; but there is only one to each body as only through its existence, the non-simultaneous emergence of different psychical processes can be explained. As regards its extension, the psychical organ is tiny and small. Besides the four elements, it is the only substance which is not infinitely big but atomic in size. That it still, like the atoms of the Elements, does not form aggregates, depends on the fact that the quality of touch i. e. impenetrability is absent in it. On account of its spatial limitation, the psychical organ may move further and its movement is either caused by the effort of the soul or by the Invisible (*adṛṣṭam*) and it succeeds with immense quickness. Finally, the psychical organ is unspiritual, because otherwise one body would shelter two spiritual entities and it would lead to a schizophrenia or splitting of the personality. Thus it is a mere tool or instrument and stands as such inservice to another, namely the soul.

After the substances follows the next category, namely qualities.[266] The classical Vaiśeṣika system knows twenty-four qualities : form, taste, smell, touch, number, extension, separateness, connection, separation, distantness, nearness, knowledge, pleasure, pain, desire, aversion, effort; further, heaviness, fluidity, humidity, preparedness or disposition (*saṃskāraḥ*) under which latter are to be understood swing, elasticity, memory-impressions; merit and guilt which are frequently summarized under the name of the Invisible (*adṛṣṭam*) and finally the sound. The common qualityness (*guṇatvam*) inheres in all these qualities. Besides, they are characterized by the fact that they inhere in the substances, while in them, neither qualities nor movement can inhere.

In general, the qualities (*guṇāḥ*) ever cling in one substance (*ekaikadravyavṛttitvam*) which they completely penetrate (*āśraya-vyāpitvam*). Only the sound and the qualities of the soul appear only in one place of their bearer (*pradeśavṛttitvam*). Further connection and separation assume a special place. They cling to more substances i.e. the substances which they join or separate (*anekāś-ritatvam*) and penetrate only a part of the same. Finally the numbers from two onwards and the separateness of several numbers of things likewise dwell in many substances.

An important classification differentiates special or characteristic qualities (*vaiśeṣikaguṇāh*) which are peculiar to particular substances and common qualities (*sāmānyaguṇāh*) which can dwell in the different substances. Among the special qualities are enumerated the old qualities of the elements—form, taste, smell, touch and sound, to which humidity and naturally the fluidity also belong ; further the qualities of the soul—knowledge, pleasure, pain, desire, aversion, effort, together with merit, guilt and the memory-impressions. The common qualities are number, extension, separateness, connection, separation, distantness and nearness with which are also joined heaviness and artificially called forth fluidity and swing or motion. Unimportant and purely mechanical is, on the other hand, the distinction of qualities which can indwell the limited substances, the unlimited substances and both.

As regards the perception of qualities, the qualities of the Elements—sound, touch, form, taste and smell are perceived each through one sense organ. The common qualities : number, extension, separateness, connection, separation, distantness and nearness, as also fluidity, humidity, and swing can be perceived through two sense-organs—through the eye and the touch. The psychical organ serves for the perception of the qualities of the soul : knowledge, pleasure, pain, desire, aversion or effort. Unperceivable are only heaviness, merit, guilt and memory-impressions.

Difficult is the doctrine of the causality of the qualities.[267] In general, the qualities can be the cause of the movement or the cause of other qualities. Causes of movement are heaviness, fluidity, swing, and again effort, merit and guilt and the particular varieties of connection viz. striking and impulse. For the assessment and arrangement of qualities, as far as they are the causes of other qualities, the old distinction between the material and the occasioning or the inducing cause is important. According to the Vaiśeṣika system, we deal with material causes when a whole arises out the parts. According to the theory of the categories, in this case, the substance of the whole arises out of the substances of the parts and the qualities of the whole out of the qualities of the parts. The substance of the parts, as it is bound with the substance of the whole through inherence, was named as an inhering cause (*samavāyikāraṇam*) ; the qualities of the parts as they inhere in the inhering substances stand in no such relation with the qualities of the whole ; they are the non-inhering cause (*asamavāyikāraṇam*). According to this view one distinguished among the qualities : qualities which are the causes of the other qualities are the non-inhering causes (*asamavāyikāraṇāni*) and the occasioning causes (*nimittakāraṇāni*). In these, non-inhering causes correspond to the old material causes. Later the idea of non-inhering cause was widened ; it extended itself to the majority of cases where the causing and caused qualities inhere in the same substance. Thus one came to the following formulation : non-inhering causes are form, taste, smell, touch (which is not hot), number, extension, separateness of isolated substances, humidity and sound. The occasioning causes are the qualities of the soul—knowledge, pleasure, pain, desire, aversion, effort, merit, guilt and memory-impressions. Besides, some qualities can be the causes of both sorts ; they are connection, separation, hot touch, heaviness, fluidity and swing. Finally there are qualities which, in general, cannot be the causes, viz. distantness, nearness and the separateness as duality etc.

Further classifications of the qualities, as far as they represent the causes of other qualities, are based on the differentiation of qualities which bring forth the homogeneous things (*samānajātīyārambhakaḥ*), from those which bring forth the heterogeneous things (*asamānajātīyārambhakaḥ*) and also those in which both hold good. Again there was the distinction of the qualities—those whose effect or operation inheres in their own bearer (*svāśrayasamavetārambhakaḥ*) from those whose effect or operation inheres in other substances (*paratrārambhakaḥ*) and those in which both cases occur. Also here lies ultimately the old distinction between the material and occasioning causes. Because the qualities, which bring forth the homogeneous, are after all the qualities of the parts which call forth the qualities of the whole and though the substance of the whole is different from the substance of the parts, these qualities bring them forth in another substance. But naturally in both cases, there are other qualities in which the same definitions prove true and therefore they break through the original classification.

Regarding the qualities considered as effect, they can be brought forth through movement or through other qualities. The connection and separation in mechanical processes are caused by Movement. In the origination of qualities out of qualities, there once more recurs the old view-point of distinction between the material and occasioning causes. One distingished between qualities—those which originate out of the qualities of the cause (*kāraṇaguṇapūrvakaḥ*) and such as do not arise out of the qualities of the causes (*akāraṇaguṇapūrvakaḥ*). Out of the qualities of the causes naturally originate the qualities of the whole, which are traced back to the qualities of the parts. The qualities, which do not originate out of the qualities of the cause, depend in the largest measure on the connection. It holds good for all the qualities of the soul, which are brought forth by the connection of the psychical organ with the soul. But it also holds good in other cases, as in the case of sound when it is caused by striking or in the case of distantness and nearness which depend on a connection with space and time. In some cases, a separation can also be the cause of a quality when, for instance, a sound is called forth by the breaking of a stick or when one separation has another separation as its cause. A special case is finally of reflective knowledge (*apekṣābuddhiḥ*) which cooperates as cause in the origination of the qualities : distantness, nearness, number and separateness.

We have, thus, said what is the most important about the causality of the qualities and about the qualities in general and we can now go over to the description of the isolated or individual qualities. In advance, it may be said that in every sort of quality a corresponding commonness inheres, which characterizes it and it is not, therefore, necessary to mention it in every individual case.

Regarding the qualities of the elements the following holds good. The Form or Colour (*rūpam*)[268] clings to the earth, water and fire. It exhibits numerous varieties, white etc. Colour is perceived with the eye, in which case the colour joins in the sense-organ. Further the colour of the substances makes possible the perception of the substances themselves, their general qualities, their movements and commonnesses.

The taste (*rasaḥ*)[269] occurs to earth and water. It can be sweet, sour, saltish, bitter, pungent and tart. It is perceived through the organ of taste, whereby again the same quality cooperates in the organ. In the form of nutrition-juice (*rasaḥ*), the taste is the basis of life, of prosperity, of strength and of health.

The smell (*gandhaḥ*)[270] is finally the quality of the earth. It is fragrant or obnoxious and is perceived through the organ of smell whereby the quality of smell cooperates in the organ.

The touch (*sparśaḥ*)[271] indwells the earth, water, fire and air. It can be cold, hot and neither cold nor hot. It is perceived through the sense-organ of skin in which the touch in the organ supports the perception and is regularly present wherever there is colour.[272]

For all these qualities, the rule holds good that they are permanent in the Atoms and impermanent in the aggregate and they perish with the aggregate. The only exceptions are the qualities of the earth, so far as they are changed by heat, as it occurs in the case of a jar.

In this case, the following process happens.[273] In an unbaked vessel when it is baked, movements originate in the atoms of which the vessel is composed, under the impact of heat. These movements cause separations which destroy the connection inhering in the atoms and through this destruction, the aggregate—the pot—disappears. As soon as it has disappeared, the hitherto existing qualities like the brown colour in the isolated atoms are destroyed through the connection with the fire, under the influence of heat, and there also arise equally through the connection with the fire the new qualities changed through heat (*pākajaḥ*). Directly thereupon originate, under the influence of the Invisible (*adṛṣṭam*) of the persons concerned through the connection of their soul with the atoms, movements in the atoms whose qualities are now changed. These movements lead to the connection of the atoms with one another and thus originates, in that way of process, above the double atoms etc., the new aggregate viz. the jar. Just as the substance of the aggregate arises out of the substance of the atoms, the qualities of the aggregate also arise out of the qualities of the atoms. As the qualities of the atom are changed through the influence of heat the qualities of the aggregate are also changed.

This theory is proved as follows: A direct change of the aggregate under the influence of fire is not possible, because the fire is not able to penetrate the unitarily extended aggregate and can only affect its surface. The fire is not also able to enter into connection with the total atoms, as long as the latter are connected with each other, because their connection admits no intervening space in which the fire could penetrate. The assumption is, therefore, unavoidable that the connection of the atoms is temporarily dissolved. Nevertheless this dissolution and the new union follow so quickly that the beholder does not notice them.

After the qualities of the Elements follows next the group of common qualities—number, extension, separateness, connection, separation, distantness and nearness.

Of these, number[271] is the cause that one recognizes the numbers and speaks of them. As number one, it indwells the individual substances and it is, like the already described qualities of the Elements, permanent in permanent substances and impermanent in the aggregates. As plurality from the number two upwards, it inheres in several substances and originates out of the number one of the individual substances under the influence of the reflective knowledge (*apekṣābuddhiḥ*) of an observer. This process happens thus:

When the eye of an observer enters into contact with two substances, there first arises a knowledge of the commonness—oneness which inheres in the quality one inhering in these substances. Then through this commonness, its connection with the quality and the knowledge of the same originates, a knowledge of the quality 'one' which is itself a unity but has a plurality to objects and looks upon them so. Under the influence of this reflective knowledge (*apekṣābuddhiḥ*), then, originates out of the number one, in both the substances, the number two.[275] Now arises again, first of all, a knowledge of the commonness two. Out of the commonness two, their connection with the quality two and the knowledge of the same, there arises the knowledge of the quality two. And out of the quality two, their connection with the substances and the knowledge of the same, there arises the knowledge of the two substances as a twoness (duality). Finally the origination of a memory-impression forms the conclusion.

The disappearance of such numbers follows through the vanishing of the observing or reflecting knowledge which has called them forth. As two knowledges cannot stand beside each other, the knowledge of the commonness two which is called forth by the number two, destroys its previous observing knowledge and with the destruction of the observing knowledge disappears also the number two. In particular, the process is as follows:

As soon as the knowledge of the commonness two arises, the observing knowledge begins to disappear and the knowledge of the quality two begins to arise. In the next moment, as soon as the knowledge of a quality two has arisen, the observing knowledge disappears and the number two as well as the knowledge of the commonness two begin to disappear, while the knowledge of the substances as two (duality) begins to arise. In the third moment, the number two disappears, the knowledge of the two substances as two (duality) arises instead, and the knowledge of the quality two begins to disappear and the memory-impresesion, which is the result of this knowledge-process, begins to arise. Finally with the rise of the memory-impression, the knowledge of the two substances also disappears. This theory makes it possible to trace back the disappearance of number two to the disappearance of the observing knowledge and still allow it to participate in the whole knowledge-process which is dissolved through it.[276]

A special case is the disappearance of number through the destruction of its bearer. When simultaneously with the knowledge of the commonness one, there arises in the parts of the things under observation, a movement which may contribute to a dissolution of the aggregate, there arises the quality of separation, simultaneously with the observing knowledge, through the movement in the parts of the things. Simultaneously with the rise of number two, the connection is destroyed through the separation, the connection which makes the aggregates out of the parts. And with the rise of the knowledge of commonness two, the aggregates disintegrate and the number two inhering in them vanishes. Still before the knowledge of the commonness, the observing knowledge is destroyed and it can therethrough lead to the disappearance of number two.

The quality of extension (*parimāṇam*)[277] is the cause of what one speaks of as mass. It is four-fold—big (*mahat*), small (*aṇuḥ*), long (*dīrgham*) and short (*hrasvam*). These—bigness, longness, smallness, shortness—are terms of daily use and the distinction between them needs no clarification.

The bigness occurs to permanent substances: ether, time, space, souls and further to the aggregates from triads (*tryaṇuka*) onwards. In permanent substances, it appears as infinite largeness (*paramamahattvam*) and is permanent. In the aggregate it is impermanent. The smallness occurs in the substance in the form of the atom, in the atoms of the Elements and in the psychical organ : and besides in the dyad (*dvyaṇukam*). In the Atoms, it has the form of infinite smallness or circularity (*pārimāṇḍalyam*) and is permanent. In the dyad it is impermanent. Really small are only atoms and dyads. When one calls some things as small in comparison with others, it is merely a metaphorical way of expression. Length and shortness occur only in aggregates—the shortness in the dyad and length in the remaining. They are, therefore, exclusively impermanent. Also the expression shortness is used in comparison with other things only in a figurative sense.

Concerning the origin of the impermanent form of the quality of extension, its cause can be threefold : a number, an extension and heaping up or an accumulation. A number is the cause of the extension when out of atoms, dyads (*dvyaṇukāni*) and out of dyads greater aggregates are formed. Because, as neither out of the circularity of atoms, the smallness of a dyad can arise, nor out of the smallness of dyads, the largeness of the rest of the aggregates can arise, another cause must be sought and that is number. When under the influence of the observing knowledge of God, the number two arises in two atoms, it brings forth, as soon as both atoms have formed into a dyad (*dvyaṇukam*), a quality of smallness in the dyad. In a similar way, largeness arises during the connection of dyads towards further aggregates out of the number of the dyads or double atoms. As the aggregates, in which there is already largeness, join themselves to form still larger aggregates, their largeness arises out of the largeness of their parts. Then we see that the largeness of the whole depends on their largeness. As finally numerous big things forms a loose heap, this largeness is conditioned through the piling up (*pracayaḥ*) of these things, that is to say, through the fact that they are conglomerated loosely or densely. On that depends the largeness of the heap, also in the case of an equal number and largeness of its parts. In the same way as smallness and largeness, shortness and longness arise in the aggregates. What finally concerns the disappearance of the impermanent forms of the extension in the aggregates, they disappear with the aggregates.

The separateness (*pṛthaktvam*)[278] is the cause of knowledge which distinguishes the things as separated from one another. So far as the separateness of individual things emerges, it inheres in the individual substances and these can be permanent substances as well as aggregates. In the permanent substances, it is permanent ; in the aggregates, it is impermanent. As separateness of several things, it inheres, like the number, on account of the observing knowledge of the observer and disappears as soon as it disappears. In these sorts of separateness, as against number, a difference exists only so far as no corresponding commonness, which would characterize them, inheres in them. They get, on the other hand, their special character through the number corresponding to them, which indwells the same things together with them.

The connection (*saṃyogaḥ*)[279] is the cause of what one knows the things as joined. It has a specially wider sphere of operation, as it can be the cause of substances, as well as of qualities and movements. According to its nature, connection consists in the union of hitherto un-united things (*aprāptayoḥ prāptiḥ*). It is threefold, according as it arises through the movement of one of the two things or of both things, or through another connection

The last is the case when a part of a whole enters into a connection and causes therethrough a connection of the whole inhering in it. Further sub-varieties of this last form of connection, according as it arises out of one, two or more connections, as Praśastapāda distinguishes them, are of no importance for the nature of connection ; so also the special case that out of one connection, two arise. On the other hand, the definition is important that there is no unborn connection (*ajaḥ saṃyogaḥ*). Because, through that a connection between infinitely great permanent substances is excluded.

This definition is connected with the idea of the occurrence of separate things (*yutasiddhiḥ*) which has been put forth in order to distinguish connection from inherence.[280] It had been, for instance, said that connection binds such things as occur separated from each other, while, on the other hand, inherence binds such things in which such is not the case. Thereby one had explained the occurrence of separated things, further, with regard to the infinitely big substances of which a spatial separation cannot take place, as a possibility to move, separated. But this explanation shows itself utilizable only there where one deals with a connection of one infinitely big substance with a finite substance. Where two infinitely great substances are concerned, it is of no use, as infinitely big substances cannot move. If then the definition of the occurrence of the separated is to be valid, a connection between infinitely by big substances must be excluded in general. Because as they are assumed, they must be permanent and uniform because a movement which can separate them is not possible in the case of infinitely big substances. So it was taught that there is no unborn connection. Whether there were also other reasons for denying unborn connection, besides these considerations, escapes our knowledge. The fact, however, is that this doctrine was formulated and such inferences were drawn. If infinitely big substances cannot join with each other, there is, for example, no connection of the soul with space and time. And one did not hesitate to draw these inferences.

In conclusion, it is to be briefly mentioned how the connection is abrogated. It is, as a rule, caused by the quality of separation, which is called forth by a movement in the things connected and as contrast to connection, it abrogates it. In isolated cases, it can find its end through the fact that the bearer itself vanishes. That is the case when aggregates are bound with each other and these aggregates disintegrate.

The quality of separation (*vibhāgaḥ*)[281] is the cause of how one knows things as separated. Its sphere of operation is essentially narrower than that of connection, as it can only come into consideration as the cause of sound or of another separation. According to its nature, it is the contrast of connection which it abrogates. It is, therefore, explained as non-association or non-union which is preceded by a union (*prāptipūrvikā aprāptiḥ*). The separation is threefold—according as it is called forth by the movement of one of the two separated things, or by the movement of both by another separation. The last is the case when in the case of a whole, through the separation of a part from any object, the separation of the whole from that object ensues, as for example, through the separation of a hand from an object which it holds, the whole body separates itself from it. Again there is a second case puzzled out by the scholiasts of the system. When, for example, a movement in a part of an aggregate contributes to the disintegration of the aggregate, it as well causes the separation of this part from the remaining parts of the aggregate as also its separation from the place in which it had been originally present. But according to the fundamental maxims of the system, both cannot be caused by the same movement at the same time. One, therefore, assumed the following : First the movement causes the separation of a part from the rest. Through this separation, the connection on which the aggregate depends is abrogated and the aggregate disintegrates. Now the part loosened by the movement separates itself from its original place. But this separation can no more be caused by the movement as some time has already elapsed in between. Its cause is, therefore, to be sought in something else, that is, in the first separation which has dissolved the aggregate and which brings forth the second separation—namely the change of place.

As regards the disappearance of the quality of separation, it not only disappears first through a new connection of the separated things, but it disappears already the next moment. One knows it only in quite a short time, as the knowledge of separation presupposes the consciousness of a previous connection. Its disappearance is, therefore, already caused by the connection into which the separated things enter with the other places of space.[282] In isolated cases, its disappearance can be caused also by the destruction of its bearer, when its bearers are namely the aggregates which disintegrate. Indeed, here again, one deals with an artificially puzzled out special case. Because the separation lasts only for one moment, the disintegration of the aggregate must result in this moment before the separation is destroyed through the connection with the next place in space. But already, the delineation of this process, the distribution of occurrences on the single moments and the binding of cause and effect into an uninterrupted chain stimulated the scholiasts of the system. The following course was therefore, assumed. Suppose a case that two aggregates are joined into a whole and that in one part of the two aggregates, a movement arises which is fit to contribute to the dissolution of the aggregate, then this movement calls forth the quality of separateness, in the part of the aggregate ; this quality of separation destroys in the next moment the quality of connection on which the aggregate depends and, therefore, the aggregate disintegrates. When now in the same moment in which the quality of separation arises in the part of this aggregate, a movement is caused in the other aggregate which in a similar way leads to the dissolution of the whole, there arises, simultaneously with the destruction of the quality of connection in the part of the first aggregate, a quality of separation in the second aggregate through a movement in that aggregate. But while this separation in the aggregate destroys the quality of connection on which the whole depends, the first aggregate already falls down to pieces and with it also disappears the separation of both of the aggregates inhering in it, before it can be destroyed through the falling to pieces of the whole and the change of place of its parts. This is quite sufficient as an example of the sportive theories in which scholiasts were involved, in order to explain the destruction of the quality of separation through the destruction of its bearer. We shall not consider the objections to it which are cited by Praśastapāda and his attempt to controvert them.

The qualities of distantness (*paratvam*) and nearness (*aparatvam*)[283] are the cause by which a man designates and knows an object as far or near. They are of a double kind according as they are conditioned by space or time. When they are conditioned by space, they are known to have a particular position in space; when they are conditioned by time, a difference of age is known.

When distance and nearness are conditioned by space, they arise thus : When two objects seen from the point of an observer in the same direction are on different distances, it is due to the fact that they are connected with the place of the observer by a greater or less number of space-points, and the observer knows the distant object in comparison with the near as far (*asaṃnikṛṣṭa*) and under the influence of this observing knowledge (*apekṣābuddhiḥ*), the quality of distantness arises in the object through the connection with the place concerned in space. The corresponding holds good for the quality of nearness. Distantness and nearness, which are conditioned by time, arise in a similar way. When in any place an older and younger man are found at the same time, what is expressed is that the older one bears the signs of old age—beard, wrinkles, gray hair, etc. and the observer knows the older in comparison with the younger one as distant and under the influence of this observing knowledge, there arises in the older man the quality of distantness through the connection with the period concerned. A corresponding thing holds good for the quality of nearness (in time).

The diappearance of the qualities of distantness and nearness ensues as a rule through the disappearance of the observing knowledge (*apekṣābuddhiḥ*) which has called them forth, in the same way as in the case of number. The process is as follows: After the rise of the quality of distantness, there first arises the knowledge of the commonness of distantness and through it the observing knowledge begins to disappear. Simultaneously the knowledge of the quality of distantness begins to arise. In the next moment, the knowledge of the quality of distantness arises and the knowledge of the distant object as distant begins to arise. In the meanwhile, however, the observing knowledge has vanished and the quality of distantness begins to disappear. And when in the next moment, the knowledge of the distant object has arisen, the quality of distantness has disappeared.

But as the qualities of distantness and nearness are not merely caused by the observing knowledge but, before all, are caused through the connection with space aud time, they can naturally be destroyed also by the abrogation of this connection. Only in that process, the movement, which abrogates the connection, must set in exactly at the right moment, so that with it the destruction comes through the abrogation of connection before the disappearance of the observing knowledge can take effect. Besides in the case of the aggregate, the destruction of the qualities of distantness and nearness can succeed through the destruction of the aggregate. Herein also, the destruction must come exactly at the right moment, before the destruction follows through the disappearance of the observing knowledge. Both are the cases which stimulate Praśastapāda to elaborate them more precisely and he has not neglected to describe the individual processes thoroughly and to adjust them with one another. But with him that is not enough. He has also included in his consideration the possibility that two of the named causes or also all the three together contribute to the destruction of qualities of distantness and nearness and he has described also in these cases the course of occurrences exactly. But these scholastic plays deserve no more than a short mention.

In the group of the common qualities are included also the special qualities of the soul. They are knowledge, pleasure, pain, desire, aversion and effort.

The knowledge (*buddhiḥ*)[284] appears in different forms corresponding to the countlessness of its objects. Still, broadly considered, two kinds are distinguished : ignorance (*avidyā*) and knowledge (*vidyā*). Each of these is divided again into four varieties. To ignorance belong doubt (*saṃśayaḥ*), error (*viparyayaḥ*), irresolution (*anadhyavasāyaḥ*), and dream (*svapnaḥ*). The knowledge (*vidyā*) includes sense-perception (*pratyakṣam*), drawing of conclusion (*laiṅgikam*), memory (*smṛtiḥ*) and supernatural knowledge (*ārṣam*) as it is ascribed to the holy seers of antiquity. We will not go into the remaining details regarding the description which Praśastapāda gives of the individual sub-varieties of the knowledge-theories of his time and much that he presents here is his own personal view. In these points, his teaching cannot therefore be considered valid as a recital of the doctrine as it prevailed, in general, in the classical Vaiśeṣika but was created out of another stream of development which later set itself up and flowed in quite a different path viz. that stream of development which contributed to the flowering of Logic and Epistemology towards the end of the classical period of Indian philosophy. We shall return to it when we deal with that stream of development in the fourth volume of our work. Here we shall only give, as an example, the doctrine of dream,[285] because it is better suited to our present context.

According to the Vaiśeṣika doctrine, sleep comes on when the body is fatigued through the activity during the day. Then, in order that the body should rest and the assimilation of the received nutrition should ensue, there is induced an effort of the soul under the influence of the 'invisible' (*adṛṣṭam*) so that the psychical organ moves to the heart and remains there motionless without any contact with the sense-organs. Through that the sense-organs come to rest; only in-and-out-breathings continue unbroken. In this condition the man sleeps. When now, in this condition, through the connection of the psychical organ with the soul and through a memory-impression mediated through the sense-organ, knowledge of any object, similar to the sense-perception arises, it is named 'dream'. Especially such a dream can have three causes. It can be caused by a specially lively memory-impression. If one has thought, while sleeping, of an object in a lively manner out of love or anger, he sees that object in a dream. Further a disturbance in the relation of the three bodily juices can influence dreams.[286] When the wind dominates, the man dreams that he flies through the air. When the bile preponderates, the man dreams of fire, of golden mountains and the like. When phlegm predominates, the man dreams of rivers, oceans, snow-peaks and many such things. Finally the happy and unhappy dreams are called forth by the 'invisible' (*adṛṣṭam*), the happy ones by merit and the unhappy ones by guilt.

Of the remaining qualities of the soul, pleasure (*sukham*)[287] is, according to its nature, satisfying. It arises, when a desired object like a wreath etc. is found nearby on account of the contact of the sense-organ with the objects under the influence of merit through the connection of the psychical organ with the soul and it produces joy, affection, brightness in the eyes, etc. In the case of past objects, it depends on memory; in the case of future objects, it depends on plans about the future (*saṃkalpaḥ*). In the case of the wise, the feeling of pleasure which arises without any object, recollection or wish-dreams, depends on knowledge, self-mastery, satisfaction and merit.

The pain (*duḥkham*)[288] by its nature is oppressive. It arises when an undesirable object like poison, etc. is found nearby, on account of the contact of the sense-organs with the objects under the influence of guilt (*adharmaḥ*), through the connection of the psychical organ with the soul and it begets ill-humour, oppressiveness and dejectedness. In the case of the past objects, serpents, tigers, robbers, etc., it depends on memory; in the case of the future, on future thoughts.

Desire (*icchā*)[289] is the desire for a thing, which one does not possess; it may be for oneself or for others. It arises through the connection of the psychical organ with the soul under the influence of the feeling of pleasure or memory. It is the cause of effort, memory, merit and guilt. The sub-varieties of desire are love, longing, passion, wish, sympathy, passionlessness, etc.

The aversion (*dveṣaḥ*)[290] or hate is, by its nature, a flaming up. It arises through the connection of the psychical organ with the soul under the influence of pain or memories. It is the cause of efforts, memories, merit and guilt. The sub-varieties of aversion are anger, hostility, rage, ill-will and ill-humour.

The effort (*prayatnaḥ*)[291] is two-fold—(i) a mere result of life or induced through desire and aversion. In the first case, it maintains in process, during sleep, in-and-out-breathing and causes, on waking, the first connection of the psychical organ with the sense-organs. In this case, it originates through a connection of the psychical organ with the soul under the influence of merit and guilt. In the second case, the cause is the human action which strives to gain the wished-for thing and to avoid the unwished-for one and besides keeps the body in maintenance. In this case, it arises through the connection of the psychical organ with the soul under the influence of desire and aversion.

With the characteristic qualities of the soul, the great groups of qualities are described. The remaining qualities follow, loosely enrolled, first the three qualities of the Elements, namely heaviness, fluidity and humidity.

Of these heaviness (*gurutvam*)[292] is the common quality of water and earth. It is the cause of falling and is inferred from falling, as it is not perceivable by the senses. It can be abrogated by connection, effort, or in a moved thing, by a swing. Like the characteristic qualities of the Elements, heaviness is permanent in permanent atoms and impermanent in aggregates.

The fluidity (*dravatvam*)[293] is the cause of flowing. It occurs to these elements : water, earth and fire. Thereby a distinction is made as natural (*sāṃsiddhikam*) and artificial (*naimittikam*). The natural fluidity is the characteristic quality of water. The artificial fluidity is a common quality of earth and fire. The natural fluidity is like the remaining characteristic qualities of the Elements permanent in atoms, and impermanent in aggregates. If in many appearances or forms of water like snow and hail, the natural fluidity appears to be abrogated, it depends on the fact that in these cases, under the influence of heavenly fire[294] (*divyaṃ tejaḥ*) heaps of water-atoms arise, in which the natural fluidity of the atoms is hindered. The artificial fluidity is produced in different forms of earth like fat, lac, etc. and in the metals which represent the appearance or form of fire, under the influence of fire. The process is the same as that during the change of the qualities of the Earth under the influence of heat.[295] First, under the impact of the Fire-atoms, the aggregate dissolves itself into its atoms. Thereupon, the atoms take on the quality of fluidity under the influence of heat. Then arise out of the changed atoms again the aggregates which also exhibit now the quality of fluidity.

The humidity or stickiness (*snehaḥ*)[296] is a characteristic quality of water. It makes possible that moist things stick to one another, that one can wash himself and some more things of like nature. Like the other characteristic qualities of the Elements, it is permanent in the atoms and impermanent in aggregates.

The next quality—the disposition or preparedness (*saṃskāraḥ*) embraces three—-the swing (*vegaḥ*), the memory-impressions and the elasticity.

The swing (*vegaḥ*)[297] emerges among the five limited substances—the four elements and the psychical organ, that is, among all substances which are capable of movement. It is generated by a movement on account of a special cause—an impulse or stroke, and causes a continued movement in a particular direction The swing is abrogated through the connection with a substance to which the quality of touch occurs, that is, through rebounding on an impenetrable object. In some cases, the swing can arise when the parts, in which it dwells, unite into a whole to which then it also occurs.

A memory-impression (*bhāvanā*)[298] is a quality of the soul which occasions a memory (*smṛtiḥ*) or a recognition (*pratyabhijñānam*) of a formerly perceived object. It is abrogated through a knowledge of another sort—through intoxication or frenzy, sorrow and such like feelings. Memory-impressions arise through the connections of the psychial organ with the soul and above all in the case of specially lively perceptions, through practice and attentiveness. When a man, for example, sees something wonderful, this perception calls forth a specially lively memory-impression. In the learning of a knowledge of a handicraft or skill by practice, the already existing memory-impressions are strengthened on account of the continuously renewed perceptions. And finally when man looks forward to any sight with special interest, the memory-impressions called forth therethrough make an especially lasting impression.

The elasticity (*sthitisthāpakaḥ*)[299] occurs in impenetrable things which consist of a union of solid or firm parts and endure for a longer time and its bearer, if it is displaced to another position, may return to its original one. Its influence is to be observed in living and non-living things as in the case of a bow, a branch and more things like them, when these are bent or rolled together. Like most of the qualities of the elements, it is permanent in permanent substances and impermanent in impermanent ones.

Both the qualities merit (*dharmaḥ*) and guilt (*adharmaḥ*)[300] which are often comprehended under the name of the Invisible (*adṛṣṭam*) are unperceivable qualities of the soul. The merit arises through the connection of the psychical organ with the soul on account of the good willing when one accomplishes duties ascribed to different castes and the stages of life. It has agreeable and profitable results and can lead to Deliverance. It is extinguished with the last feeling of happiness brought about by it. The guilt arises through the connection of the psychical organ with the soul on account of the bad willing when a man does the opposite of what the merit leads to as consequence, when he neglects the prescribed duties and allows himself to be guilty of errors out of frivolity. It has disagreeable and unprofitable consequences and is extinguished with the last sorrowful experience brought about through it.

In connection with the qualities, merit and guilt, Praśastapāda presents briefly his doctrine of Deliverance.[301] The last cause of entanglement in the cycle of being is ignorance. On it depend the passions, desires and hate. When a being, caught in ignorance and ruled by desire and hate, gains merit with which only slight guilt is mixed, he is reborn in the world of gods or in the human world and attains a body, sense-organs and objects which prepare happiness for him. If on the other hand, he saddles himself with guilt with which only slight merit is mixed, he is reborn in the animal-world or in one of the hells and gets a body, sense-organs and objects, which prepare sorrow for him. Thus merit and guilt lead to new rebirths in a beginningless cycle of being. A deliverance out of it is possible only in the following way : He, who is born in a pious family through knowledge and selfless acts, seeks after a way out of the sorrow of existence, and on that account goes to a teacher and receives from him the true knowledge about the six categories by which the ignorance goes out and with the ignorance also vanish desires and hate. Consequently merit and guilt which are caused by desire and hate can no more arise and what existed from former times is cancelled through retribution. Only a pure form of merit still arises, which brings forth the feeling of joy begot by the view of the highest truth and then goes out. When it is extinguished and finally the body also disintegrates with death, there is no new rebirth and man attains the Deliverance, because he comes to rest and calmness like a fire, the fuel of which is consumed.

The last quality, the sound (*śabdaḥ*)[302] is a quality of the Ether and is perceived through the ear. It is limited in place and has the duration of only a moment. The sound can be called forth by connection, separation or through another sound. Every sound is destroyed by the following, with the exception of the last sound of a series of sounds, which is destroyed by the previous sound.[303] This is a forced and a very questionable theory which has been formulated, because no other way out was known.

The sound is two-fold—syllabic sound (*varṇaḥ*) and sound (*dhvaniḥ*). Under syllabic sounds are to be understood the speech-sounds. The sound is brought forth through an instrument. The origination of the speech-sounds ensues as follows : Through the connection of the speech-organ with the soul and under the influence of memory there is awakened a wish to utter the syllabic sound. Thereupon, arises in the soul an effort and under the influence of this effort there arises a movement in the speech-air, through the connection of the soul with the speech-air. This moves upwards and hits the throat and the remaining instruments of speech. And under the influence of the connection of the air with the instruments of speech there arise the speech-sounds through the connection of speech instruments with the Ether.[304] The sound (*dhvaniḥ*) arises, for example, under the influence of the connection of the drum and the stick, through the connection of the drum with the ether, or when a man breaks a stick, under the influence of the separation of the parts of the stick from one another through the separation of the stick from the ether.

The propagation of sound follows in this way : evey sound while vanishing generates another sound in its direct neighbourhood, so that there arises a chain of sounds which reaches the ear of the hearer like a wave. Because neither the ether of the ear nor the sound lasting for only a moment can move itself, a perception is not possible if the sound does not reach the ear ; there remains no other possibility than the assumption of such propagation of sound.[305]

The third category the movement (*karma*)[306] is divided into five sub-varieties : raising, lowering, bending, stretching and going. Commonness of movementness (*karmatvam*) occurs in all these sub-varieties. Besides, each is characterized through its special genus.

The place of movement inside the categories is due to the fact that, like the quality, it necessarily presupposes a substance as bearer, while it itself can neither be the bearer of a movement nor of a quality. Every movement, therefore, inheres only in one substance. This substance must be limited as movement denotes a change of place, which is only possible in the case of limited things. Again, it is important that every movement has only the duration of a moment.[307]

Regarding the causality of movement, it is called forth by heaviness, fluidity, effort or a connection. It, itself, without the assistance of a further cause, brings forth a connection, separation. Thereby, the connection brought forth by it makes an end of action itself. According to the scheme of ideas of the Vaiśeṣika, the movement is a non-inhering cause (*asamavāyikāraṇam*). It shares also with others in the origination of the aggregates but thereby, it brings forth neither the substance of the whole, because that is the result of the connection called forth by it, nor does it bring forth a homogeneous result, that is to say, another movement. It causes, on the contrary, only during the rise of the aggregate, the connection and, in its destruction, causes also the separation of its parts ; it therefore brings forth a quality which inheres partly in its bearer and partly in another substance.

Of the sub-varieties of movement, raising (*utkṣepaṇam*) is a movement which ensues in such a way that the parts of the body and things connected with them join themselves with places, in space situated upward and separate themselves from those placed downward. The lowering (*apakṣepaṇam*) is the opposite thereof. The bending is a movement through which the end of a straight thing separates itself from its place in space and joins with the place in the beginning so that the whole becomes curved. Stretching (*prasāraṇam*) is the opposite of that. The going (*gamanam*) finally causes the connection with the places not fixed in the space and also the separation from them. It is, therefore, an indefinite movement.

A further classification of movement is as follows : movement can happen in the parts of the body and in objects which are in connection with it i.e. in things which stand under the influence of the soul and movements can happen in things which do not stand under the influence of the soul. In the first case they can be conscious (*satpratyayaḥ*) or unconscious (*asatpratyayaḥ*). In the second case, they follow without any connection with consciousness (*apratyayaḥ*). In this frame, Praśastapāda describes all the cases of movement which had been dealt with by the old nature-philosophy.

In order to begin with a movement which stands under the influence of the soul, it—for example, the raising of the hand—ensues thus : When a man wishes to raise the hand, there arises effort on the part of the soul connected with the hand. Under the influence of this effort, a movement arises in the hand through the connection of the soul with the hand. And this movement moves the hand upwards. Things are more difficult when man, for example, pounds in a mortar with a pestle.[308] Also in this case, there first arises the wish to raise the pestle. Out of that arises an effort and under the influence of this effort, there arises a movement in the hand, through the connection of the soul with the hand, which raises it upwards. But at the same time, there also arises, under the influence of effort, similar movement in the pestle through the connection of the pestle with the hand. Now it proceeds further. If the pestle is raised high enough, the wish to raise it ceases and in its place steps in a wish to lower it. Thereupon arises again in the way mentioned already the movement of lowering in the hand and the pestle though effort and through the connection of the soul with the pestle. The last moment of this movement leads to the impulse named connection between the pestle and the mortar. This impulse sets up again a stimulus under the influence of a swing (*vegaḥ*) indwelling the pestle, to generate an unconscious movement in the pestle which makes it fly upwards. This movement brings forth a swing in the pestle under the influence of an impulse of the pestle. And under the influence of the swing, there arises an unconscious movement upwards in the hand through the connection of the pestle and the hand, until by and by, after wish and effort, again the conscious movement sets in.

This example may be enough to show how Praśastapāda treats his material. In a similar way, he speaks of the movement of the objects, which are thrown with the hand or with some device e.g. the movement of an arrow which is shot from a bow. Then he goes on from the movements which stand under the influence of the soul to those which do not stand under the influence of the soul.

Such movements take place in the four elements. As causes, there come into consideration a thrust (*nodanam*), a stroke (*abhighātaḥ*), the connection with something already joined (*saṃyuktasaṃyogaḥ*), that is to say, the connection with an object, which is hit by a thrust or a stroke—where we speak of a propagation of a thrust or impulse; heaviness, fluidity which cause the falling and flowing named as movements and finally the swing of a moved object. Here also Praśastapāda speaks of different examples, according to his manner, in details, in the light of the doctrine of categories. In connection with the movement of the four Elements, he mentions, as a special case, the movement of the breath-air. In a waking state, it is caused by a connection with the soul, in which an effort also cooperates, which, on its side, goes back to a desire or aversion, why, even the course of breathing can be consciously regulated. In sleep, the connection with the soul is also the cause of breathing ; still in that case the effort depends on the life (*jīvanam*) called the connection of the psychical organ with the soul.[309]

After the movement in the four Elements, Praśastapāda describes the relation of movement to the remaining substances. Of these ether, time, space and soul fall away, as they are not limited, a change of place being impossible in their case. On the other hand, the movement in the case of the psychical organ is important as its whole work depends on it. As long as life lasts, the movement of the psychical organ makes possible, above all, the connection of the soul with the different sense-organs ; its movement is caused by the union with the soul and follows under the influence of effort. This depends, during the waking state, on the will of a man as the perception occurs voluntarily through the sense-organs. Only the first perception, after waking out of sleep, is involuntary and in this case, therefore, the effort is occasioned through the life named as the connection of the psychical organ with the soul. At the end of life, the movement of the psychical organ causes the departure from here and rebirth in a new embodiment. As the infinitely big soul cannot wander, it is the psychical organ which binds the soul to the temporary body, and thus leades to rebirth. It happens thus in the following way : When merit and guilt, which condition a particular existence and thus cooperate with the life (*jīvanam*), are exhausted through retribution, the effort, which keeps breathing-in-process called forth by life, ceases, its operation is suspended and breath stops. But now a man has again gained in this existence new merit and new guilt. These now come into activity and contribute, together with the connection which binds the psychical organ with the soul, to the fact that the psychical organ departs from the body and with it death ensues. Thereupon there again originates, through merit and guilt, a fine transmitting body (*ātivāhikaśarīram*)[310] which receives the psychical organ and makes wandering to the place of next birth possible. There it enters into a new body which is commensurate with the merit and guilt of man and then begins the new existence.

These are the most important functions of the psychical organism which are rendered possible by movement. It is still to be mentioned that a Yogī, through the wonderful power of the psychical organ, can also wander to any place outside the body and can again enable it come back. Finally Praśastapāda notes that during world-creation the movement, which leads to the connection of the psychical organ with the newly born body, is conditioned by the 'Invisible'. It gives him the occasion to point out that in general all movements for which no other reason can be definitely fixed are to be traced back to the 'Invisible'. With this, there has ended what Praśastapāda has to say about the category of movement and he goes on next to the description of the next category of commonness.

The commonness (*sāmānyam*)[311] which remains undivided[312] and uninterrupted in its bearer, is the cause why man recognizes the agreement (*anuvṛttiḥ*) with one another; when a man, for instance, observes an object in which a definite commonness dwells, there originates, on account of a memory-impression which has been called forth by the earlier preception of similar objects, a knowledge on the basis of the memory of the earlier perceptions that here lies something of a like sort. And it is what lies at the bottom as cause of this knowledge—the commonness.

As the commonness, according to this definition is different from substances, qualities and movements, it is an independent category. There are numerous commonnesses, because every commonness clings to a particular group of things and calls forth a special idea. Thereby the commonnesses are permanent. As they are different from their bearers they do not perish even though these bearers perish. But of every kind, there is only one unique commonness because its characteristic is the same in all its bearers and a distinctive mark is absent. This one commonness indwells undivided in every bearer. It, no doubt, exists everywhere in all its bearers but particularly also only in its bearer. Though the commonnesses are not restricted spatially, the conditions for their existence are only given in their bearers. In other places in between they cannot exist and are, therefore, ungraspable there (*avyapadeśyaḥ*).

There are two sub-varieties of the category of commonness, the highest one and the lower one. The highest commonness is the existence (*sattā*). It is, exclusively, commonness and the cause by which a man knows all things as agreeing with one another. Just as leather, woollen and linen clothes, dipped in blue colour, can be recognized, according to universal agreement, as blue in spite of their difference otherwise, even so substances, qualities and movements in spite of their difference otherwise, are recognized and there is a universal agreement that they exist. This knowledge of universal agreement must depend on another cause different from substances, qualities and movements themselves. This cause is commonness-existence.

Among lower commonnesses are counted substances (*dravyatvam*), qualityness (*guṇatvam*) and movementness (*karmatvam*). It is the cause that things partly agree with one another, and partly deviate from one another and is, therefore, commonness (*sāmānyam*) as well as particularity (*viśeṣaḥ*). Thus substanceness is the cause that earth, water, fire etc., in spite of their differences otherwise, agree with one another as substances and it is therefore the commonness. But it is also the cause that things distinguish themselves from qualities and movements and is in this sense a particularity ; a corresponding state holds for qualityness, movementness and all further lower commonnesses. They are all, because of their wide spheres, at bottom (*prādhānyena*) assumed as commonnesses. Because they distinguish their bearer from the heterogeneous one, they are designated in a metaphorical sense (*bhaktyā*) as particularities (*viśeṣaḥ*).

The category of particularity (*viśeṣaḥ*)[313] embraces the last particularities (*antiyā viśeṣāḥ*). These indwell the permanent substances—the atoms of the four Elements—ether, time, space, the soul, and the psychical organ.[314] One such particularity indwells every individual substance and differentiates it from all other homogeneous and heterogeneous things. These particularities are not perceivable by ordinary men and are only seen by Yogīs in their condition of contemplation. As, for instance, ordinary men distinguish a cow on the ground of the commonness, qualities and movements indwelling it, as something different from a horse, so also the Yogīs are able to distinguish from one another the atoms, the released souls and the psychical organs, in spite of the fact that they are like one another according to the commonnesses qualities and movements indwelling them and they are also able later to recognize them again. But as other causes are not proved, it can only depend on the fact that a characteristic entity indwells every one of these substances and distinguishes them from all homogeneous and heterogeneous things. This entity is the particularity (*viśeṣaḥ*).

In this case, no other explanation is thinkable. Because, in spite of their supernatural powers, the Yogīs are able only to distinguish these substances, when something which renders the distinction possible indwells them. It cannot also be asserted that these substances are different from one another, of themselves, as no further particularities which can distinguish them from others can indwell the particularities (*viśeṣaḥ*). Because, in the case of particularities, this difference constitutes their nature. In the case of other things, however, in which this is not the case, they must depend on the influence of other entities. Thus a lamp, which is, by its nature, illuminating, illuminates itself. Other things, on the other hand, must be illuminated by it. Or to use another example, according to the Hindu prescriptions regarding purity, cow's flesh or horse's flesh is, by nature, impure, while other eatables become impure through contact with it. In the present case, the relation of permanent substances and the last particularities is to be thought of in a similar way.

The last category of inherence (*samavāyaḥ*)[315] is a connection which calls forth the idea of 'here' in the things occurring not separated, which stand in the relation of the bearer and the borne (*adhāryādhārabhūta*). As among things occurring separated, for example a jar and milk, an idea arises, on the ground of their connection: 'Here in the jar there is milk'. So also a similar idea on the basis of inherence arises among things occurring not separated. Thus a man knows, for example, when he deals with a whole and its parts: "Here in the threads is the cloth contained". Among the substances, and their qualities and movements, one recognizes : "Here in the substances, there exist qualities and movements." In the case of substances, qualities, movements and commonnesses inhering in them one knows: "Here in the substances, qualities, movements, existence is present; here in the substance there is substanceness, in the quality, qualityness; in movement, movementness". In the case of the substances and the last particularities one knows: "Here in these permanent substances are the last particularities existent".

From connection (*saṃyogaḥ*), the inherence is distinguished by the fact that the things which it joins can never occur separated. Therefore, it cannot be called forth like connection through movement. It cannot be also destroyed by separation. Besides, the things, which it joins, occur exclusively as the bearer and the borne.

That inherence (*samavāyaḥ*) is a separate category, arises out of the speciality of the characteristic in which man recognizes it. As one knows different things as of a like sort on the ground of commonness and out of that infers the existence of a further entity namely, the commonness, so also, one is led to recognize among the five categories the idea of 'here'—the existence of a further category—namely, inherence.

In contrast to the quality of connection, which emerges as plurality, there is only one single Inherence. Because the characteristic, out of which we infer it, is everywhere one and the same and a starting-point is absent out of which one could infer or conclude plurality. Also inherence in contrast to connection is permanent, because it is not caused, as no cause can be proved. As far as the existence of inherence in the remaining categories is concerned, there is no need of a further connection or inherence, as the inhering forms its own nature. Finally the inherence is not perceivable by the sense because it inheres in no sensuously perceivable things and is not reflected in knowledge; on the contrary it is inferred out of the idea of 'here'.

With the description of the category of inherence, the work of Praśastapāda concludes. Simultaneously ends with it the history of the Vaiśeṣika of the classical time which has found in this work its concluding presentation. Since then, something really new was created in the sphere of the theory of knowledge and logic and here the lead was soon assumed by the Nyāya, while the Vaiśeṣika moved into the background. Inside the Vaiśeṣika itself, one restricted oneself to working through the doctrine transmitted in the commentaries and to shaping out further the individual things. Really new features do not come forth. Only first, about the turn of the millennium (the first thousand years A.D.) the new School of the Nyāya—the Navya Nyāya—strikes a new path ; still it works back to the Vaiśeṣika and leads to the stronger changes of the old doctrine.

With this, we have provisionally reached the conclusion and it is therefore time to direct back our gaze. It is a long and rich development which we have known, a development which extended itself over eight centuries. Its importance lies above all in the fact that here we get acquainted with a kind of philosophising which is something rare in the Indian soil and which one, according to the usual ideas of Indian philosophy, would not expect. Here is the view directed not on the beyond and no striving after Deliverance is the motive of this philosophy. The interest, on the contrary, is on this existence and its root is the pure striving for knowledge—the striving to understand and explain the world of phenomena. The doctrines, which were thereby arrived at, may appear to us today primitive and laughable. But in order to be just to them, we need not start from the views of modern science. We must, on the other hand, include in our comparison what was created under similar presuppositions and conditions and these are the doctrines of Greek Philosophy. Then we can say that the nature-philosophy of the Vaiśeṣika, so far as its traditionally handed down material allows us to gain its distinct picture—its Atom Theory, its doctrine of Perception, its Psychology, as well as its Theory of Categories, can be well compared with the corresponding doctrines of the old Greek thinkers. And we have had repeated occasions to point out the unusual sharpness and consistency of thought by which the Vaiśeṣika is distinguished. Thus seen, the philosophy of the classical Vaiśeṣika represents a most highly considerable phenomenon. Now the question raises itself, why it did not attain more and more growth but soon grew stiff and numb, and why it, in the form in which it is shown handed down to us, produces, in spite of everything, an unsatisfactory, why, in many view-points, an unpleasant effect.

During the second great philosophy of the classical time—

i.e.—the Sāṃkhya, we have said[316] that its ancient doctrines must have appeared obsolete and out-distanced in later times and were therefore rejected. That does not hold good for the Vaiśeṣika. Its theories were as well rejected by the opponents and passionately contested but they were never felt to be obsolete. Here the reasons which led to the arresting of development and to its torpidity are to be sought elsewhere. To the classical Vaiśeṣika, the fresh sources of observation, which gives life to scientific knowledge, were lacking. Its nature-philosophy, therefore, dried up and died. A similar case happened to the doctrine of categories. It worked with a few ideas once gained and lost itself in an unfruitful scholastics. But that passed a sentence on the system. In spite of shining beginnings, the living stimulus, which always produces an impregnating effect, was missing in it. Therefore, it is intelligible that it gradually grew stiff and numb and was bound to step in the background against other schools.

In spite of that, the historical significance of the Vaiśeṣika is immensely great and the influence, which it has exercised, can be hardly over-estimated. The manner to think—which it has created in the doctrine of the categories, has shone out far and wide and has influenced the new school of the Nyāya until the present times. The opponents of the Vaiśeṣika also could not escape its influence. They have developed and formed a large part of their doctrines in the discussions with the Vaiśeṣika. So in spite of its weaknesses or foibles, this system represents a significant limb of Indian philosophy which assumes an important place inside the whole and without which the remaining would never be fully intelligible.

8. THE SYSTEM OF THE JAINA

In the last section we have dealt, in connection with the origin of the Vaiśeṣika system, with the development of the old Indian Nature-philosophy in general, so that it is not necessary to describe, besides, the individual doctrines. Only in one case we must make an exception—in the case of the Jaina ; that is the fully developed philosophical system which developed, in the course of the period with which we have dealt, out of the simple ancient doctrines of the Jina. This stands apart from the general development and exhibits so many original features that we must deal with it separately. Still it is not necessary, to deal with it as much exhaustively as we did with the Vaiśeṣika. Because, the system of the Jaina cannot be compared with the Vaiśeṣika in point of philosophical importance and effect. Besides, its detailed historical representation through periods is not possible. This is due to the constitution of the tradition as also to the present position of research. Before we speak of the condition of the tradition (or the material handed down), we must speak a few words about the external history of Jinism, so far as it concerns the development of the doctrine and is, therefore, important for us here.

In the case of the representation of Buddhism, we shall see that a large number of schools were formed early on its soil from which different important systems were created which differed from one another in essential features. Anything comparable to it is absent in Jinism. We hear, no doubt, in the old period, of different schisms.[317] Interesting opinions about the doctrine are also mentioned. Thus, the founder of the sixth schism is supposed to have represented a doctrine of categories similar to that of the Vaiśeṣika. But apart from the uncertainty of information, these schisms have not led to the foundation of lasting schools and to any formulation or development of important doctrines. For us, the historical fact which is of practical importance is only the great split of the Jaina Church in two branches—the Digambara and Śvetāmbara. What is reported by legend about this split is worthless and is of no interest for us. The fact is that we must reckon with this split in the first post-Christian Centuries. As the names Digambara ('sky-clad') and Śvetāmbara ('white-clad') show, they deal originally with a difference in the ways about the life of the monks. Differences in the opinion about the doctrine seem to have been formed gradually and were never very great. Still the following thing is important. Through the fact that both the branches of the Church led their own lives, its result was that the changes, to which the holy tradition was naturally subjected in course of time, followed in the two branches in different ways so that gradually traceable differences were developed. Only the Śvetāmbara have maintained the old canon, while it was given up by the Digambara and was replaced by the later dogmatic works. Also from the point of contents, differences of all sorts appeared forth.[318] Further the separation resulted in the Śvetāmbara and the Digambara developing their own literature and many times going their own manifold, different ways. These differences, however, played a great role only in later times and we shall have to deal, in the representation of the Knowledge Theory, with the Digambara and Śvetāmbara separately. In the period with which we have to do here, the differences are without any great importance and we can, therefore, leave them out of consideration.

Now, regarding the constitution of the handed-down tradition: When we try to describe how out of the simple doctrine of the Jina, the doctrinal system of the Jaina developed, as it is represented to us at the end of the classical period of Indian philosophy, there stand before us, for our disposal, several masses of tradition. Among them in the first place, the writings of the Jaina Canons are to be named. As we have already said during the description of the doctrine of Jina,[319] the oldest tradition of the Jaina is contained in the canon of holy writings, of which we have already spoken briefly. On that occasion we have already pointed out that this canon consists of very heterogeneous constituents, that, beside very old texts, there stand such as are younger or later by many centuries and that it is difficult to peel away and get at the oldest kernel which forms a certain foundation for the presentation of the teaching of Jina. Already this composition of the Canon out of the layers of different times could give precious starting points for the development of the doctrine and could hand down precious material for a presentation such as we attempt here. But with this aim, the composition of the canon itself must be clearly presented; its different constituents must be separated and arranged from the point of time. But hardly the first steps have been taken towards it.

One does not fare better with the next mass of tradition viz. the commentaries on the canonical writings. On the Jaina-canon, we possess a rich commentary-literature, the production of which belongs to the period here dealt with. The oldest among these works are called *'nijjutti'*. They are composed in verses and give, in the shortest form, the keywords for the orally handed down explanation of the holy texts. Later these works were supplemented with interpolated verses, and were finally enlarged into extensive metrical commentaries which were named *'Bhāsa'*. Connected therewith are further prose commentaries called *'Cuṇṇi'*. All these works are composed in Prakrit and form the foundation for the later exhaustive commentaries in Sanskrit. Rich material may be necessarily found in these works for the history of the Jaina doctrine. But they are printed only in small parts and their evaluation has yet hardly begun.[320]

There remains, therefore, only the third mass of tradition—the group of independent doctrinal writings. Such writings were already composed in the period with which we are dealing. Of all, there are the works of two authors, which are to be considered here. They are the works of Umāsvāti and Kundakunda. Of these, Umāsvāti was the pupil of Ghoṣanandī and Mūla, was active in Pāṭaliputra and is supposed to have lived in the first post-Christian centuries. Of his works the most important are the *'Tattvārthādhigamasūtrāṇi'* ('aphorisms about the knowledge of the meaning of truth') on which he himself composed a commentary.[321] The Sūtras were recognized as authoritative by the Śvetāmbara as well as the Digambara ; the commentary, on the other hand, only by the Śvetāmbara. The second author Kundakunda is counted as the Digambara. About his person, reliable information is missing. Still he is supposed to have been a native of the Deccan and must have belonged to a time not much later than Umāsvāti (about 300 to 400 A.D.). Numerous works are ascribed to him, of which *'Pavayaṇasāro'* ('the kernel of proclamation or preaching')[322], the '*Pamcatthiyasamgaho*' ('summary of the five masses of existence)[323] and the '*Samayasāro*' ('the kernel of the doctrine')[324] are the most important.

The works of both these authors give us a sufficient picture of the doctrinal system of the Jaina upto their time. The difficulty lies in the fact that in the present state of our knowledge regarding that time, their works appear not as parts of a connected literary development but stand by themselves alone. They do not allow the Jaina doctrine to appear in its development but recite only the condition upto their particular period. In spite of that, our knowledge of the general development renders possible the essentially true assessment and arrangement of information offered by them. We, therefore, hope to give, at least in the ground features, a correct picture of the Jaina doctrine of the classical period. In doing so, I proceed thus: The work of Umāsvāti gives, in the most concise form, the dogmatics of Jainism. It embraces the entire range of the doctrine. But it presents only the dry, short maxims. The philosophical thought comes in them very briefly. Besides, it enters incomparably at great length into things which are philosophically of only little interest—such as the construction of the world, which the Jainas delineate in all particulars in a phantastic way, or the directions of conduct for the monks. Reverse is the case of Kundakunda whose work is dominantly characterized by philosophical interest. He deals especially with the theoretically important fundamental questions. He handles them at length and in a well-thought-out way. Consequently, he neglects the external particulars. Under these circumstances, I choose for my presentation the following way : I accept, as the basic foundation, the aphorisms of Umāsvāti but touch only very concisely what is philosophically unimportant. For that, I seek the explanation of Kundakunda to illumine the philosophically important problems in hand. Besides, I give this stuff or material the arrangement which corresponds to our hitherto offered presentation of the Nature-philosophical doctrines.

In this way, the doctrinal system of the Jaina in the classical period of Indian Philosophy represents itself like something as follows :

There are five masses of existence (*astikāyāḥ*), space (*ākāśam*), impulse (*dharmaḥ*), hindrance (*adharmaḥ*), souls (*jīvāḥ*), matter(*pudgalāḥ*). They are permanent and firmly fixed in number. Out of them is composed the world (*lokaḥ*) which is only one and limited according to the Jaina doctrine. The first three masses of existence : space, impulse and hindrance are only existing as one each. They are incorporeal (*arūpī* or *amūrtaḥ*) and immovable (*niṣkriyaḥ*). The space is infinitely great; it stretches not only over this whole world but also far beyond it over the non-world (*alokaḥ*). It consists of endlessly innumerable points of space. Impulse and hindrance are restricted to the world, as they can be effective only in this world, but they fill it entirely.[325] They consist of innumerable space-points. The existence and operation of space consists in the fact that it preserves space for things and receives them in itself. The efficacy of impulse and hindrance consists in the fact that through them are rendered possible the movement and rest in things.

Beside these three masses of existence, there is also named, in general, the time (*kālaḥ*)). It was not received into the list of masses of existence. But one soon saw himself compelled to explain, when difficulties presented themselves.[326] First, one defined Time (*kālaḥ*), just as he described three masses of existence, according to its efficacy, as it was stated that Time is that which renders possible the mutation (*vartanā*) of things.[327] Then it was naturally clear that the Time is incorporeal. But now already begin the difficulties. While the remaining masses of existence were defined according to their relation to space and it was declared how many space-points they take, one was, on the other hand, compelled to say in regard to time that it has no space-points. But with it the question arose, in which form it then existed. In order to answer this question, it was explained that the Time stood leaning upon (*pratītya*) the variable masses of existence : souls and matter. Slowness and speed in the mutation of things, it was said, are not possible without a mass (*mātrā*). The mass again cannot be independent of variable or mutable things. It stands only in dependence on them. But can one, under these circumstances, characterize time as material or object as substance? Views wavered on this point. Kundakunda and the Digambara in general decided in its favour. Umāsvāti allows the question open. The following was also to be further considered : What depends on the variable or mutable things is naturally not the time in general but only the present, the moment (*samayaḥ*) This moment is transitory and originates and vanishes in the same moment. It is the time which an atom requires in order to cross one space-point. Only that, which earlier and later is connected with it, is, as one taught, the time (*kālaḥ*) in general. Umāsvāti and Kundakunda explained this question somewhat like this.

Now remain still the two most important masses of existence: souls and matter. Both are different from the hitherto described ones through the fact that they are a plurality and are mobile. For, the souls are incorporeal and alone spiritual (*cetana*) among all the masses of existence. The particles of matter are unspiritual or insentient but they alone are corporeal (*rūpī* or *mūrtaḥ*) among all the masses of existence.

The characteristic of the souls is, according to Umāsvāti, that they influence one another (*parasparopagrahaḥ*)[328]. Far more important and characteristic of their nature is, however, their activity (*upayogaḥ*), which depends on their spirituality or sentience and consists of knowledge and sight or view.[329] Further the soul is not only a sentient or spiritual knower, it is also a doer, enjoyer and master (*prabhuḥ*). It is the doer (*kartā*) so far as it accomplishes actions which determine its fate in metempsychosis. It is the enjoyer (*bhoktā*) because it enjoys the fruit of its works. It is the master (*prabhuḥ*) because its fate in metempsychosis as well as its Deliverance lie in its hands and depend on itself only. In these definitions, the comprehension of the soul as a doer created some difficulties.[330] The Jaina designate, as we have already said in the description of the doctrine of Jina,[331] action or *karma* as a material stuff which streams in the soul through the activity of the soul, fixes itself firmly and binds it. Now naturally one cannot say that the soul brings forth this material stuff, this action. Only the condition of the soul (*bhāvaḥ*) which brings forth the instreaming stuff, is caused through its action. Besides, one can, in a certain sense, assert that it is the material stuff which is brought forth by the work or action and the condition concerned. But in another sense, the soul itself is the cause of this condition. Thus its activity properly consists in doerness. All the named qualities of the soul, it may be remarked here, occur to it in full measure but only in the state of Deliverance. In the case of the wandering souls, they (qualities) are restricted by the in-streaming *Karma*-stuff in different ways and come into validity only when this *Karma* is destroyed (*kṣayaḥ*) or is brought to rest (*upaśamaḥ.*)

Concerning the extension of the soul, it embraces as many points of space as also the World-space. It can, therefore, fill the entire world. But it can also, on account of its subtleness or fineness and because it is not impenetrable, draw itself together to any small space as it likes. The embodied soul has the size as large as that of a body in which it is embodied and to which it adjusts itself. This adjustment is elucidated by the example of light which in a similar way fills space, may it be great or small.

The matter (*pudgalāḥ*) is, as we have said, insentient and corporeal in contrast to the souls.[332] Its operation consists therein that the body, the speech, the psychical organ and the breath are formed out of it and further that it causes pleasure, pain, life and death.[333] As regards its extension, it is to be distinguished as atoms (*aṇavaḥ*) and aggregates (*skandhāḥ*). Of these, the atom takes one point of space, the aggregates as many as they like, according to the number of their atoms. But they have a particular size only in the form of gross matter. In the form of fine or subtle matter, as many atoms as one likes are crowded together in any small place.

The origin of aggregates (*skandhāḥ*) ensues through the conglomeration of atoms and small aggregates or through the disintegration of the big ones. Atoms arise only through the disintegration of aggregates. The amalgamation of the atoms in the formation of an aggregate depends on the quality of touch which occurs to the atoms.[334] Thus touch is either rough (*rūkṣaḥ*) or smooth or sticky (*snigdhaḥ*).[335] Besides, both sorts of touch occur in different degrees from the least roughness or stickiness or smoothness to the highest one. When the atoms which possess the quality of touch in different degrees occur together, though they may be homogeneous or heterogeneous, they join themselves with one another. This theory was supplemented with some definitions which remain provisionally unintelligible to us regarding their origin and proof. For example, it was asserted that atoms, which possess these qualities in the smallest degree, generally enter into no connection. In the case of those which enter into connection, there must be a difference of two degrees in the strength of their qualities upon which after the entry of the connection an equalization follows.

The doctrine of qualities is formulated in an original way. Here also atoms and aggregates are distinguished. The old qualities of the elements occur in the atoms : touch (*sparśaḥ*), taste (*rasaḥ*), smell (*gandhaḥ*) and colour (*varṇaḥ*). The qualities of the aggregate are, besides, sound (*śabdaḥ*), connection (*bandhaḥ*), subtleness or smallness (*saukṣmyam*), grossness or bigness (*sthaulyam*), form or shape (*saṃsthānam*), separation (*bhedaḥ*), darkness (*tamaḥ*), shadow (*chāyā*), radiation of warmth (*ātapaḥ*) and illumination (*uddyotaḥ*). In these, for example, with sound, they held fast, in the ancient manner, to the material character of this quality. In the qualities of the elements, further sub-varieties are distinguished. The touch is eight-fold: hard, soft, heavy, light, cold, warm, sleek, rough. The taste is five-fold : bitter, pungent, acrid, sour and sweet. The smell is two-fold : fragrant and obnoxious; and the colour is five-fold : dark, blue, red, yellow and white.

It is now remarkable that according to the Jaina doctrine, these qualities are not distributed according to the elements on the atoms but that they occur to all the atoms equally symmetrically. Every atom possesses a taste, a smell, a colour, and two kinds of touch. In the atoms, therefore, there is no difference of Elements. Only in the formation of the aggregate, through the change (*pariṇāmaḥ*) to which all material things (*pudgalāḥ*) are continually subject, the particular qualities arise forth, others step back and there arises the difference of Elements. It is this basic difference which distinguishes the atom-doctrine of the Jaina from that of the Vaiśeṣika and which, perhaps, is conditioned by the Jinistic doctrine of relativity of which we shall come to speak.

To the doctrine of masses of existence, Umāsvāti joined the doctrine of categories : As we have already mentioned, the Jaina know only three categories : substance (*dravyam*), quality (*guṇaḥ*) and condition (*paryāyaḥ*). They have not formulated the theory of categories in the way of the Vaiśeṣika. We, therefore, find no enumeration and full description of all substances, qualities and conditions from the stand-point of the doctrine of categories. Umāsvāti, on the contrary, satisfies himself with a short mention and definition of a few individual categories.[336] He says : "A substance is that to which cling qualities and states". "Qualities have substances for their bearer and are themselves without qualities". "The constitution of the substances and qualities" finally "is its change (*pariṇāmaḥ*)" or its condition.

Though in the Jaina doctrine one renounced the formulation of the category-doctrine after the manner of the Vaiśeṣika into a frame in which the whole traditional Nature-philosophy was included, it was sought to make it fruitful in another way. Through the attempt to define more exactly the nature of the categories and their relation with one another, one reached a comprehension of the nature of things which created the philosophical foundation or groundwork for the Jinistic theory of relativity according to which the constitution of things admitted a plurality of comprehensions and assertions or expressions. We see this already in Kundakunda.[337] He first inquires into the nature of substance and finds it in existence (*sattā*). Thereby he considers as existing that which according to its nature is a given fact (*sahāvasiddham* or *avatthitaṃ sahāve*). The existence consists now in origination, disappearance and preservation or persistence. This triad appears bound with each other ever and indissolubly. There is no origination without destruction, no destruction without origination and both not without persistence. The substance whose nature consists of existence is, therefore, continually adhered to by origin, destruction and persistence and with all together. Consequently it is subjected to continual change in which it still persists imperishable. This apparent contradiction is explained through the relation of the substance to the qualities and conditions. According to the Jaina doctrine, the substance is not only their bearer but it is, by its nature, inseparably bound with them. There is no substance without qualities and conditions and no qualities and conditions without substance. It is not to be understood in the sense of the Vaiśeṣika that substances, qualities and conditions cannot occur separated from one another. But therewith a unity of its nature is supposed to be asserted by it (*doṇham aṇaiṁṇabhūtaṃ bhāvaṃ*). This explains the union of change and persistence in the nature of a substance. What originates and disappears is not the substance itself but its qualities and conditions. Its existence, on the other hand, persists. In the case of the origination and disappearance of things, one need not speak, after the fashion of the Vaiśeṣika, of the origination of the non-existent but the things, according to their qualities and conditions, are subjected to origination and disappearance.

Kundakunda explains this doctrine in the example of the soul.[338] The soul possesses different qualities like sentiency and activity. And it appears in different forms of existence in different conditions as god, man, denizen of hell or animal. When a man dies and is reborn as god, or in any other form of existence, it is not the soul that dies and is reborn but it is only the condition as man and god that dies and is reborn. One can, therefore, speak of no disappearance of the existent and the origination of the non-existent but only of a change of the condition of the soul.

With this we have said, in the sense of the Nature-philosophy as well as from the stand-point of doctrine of categories, what is most necessary about the factors out of which the doctrinal system of the Jaina forms its world-picture and can now go on to consider the world-picture itself. In that we meet with many remarkable ancient features beside the unbridled phantasy-building in the delineation of individual things.

Regarding the construction of the world,[339] the Jaina know only one world which floats in empty space. It is, below, the broadest, narrows itself towards the middle, then again gets broader, until finally to become narrow again. Occasionally its shape is compared to a human being who stands with spread-out legs and it is perhaps a very old idea. In the lower parts of the body of this world-man, the hells are found, in the middle is the human world and in the upper part and the head the heaven and finally the place or spot of the emancipated.

This whole world is surrounded by many covers or veils : first of all, by empty space, then by thin air, then by thick air and finally by thick water.

The hells which occupy the lowest part of the world are seven in number and are situated like storeys over one another.

In them, the creatures, which are born therein, on account of their bad deeds, suffer terrible torment which is partly inflicted by them mutually but partly also inflicted by hellish demons.

Above the hells, the human world is situated. In its middle is found the continent of Jambudvīpa like a mighty disk, around which there are, in continually larger rings, the alternating oceans and other continents. It is divided in seven zones through six chains of mountains which go through it from the west to the east. The southern-most is India-the Bhāratavarṣa-which is separated in the north from other remaining continents by Himavān or Himālaya the first of the named mountain-chains. In the middle of the whole Jambudvīpa, Meru, the mountain of the gods, raises itself as a gigantic cone. It is remarkable that only the Jambudvīpa, the first of the continents. surrounding it and the inner half of the second are inhabited by men. And only a part of this sphere is the place of works (*karmabhūmiḥ*), that is, only in it, the good and bad works could be accomplished and eliminated and only in it is Deliverance possible.

Above the human world are the heavenly worlds. The gods, of whom there are four classes, in no way, inhabit only the heavenly worlds. Both the lowest classes, among whom the Jaina include the half-gods and demoniac creatures of popular superstition, live in the human world or the underworld or partly in heaven. Also the third class—the stargods who circle around the divine mountain and create the division of time, belong to the human world. Only the fourth class represents the proper denizens of heaven. Their numerous worlds are again situated one above another storey-like and fill the above or upper part of the entire world. Above them, there is only a thin space— the spot of the Delivered. All gods live in happiness and magnificence. Thus the higher are superior to the lower in life-duration, power and bliss. Nevertheless, their sphere of influence, their size of the body, their possession or property, their pride are smaller, as their earthly bondages are smaller.

The whole world holds good as permanent for the Jaina. As distinguished from other systems, the Jaina know no continually recurring world-originations and world-destructions. Evidently their doctrine had early assumed so firm a shape that this idea could no more penetrate them. On the other hand, they know the old idea of the alternation of world-ages, though in a peculiarly recast form. According to them a very good (*suṣamasuṣamā*) world-age is followed by a good one (*suṣamā*); after that there follow a good-bad (*suṣamaduḥṣamā*) age, a bad-good (*duḥṣamasuṣamā*) age and finally a bad (*duḥṣamā*) age. Then begins again an ascent. The world-ages recur again in a reverse sequence. Thus up and down they join themselves with one another in permanent alternation.

The most important events in these world-periods recur permanently and the Jaina believe that they can specify it to a detail. In every cycle of six world-ages, according to their opinion, 63 great men appear—24 Prophets (*tīrthaṃkarāḥ*), 12 Kings ruling over the world (*cakravartinaḥ*) and 27 great heroes. The last consist of 9 groups, of 3 each, which are characterized by the names Baladeva, Vāsudeva and Prativāsudeva borrowed from the Kṛṣṇa legend. The history of these 63 great men forms the world-history of the Jaina. Towards their compilation the whole legend-and-fairy-tale-world of India has been requisitioned. Thus the history of the 8 hero-triads corresponds to the Rāma-legend. Then the 8th Baladeva is Rāma or as the Jaina call him Padma from whom his consort Sīta was carried away by Prativāsudeva, the demon-prince Ravana and she is won back in an adventurous struggle. The 9th Vāsudeva is Kṛṣṇa who kills the bad King Kaṃsa and vanquishes the Prativāsudeva Jarāsandha, the father-in-law of Kaṃsa, who was interested in his vengeance. With the Kṛṣṇa-saga is connected the main story of the great heroic epic Mahābhārata—of the internecine strife of the two princely houses of the Kaurava and Pāṇḍava. And the most famous fairy-romance of ancient India—the Bṛhatkathā of Guṇādhya, was also, along with them, pressed into service. In such a way the Jaina have sketched a comprehensive picture of the whole world-occurrence. For them it had this advantage that they produced, before their followers, the total legend-tradition remodelled in their spirit or sense and could make them therethrough serve the religious aim. Indeed we need not conceal the fact that the Jaina-works which describe the world-history show more a well-meant edifying tendency than poetical power. But the world-history is a remarkable and characteristic constituent of the Jaina-doctrine and as such it deserves a short mention at least in a work about Indian philosophy.

Regarding the beings which people the described world, they were classified from different points of view.[340] At bottom are all the beings of the Souls of whom the largest part is involved in metempsychosis. That gives rise to the division of the released and the wandering souls. The wandering souls were divided, according to the number of the sense-organs, according as it was connected with the sort of their entanglement (in birth). Of the sense-organs, the usual number of five was known: the senses of touch, taste, smell, eye and ear to which the objects of touch, taste, smell, colour and sound were juxtaposed. The plants have only one sense-organ and also element-beings have one sense-organ. According to the Jaina doctrine, souls are connected not only with the plants but also with all elements. Of them, the souls connected with parts of Earth and Water as well as the plants are motionless, while those in the parts of Fire and Air are mobile. To them all occurs as sense-organ the sense of touch or contact. Of the animals, the lowest ones possess the two sense-organs of touch and taste. Among the ants, there occurs already the sense of smell. In the bees and other higher insects, there occur the eye. Among all further animals, among the beings of hell, men and gods, there is also the ear. They possess, therefore, all the five sense-organs. Besides the sense-organs, the souls are also connected with the psychical organ (*manaḥ*). It is the case, in respect of beings in hell and gods and in respect of men when they have left the mother's womb and in respect of a part of the animals.

Another classification of living creatures is the otherwise wide-spread division according to their origin.[341] Of them the Jaina know three sorts : a sudden appearance into view (*upapātaḥ*), begetting (*garbhaḥ*), and coagulation i.e. the self-active conglomeration of element-parts (*sammūrchanam*). A sudden appearance into view is found among gods and beings of Hell. The begetting leads to three sorts of birth, according as the creature is born in an egg (*aṇḍajaḥ*), from the embryo in the womb (*jarāyujaḥ*) or as a living young one (*potajaḥ*).[342] Those born from the egg are birds, reptiles and fish. From the embryo in the womb are born mostly higher quadrupeds and human beings. As living young ones are born into the world not only some higher quadrupeds like elephants but also hares, ichneumons, mice and bats. Through coagulation or conglomeration (*sammūrchanam*) originate finally the remaining living creatures.

What Umāsvāti has to say about the constitution of living creatures in the different worlds, about their duration of life and such other things, is a pure web of phantasy and is philosophically of no interest. I restrict myself, therefore, in the following, in essentials to the theory or doctrine of men. The man, as a soul entangled in the cycle of birth, consists of soul and body, according to the Jaina doctrine. Thus, however, many bodies are to be distinguished.[343] As we already know, the Indian philosophy knows, since old times, not only the usual gross body. We have, for example, in the presentation of the Sāṃkhya, known of the fine body (*sūkṣmaṃ śarīram*) which is the bearer of the transmigration of the soul.[344] We have also heard, during the description of the Yoga, of a mental body (*manomayaḥ kāyaḥ*) which the Yogī separates from his gross body and which serves him for the practice of wonder-powers.[345] Artificial bodies (*nirmāṇakāyāḥ*) are also mentioned, which are created by ascetics through their super-natural power, for different aims. The Jaina have seized all these suggestions and systematically built out of them. Accordingly, they distinguish, in all, five bodies : a gross body (*audarikaṃ śarīram*), a transformation-body (*vaikriyaṃ śarīram*), a transference-body (*āhārikaṃ śarīram*), a fiery body (*taijasaṃ śarīram*) and a *karma* body (*kārmaṇaṃ śarīram*).

The gross body is the usual body among men and animals who originate through begetting or through coagulation. Among gods and creatures of hell who appear forth directly, the transformation-bodies emerge into their place. These bodies can also be acquired by ascetics as a result of perfection (*labdhiḥ*) and serve the practice of miraculous powers.[346] The transference-body is also the result of perfection. It consists of good and pure stuff, encounters no resistance on account of its fineness or subtleness and is created in order to bring information about important questions from a teacher who is in another place. According to Umāsvāti, the ability to create such a transference-body was restricted to the old ecclesiastical teachers who were still in possession of full holy knowledge. The assumption of a fiery body is based on the old idea of a magical lustre which an ascetic acquires through his self-mortification and through which he may be able even to burn his enemy. According to the Jaina doctrine, it is an independent body which causes the shining out of lustre and splendour. Partially, this body is considered as a result of Perfection which is acquired by an ascetic. Partially, one was of the view that it occurs to all creatures from the beginning and one sporadically assumes that it influences digestion. The *Karma*-body finally is a result of the *Karma*-stuff clinging to the soul. This *Karma* brings forth the *Karma*-body as well as other bodies just as the sun lights itself up as also other things. As an instrument of entanglement in the cycle of birth, the *Karma*-body accompanies all beings from eternity until the moment when they attain Deliverance.

Of the bodies enumerated, the following is always finer than the preceding one and consists of a conspicuously large number of points (*pradeśāḥ*). The last two bodies, the fiery and *karma* bodies are so fine that they can reach any limit of the world without encountering resistance. Of these bodies, every creature possesses several, but four at the most. It holds good also for men. A man possesses in every case the gross-and-*Karma*-bodies. The fiery body can further occur in addition to them. Besides he can also gain the transformation-body or the transference-body but only one at a time, because these both exclude each other.

Among men, the four life-forces (*prāṇāḥ*) are bound up with the bodies.[347] These are the life-force of the senses (*indriyaprāṇāḥ*), the life-force of strength (*balaprāṇaḥ*), the life-force of life (*āyuḥprāṇaḥ*) and the life-force of in-and-out-breathing (*ānāpānaprāṇah*). The life-force of the senses embraces the five sense-organs. Under the life-force of strength are to be understood the body (*kāyaḥ*), speech (*vāk*), the thinking (*manaḥ*). The life-force of life is the cause which preserves the existence. About in-and-out-breathing, nothing is further to be remarked. All these life-forces are of a material nature. Among them only the group of the sense- organs has a great importance and about this something is more to be said.

Regarding the working of the sense-organs, Umāsvāti does not go so much into it deeply. We have already mentioned the most important considerations in the general presentation of old Nature-philosophy. We can, therefore, exclude them. Remarkable and worth mentioning are *still* the different forms of phenomena which the Jaina distinguish under every sense-organ.[348] Here also lie at the bottom, as in the doctrine of different bodies, old ideas which have been seized upon, supplemented and finally brought into a regular system by the Jaina. Old and generally widespread is the distinction between the proper sense-organs and the parts of the body which represent their bearers. The Jaina include, under consideration, further, the part of the soul which operates in the sense-organs. Besides, they distinguish, corresponding to their categories, between substance and condition. They arranged these ideas systematically and came to the following doctrine :

Among the sense-organs, there is a two-fold distinction : the sense-organs as substance (*dravyendriyam*), the sense-organs as condition (*bhāvendriyam*). The *sense-organ as substance* is divided into talent or tendency (*nirvṛttiḥ*) and an instrument of doing (*upakaraṇam*), of which again each one can be inner (*abhyantaraḥ*) and outer (*bāhyaḥ*). The inner tendency consists of the points of the soul which, arranged in a definite form, are active as sense-organs. The outer tendency (*bāhyanirvṛttiḥ*) consists in the particles of matter which join themselves together under the influence of *Karma* in conjunction with these points of the soul in the same form. Under instrument of activity (*upakaraṇam*), the bodily organ is to be understood ; in the sense of sight, for example, the eye-ball is as the inner instrument, while the eyelid, the eyelashes are as external instruments. In the case of the sense-organs as condition, ability or capacity (*labdhiḥ*) and activity (*upayogaḥ*) are distinguished. The capacity is produced through the destruction (*kṣayaḥ*) or the coming to rest (*upaśamaḥ*) of *Karma* which stands in the way of the corresponding activity of the soul. The activity (*upayogaḥ*) is the change (*pariṇāmaḥ*) of the soul which eventually appears forth.

The psychical organ (*manaḥ*) is twofold : as substance (*dravyamanaḥ*) and as condition (*bhāvamanaḥ*).[349] In the first case, it consists of the matter which has conglomerated together into a psychical organ under the influence of *Karma*. In the second case, is to be understood, thereunder, the adaptation of the concerned parts of the soul which appear forth on account of the destruction of the hindering *Karma*. About the activity of the psychical organ, Umāsvāti has little to say. It is the bearer of the reason or judgement and examines what is useful and harmful in order to strive after it or avoid it. He also observes that it is operative in the usual form of knowledge and in the sense-perception besides the sense-organs and as a single organ in knowledge through communication.

This small survey of the mind has its good reason or motive. In the doctrine of the Jaina, the soul has preserved its old constitution. One, as before, held fast to the view that it is of a restricted size and denies the doctrine of the infinity of the soul assumed by the Vaiśeṣika. One also participated as little in the other changes which this doctrine in the Vaiśeṣika underwent in future —above all, concerning the qualities of the soul. For the Jaina, the qualities of the soul are, in the first place, knowledge which, by no means, something external, is joined to the activity of the organ, especially of the psychical organ and vanishes as soon as the soul stands alone by itself. The qualities belong, on the contrary, firmly to its nature and occur to it also after Deliverance. Consequently Deliverance does not represent, as in the Vaiśeṣika, a state of absence of consciousness. The Released one possesses, on the contrary, all the qualities of the soul to an unlimited and in the highest degree and he is, above all, omniscient. But out of this it follows that the psychical organ is not an indispensable presupposition of all knowledge-processes. It, on the contrary, appears as by far unnecessary or a thing to be dispensed with. Therefore, it is conceivable that it played only a modest role in the epistemology of the Jaina.

With these considerations about the psychical organ and its working, we have already reached what forms the kernel of human nature, according to the Jaina doctrine, in respect of the soul and its qualities. As already described before, the Jaina consider the soul as the bearer of different qualities. Among them, knowledge is the most important and therefore Umāsvāti deals with it more closely.[350] He distinguishes between five sorts of knowledge : experience (*matijñānam*), communication (*śrutajñānam*), supernatural perception (*avadhijñānam*), knowledge of other men's thoughts (*manaḥ-paryāyajñānam*) and omniscience (*kevala-*

jñānam).[351] Of these, the first two are natural forms of knowledge. They ensue with the help of the sense-organs and of the psychical organ and are therefore indirect (*parokṣaḥ*). The remaining three deal with the supernatural forms of knowledge. They depend exclusively on the knowledge-faculty of the soul and are therefore, direct (*pratyakṣāḥ*). This division shows the one-sided interest which governs the epistemology of the classical Jaina system. All usual knowledge-processes—sensuous perception, conceptual thought and memory are summarized in a word simply as experience (*matijñānam*). The communication (*śrutajñānam*) is only conceded on account of its special position, as the knowledge of the Jaina doctrine depends on communication. The next two forms of knowledge are important for the ascetic who has trodden the way of Deliverance. The omniscience (*kevala-jñānam*) which forms the conclusion is for the Jaina an essential characteristic of the Released.

With regard to the different kinds of knowledge, in particular, the following is to be observed :

The experience (*matijñānam*) passes through four stages. It begins with a first fleeting notice (*avagrahaḥ*). It is followed by a wish (*īhā*) to know the noticed object more exactly. That leads to the clarifying of the real state of things (*apāyaḥ*) and finally to the final ascertainment of the object concerned (*dhāraṇā*). In the case of the first notice (*avagrahaḥ*), there is only an unparticularized impression. The remaining steps, on the other hand, comprehend already the object concerned. Perception through sight and thought forms an exception. They are never entirely unparticularized or indefinite. In them, on the contrary, the first notice (*avagrahaḥ*) comprehends the object.

The communication (*śrutajñānam*) is based on experience (*matijñānam*). It can be of two sorts, according as it is, according to its contents, contained in the holy writings of the Jaina canon or not. In the first case, it is twelve-fold according to the number of holy writings. In the second case, it can be of the most different kinds.

The supernatural perception can be innate but it can also be caused by the destruction or coming to rest of the opposing *Karma*. The first case is of the Gods and creatures in Hell, the second of the remaining beings. Umāsvāti distinguishes, besides, six varieties of supernatural knowledge accordingly as it vanishes on change of place or not, whether its sphere of operation decreases or increases, and whether it is changeable or not.

In the case of knowledge of others' thoughts (*manaḥparyāyajñānam*), Umāsvāti distinguishes between simple and all-comprehensive forms, the second being characterized by greater clarity and permanence. In the case of omniscience (*kevalajñānam*), no varieties are distinguished.

Objects of experience (*mativijñānam*) and communication (*śrutajñānam*) are all substances but not in all conditions (*paryāyāḥ*). Objects of supernatural knowledge and of the knowledge of others' thoughts are only the material object (substances) and these also not in all conditions. Only the omniscience has as its objects all substances in all conditions.

As conclusion, it may be mentioned that Umāsvāti, besides the mentioned forms of right knowledge, considers also false knowledge. This appears in three forms which are the counterparts of right experience, communication and supernatural perception and consists in the fact that a man like a lunatic knows without any distinction the true or the right and the untrue or the wrong, as the chance may be.

The Theory of Knowledge of the Jaina : Umāsvāti tries to put the described sorts of knowledge in relation to the means of right knowledge which the other philosophical schools taught and strives to connect them with the epistemological doctrines of these schools. But his attempt is mechanical and inadequate. The Jaina created a real Theory of Knowledge and Logic only late, when the Theories of Knowledge of other schools also reached their highest flowering. We shall return to it, during the presentation of that period. Besides the means of right knowledge, the Jaina have also continually dealt with the doctrine of the various ways of consideration (*nayāḥ*) and in this there sticks an old kernel which perhaps goes back to the first beginning of Jinism. Into this doctrine we must go at this place at least slightly.

Already in the oldest parts of the Jaina canon, it is reported that the Jina had the habit to answer the questions which were put to him, not simply, in short, in a definite sense but he pointed out that one could see things differently from different sides and that, accordingly, different answers may be possible. Jinism held fast to this view and built it gradually systematically. For instance, a number of view-points were posited, according to which one considered the things and four view-points were distinguished according as man directed his attention to the name (*nāma*), presentation (*sthāpanā*), the substance (*dravyam*) or the condition (*bhāvaḥ*) of a thing.[352] More important is the already mentioned doctrine of the different ways of consideration (*nayāḥ*) to which a thing can be subjected. It was especially carefully elaborated and gained, in the later theory of knowledge of the Jaina, a firm place beside the doctrine of the means of right knowledge (*pramāṇāni*). But philosophically it is most important that through this manner, one came to consider the things and attribute to them a manifold composite nature which made them appear now this way, now that way, according as a man looked at it from this or that side of its nature. This comprehension of things which was designated as the doctrine of relativity (*syādvādaḥ*), we already meet with in the Sāṃkhya and the Mīmāṃsā.[353] But nowhere did it get so much importance and nowhere it was so systematically worked out as in the Jaina. All the mentioned thoughts developed slowly in course of time. They attained their full shape, however, only in the last period of the classical period of Indian philosophy when the theory of knowledge stood in the forefront of interest. There we shall occupy ourselves with it more exactly. Only the doctrine of the ways of consideration (*nayāḥ*) with which Umāvāti deals more closely, will be here, in short, recited in the form in which Umāsvāti puts it forth.[354]

According to Umāsvāti, there are five ways of consideration : the one in current use (*naigamaḥ*), one in which things are summed up (*saṃgrahaḥ*), one which is customary (*vyavahāraḥ*), one which is rectilineal or straightforward (*ṛjusūtraḥ*), and one in linguistic use (*śabdaḥ*). Of these, the first is divided into two and the last into three sub-varieties.

The way of consideration as in current use (*naigamaḥ*) concerns itself with the objects of the words used in usual life and with the knowledge of these objects. The two sub-varieties are : first, when a man has a special object before his eyes, the second when he has the object of a like sort. Still one makes no difference in them in particular. The way of consideration which is a summing up (*saṃgrahaḥ*) considers one or many objects which are characterized according to the above-mentioned four view-points in a general comprehensive way, whether they be present, past or future. The customary way of consideration (*vyavahāraḥ*) takes in the things by large as they are comprehended in the same way by the ordinary men and by the experts and as they come in use in daily life. The straightforward way of consideration (*ṛjusūtraḥ*) knows the things according to their naming, in so far as they are at hand and present. The linguistic way of consideration (*śabdaḥ*) can be as concerning the present (*sāṃprataḥ*), when the objects are present and are known through words which comprehend one of the above-mentioned four view-points and are known from previous or earlier time. It can be bound (*samabhirūḍhah*) when it holds itself to an object at hand in particular and goes over to none else. It is named finally as thus constituted (*evambhūtaḥ*) when it directs itself to the mutual connection of expression and the object.

We have now described a large part of the classical system of the Jaina. We have dealt with the factors out of which the world is built, the world-edifice and the beings which people it. With it is the stage set, on which the world-event happens. This itself consists, as for Indian doctrines of Deliverance, as well as for the Jaina, in the course of cycle of births which endures permanently as long as one does not succeed in escaping from it through Deliverance. The law of metempsychosis and the way of Deliverance are yet to be described.

The Jaina doctrine of Deliverance : The doctrine of Deliverance belongs to the oldest constituents of the Jaina system, because what the Jina proclaimed was, in the first place, the doctrine of Deliverance. What we have already said during our presentation of the teachings of Jina holds good, therefore, in its basic features.[355] The later period has, above all, added what I name as the scholastics of Deliverance. That is to say, one inquired what is useful for Deliverance and what stands in its way, enumerated virtues and vices, gave directions and prohibitions and was absorbed in externalities and secondary things but knew to give to the whole an outlook of a stately and well-organized doctrinal edifice. Umāsvāti has summarized in his aphorisms the whole Deliverance-scholastics and it forms a large part of his work. It is philosophically utterly unimportant and produces a dry effect with the arid systematics of the aphorisms. I give it only roughly in broad features. It exhibits something like the following picture :

From the standpoint of the doctrine of Deliverance, Umāsvāti distinguishes seven basic truths—souls (*jīvāḥ*), non-souls (*ajīvāḥ*), instreaming (*āsravaḥ*), bondage (*bandhaḥ*) warding off (*saṃvaraḥ*), cancelling (*nirjarā*) and deliverance (*mokṣaḥ*). We have already spoken about the souls and the non-souls and need now speak only about the remaining basic truths which directly concern Deliverance.

The entanglement of souls in the cycle of births depends on different causes—on false belief (*mithyādarśanam*), non-observance of moral commands (*aviratiḥ*), negligence (*pramādaḥ*), passions (*kaṣāyaḥ*) and activity (*yogaḥ*).[356] Of these Umāsvāti deals in details with the non-observance of moral commands.[357] These are the five basic moral commands (*vratāni*): Cessation from injuring the living (*hiṃsā*), from falsehood (*anṛtam*), theft (*steyam*), unchastity (*abrahma*), and from striving after possession (*parigrahaḥ*). According as they are practised in a restricted or full measure, they are designated as small or great. Their observance is facilitated through the practices of the following kind: One considers that the injury to living creatures, etc. brings here and in the next world harm and disgrace and that it is exclusively sorrowful. One, therefore, applies himself to the well-wishing towards all beings, rejoices in the advantages or benefits of another, shows compassion for the unhappy and equanimity towards the incorrigible. One considers the constitution of the world and of his own body in their aspect of futility in order to promote the pious ardour and passionlessness. The monk or the houseless one is obliged to observe the great moral commands or vows. The small ones hold good for the laymen or the householders. Further, the laymen can also take up additional vows.[358] Umāsvāti elucidates all these commands more exactly. Injury to a living creature is said as robbing a being of its life by deluded action. One offends against this vow of non-injury to a living creature not only when he kills another creature, but also when he binds, strikes, injures, heavily belabours another creature or deprives him of food and drink. Falsehood is uttering something that does not exist. As untruth are enumerated also false information, secret rumours, falsification of record, appropriation of confided goods and betrayal of secrets. Thus and in a similar way, all the vows are described by Umāsvāti.

The non-observance of vows represents only one cause of the entanglement in metempsychosis. By far more important is that every activity of the body, speech and the psychical organ leads to entanglement as its consequence. Because, through activity, there stream into the soul the suitable relevant particles of matter and fix themselves as *Karma* in it and bind it, as merit when it is instreaming through good activity and as guilt when it streams in through bad acts. This instreaming (*āsravaḥ*) of the *Karma* stuff is the third basic truth and is accordingly described at length by Umāsvāti who distinguishes in it numerous sub-varieties.[359]

First of all, it should be distinguished whether the activity, which entails instreaming, is conditioned by passions (*kaṣāyaḥ*) or not. Only in the first case, the instreaming matter clings to the soul in an enduring manner, while in the second case, it is immediately separated and has no further consequence. In the first case, the instreaming can be caused through the five-fold non-observance of moral commands on account of the four passions: anger (*krodhaḥ*), pride (*mānaḥ*), deceit (*māyā*) and greed (*lobhaḥ*), through the five-fold negligence of the senses, and through the twentyfive kinds of actions. Further, different sorts of instreaming are distinguished, according to the make-up or constitution of activity, which entails it, whether it is strong or weak, conscious or unconscious, whether carried out with energy or its object is living or lifeless. Therewith are joined again numerous distinctions of further sub-varieties. Finally, the instreaming can be divided according to eight kinds of *Karma* which it has for its result. It is as follows:[360]

The instreaming *Karma* matter sticks, as we have said, to the soul and binds it. This bondage (*bandhaḥ*) is the fourth basic truth. It is formed or organized according to the constitution of *Karma* which has entered the soul and it is divided into eight kinds. They are namely the *Karma* causing the veiling of knowledge (*jñānāvaraṇam*), *Karma* which envelops insight (*darśanāvaraṇam*), emotional (*vedanīyam*) *Karma*, bewildering (*mohanīyam*) *Karma*, *Karma* of life-prolongation (*āyuṣkam*), *Karma* of the name the individuality (*nāma*), *Karma* of the social position (*gotram*) and the hindering *Karma* (*antarāyam*).

The knowledge-veiling *Karma* is five-fold according to the five sorts of knowledge which it hinders. The insight-enveloping *Karma* is nine-fold. The insight, which it hinders, can be through the eye or not through the eye, or through supernatural sight or the sight of the all-knowing. Further the insight-enveloping *Karma* can call forth the unconsciousness of sleep which can be absorbed in by stages, such as going and standing or acting in sleep. The emotional *Karma* is two-fold, according as it leads to happiness or unhappiness. Of the bewildering *Karma*, there are 28 kinds. They can perplex the belief or the conduct. In the first case, it is threefold, according as the belief is right, erroneous or partly right and partly erroneous. In the second case, it is to be distinguished whether it depends on passion or not. If it depends on passion, it gives rise to sixteen sorts, as there are four passions of which each can emerge in four degrees. In that which does not depend on passion, the causes are laughing, pleasure, displeasure, fright, application, horror and consciousness of sex as man or woman or being without any sex-distinction—which comes to nine kinds. In the *Karma* of life-prolongation there are four kinds which are to be distinguished, each according as it respectively deals with beings in hell, animals, men or gods. The *Karma* of individuality exhibits the most numerous kinds viz. 42 kinds. They condition the individuality of a being in the most diverse respects, above all, according to the stage of being, class, formation of the body and bodily functions. The *Karma* of the social position can be high or low, of which again there are numerous varieties. The hindering *Karmu* finally is of a five-fold kind: it hinders the activity of giving, taking, eating, using and willing.

Besides the kinds of *Karma*, Umāsvāti also describes its duration, its operation or ripening (*maturity*) and its multitudinousness. Thus he gives, how long each sort of *Karma* endures at its highest or lowest. He mentions how far a change in the operation is possible. And he discusses the relation of the points of *Karma* to the points of the soul.

All sorts of *Karma* bind the soul in the most diverse forms and fix its fate in the cycle of births. Besides, they influence the constitution of the soul itself in an incisive way. The Jaina have distinguished and described, according to this influence, different conditions (*bhāvāḥ*) of the soul.[361] Accordingly there are five such conditions: the condition of the coming to rest of *Karma* (*aupaśamikaḥ*), the condition of the destruction of the same (*ksāyikaḥ*), the mixed condition (*kṣāyopaśamikaḥ* or *miśraḥ*), the condition of the operation of *Karma* (*audayikaḥ*) and the conditioning of the quality of *Karma* (*pāriṇāmikaḥ*). In the condition of the coming to rest, the *Karma* is no doubt present but it has come to rest and does not operate. As a result, there is the emergence of right belief and right conduct. In the condition of destruction, the *Karma* has completely vanished. The soul rejoices in the full knowledge and view and in the unhindered activity of giving, taking, enjoying, using and willing. In the mixed condition, where *Karma* is partly brought to rest or partly destroyed, there stand, beside knowledge, also ignorance, further, restricted view, giving, taking, enjoying, using and willing, right belief and right conduct and partly self-discipline, all to a limited extent. In the condition of the operation of *Karma* there emerges membership of or participation in the four forms of existence, as denizens of hell, animals, men or gods; further the four passions—anger, pride, deceit and greed—the three sexes, false belief, ignorance, deficient self-discipline, impiousness and the six colours of the soul (*leśyāḥ*) yet to be spoken of. The condition of the quality of *Karma* finally implies the condition or constitution which occurs to the soul by nature without regard to *Karma*, namely, sentiency (*jīvatvam*), potentiality of deliverance (*bhavyatvam*) or the absence of potentiality of deliverance (*abhavyatvam*) and others.

At this stage, it is the proper place to mention, in short, the doctrine of the colours of the soul, which Umāsvāti touches many times. According to the old Jaina doctrine, the *Karma* lends the soul a definite character which shows itself in taste, smell, touch but above all in colour. There are six such colours of the soul: dark (*kṛṣṇaleśyā*), dusky or blue (*nīlaleśyā*), grey (*kapotaleśyā*), yellow (*tejoleśyā*), rosy (*padmaleśyā*), and white (*śuklaleśyā*). These colours of the soul change continually, each according to the actions of beings and according to their fate in the cycle of existence. The souls of the denizens of hell, and of lower animals have only dark, dusky or blue and grey colours. The gods can also possess the bright colours, the highest gods exclusively those only. Among men and animals, having five senses, all colours of the soul are possible. This doctrine of the colours of the soul is only loosely connected with the rest of the doctrine of the Jaina and makes the impression of being a foreign body. And it is possible that the Jina has taken it from the chief of the school of the Ājīvika, Maskarī Gośālīputra.[362]

With this we have described the third and the fourth basic truths—the instreaming of *Karma* in the soul and the bondage of the soul conditioned by it. But how is freedom from this bondage possible? The two following basic truths, warding off (*saṃvaraḥ*) and cancelling (*nirjarā*) point it out.[363] Of these (*saṃvaraḥ*) 'warding off' implies the hindering of new *Karma* streaming in the soul, and cancelling (*nirjarā*) implies the destruction of the already penetrated *Karma*. In the description of both these basic truths, we can understand that Umāsvāti has recited in a large part the same which we described in the presentation of the doctrine of Jina. Only he inserts some things more and carries forth the doctrine further, in some particulars

As the warding off of new *Karma*, first of all, different forms of moral behaviour and spiritual practices serve as means. Such are three kinds of discipline : discipline (*guptiḥ*) of the body, of the speech, and of thought ; further the fivefold cautiousness or wariness (*samitiḥ*), the ten duties (*dharmāḥ*), the twelve considerations (*anuprekṣāḥ*) and the enduring of 22 miseries (*pariṣāhāḥ*).[364] Besides, there is the five-fold conduct (*caritram*) : the plain pious conduct, the conduct of a monk after receiving the consecration, the conduct of a monk who has expiated for a fault, the conduct in which only a quite little remissness occurs, and finally the faultless conduct as it corresponds to the ideal picture already sketched.

As the next, follows the penance (*tapaḥ*). This serves as not only the warding off of new *Karma* but also of the cancelling of the old. It is two-fold : external and inner penance. The external penance consists in the omission of meals, diminishing of nutrition, restriction to a particular diet, renunciation of dainty food, choice of a lonely resting-place and mortification of the body. The inner penance consists in confession and penitence, reverential behaviour, intentness on serving, study, renunciation and mediation. Umāsvāti again distinguishes a large number of sub-varieties. By far the most important among them is the mediation (*dhyānam*). It consists in the collection and suppression of thought and can last up to nearly an hour. The meditation can be of four kinds : (i) mournful, (ii) malignant, (iii) pious and (iv) pure. The mournful meditation consists in lively thinking on the disagreeable which one has suffered, in order to be free from it, and on the agreeable, in order to attain it. Among beings, it occurs to those who are not abstemious, partially abstemious, or are negligent in self-discipline. The malignant meditation aims at murder, falsehood, theft and the preservation of earthly goods and is practised by creatures who are unabstemious or partially abstemious. The pious meditation helps towards the understanding of the holy doctrine, of the aberrations of beings, of the results of actions and of the world-construction. It can be reached by those who are not remiss in self-discipline, and by such whose passions have come to rest or are destroyed. For the beings of this kind there are accessible the first two steps of the highest form of meditation with which we have been already, in particular, familiar in the doctrine of Jina.[365] The last two steps of pure meditation are, however, reserved for the omniscient one.

All the named forms of penance help towards the cancellation of *Karma*. Still their working is different, according to the beings who practise it. They operate much more energetically in the case of monks than in the case of laymen. In the case of the monks also, the success is determined by the moral stage which they have reached.

With the destruction of *Karma*, there ensues the deliverance.[366] First disappear the bewildering (*mohanīya*), knowledge-veiling and insight-enveloping (*jñānāvaraṇa* and *darśanāvaraṇa*) and the hindering (*antarāya*) *Karmas*. Through their disappearance is unfolded the true nature of the soul unhindered and the omniscience (*kevalam*) appears, which consists of full knowledge and insight. The emotional *Karma*, the life-prolonging *Karma* and the *Karma* of individuality (*nāma*) and the *Karma* of the social position (*gotra*) still continue and therethrough the existence continues. Finally disappear also these forms of *Karma*, then the existence comes to an end and the final Liberation emerges. The soul, an account of its natural lightness, ascends up to the highest part of the world, where it remains in permanent blessedness.

Umāsvāti represents the Deliverance-doctrine thus. His presentation is a typical example of Jainistic Deliverance-Scholastics and produces not a very satisfactory impression. But happily that is not the only way in which the subject-matter has been dealt with by the Jaina. The second author, whom we have chosen for our presentation i.e. Kundakunda, offers an example of an entirely new way of consideration. Kundakunda cares little for everything which is external or mechanical. He is not occupied with the classifications and enumerations. He knows them but they remain in the background. He seizes the essentials and pursues the philosophical thought to its depth, entirely in contrast to Umāsvāti who clings to the superficial. We could observe it up to now many times. But nowhere it is seen so strongly as in the doctrine of Deliverance. We shall give, therefore, a short sample of that at least.[367]

In the attempt to reshape the handed-down form of the Deliverance Doctrine according to a uniform broad basic view, many old maxims present difficulties. In order to circumvent them, Kundakunda chose the following way.[368] He says that two ways of consideration must be distinguished, in considering things—the pure (*śuddha-nayaḥ*) or the final (*niścaya-nayaḥ*) consideration and the common-place (*vyavahāra-nayaḥ*) consideration. The common-place consideration (*vyavāhara-nayaḥ*) is necessary in order to make the doctrine intelligible to ordinary men. One can only come to an understanding with a foreigner when one uses his speech.[369] But one must be clear about the fact that it has validity only in a certain sense. It should necessarily supplement the pure way of thought which alone brings full truth. As he interprets, therefore, these maxims in this sense, he understands them in such a way as to bring them in unison with his comprehension.

Concerning the Deliverance, Kundakunda employs the

traditional views with a few changes as the basic structure of his presentation. The last cause of entanglement in the cycle of being is the three stains or pollutions (*āsravaḥ*):[370] desire, hate and delusion. On them depend the four causes of action : wrong belief (*mithyātvam*),[371] ignorance (*ajñānam*), indiscipline (*aviratiḥ*) and activity (*yogaḥ*). These call forth the material *Karma* (*pudgalakarma*) which clings to the soul. The decisive cause is, however, the delusion or the ignorance (*ajñānam*) of the true nature of the soul. This consists in the fact that one regards foreign things as the 'I', because he thinks, "I am it ; It is my I. I belong to it ; it is mine." But only a fool makes these wrong ideas of the 'I' and designates the material things as mine. Because, how can the soul, as the omniscient have viewed it, be a material thing, so that one could designate it as mine ?[372] The soul, on the contrary, is mere activity (*upayogaḥ*),[373] pure view (*darśanam*), knowledge (*jñānam*) and morality (*cāritram*). Neither the base quality like delusion, nor the good quality like the piety can occur to it.[374] In general, the material qualities have nothing to do with the soul, beginning from the qualities of the Elements to the psychical conditions which are brought forth through the instreaming *Karma*. When such qualities are ascribed to the soul, it depends only on the above-mentioned common-place or habitual way of consideration (*vyavahāranayaḥ*). From the standpoint of the final way of consideration (*niścaya-nayaḥ*) it is not justified. The connection of the qualities with the soul resembles a mixing of water and milk.[375] But they belong, on that account, not to the soul. Its single quality is, on the other hand, the activity.[376]

Now how does Deliverance ensue? When man knows the fateful mistake which confounds the soul and matter together, as one knows of property not belonging to him: "it is not mine," and gives it up, so also one knows of the matter and its qualities: "It is not my I, it is not mine", and separates himself from them. Simultaneously, one is supposed to observe the soul according to its true nature as view (*darśanam*), knowledge (*jñānam*) and morality (*cāritram*). Then an ascetic who practises this contemplation of the soul in continuous endeavour, reaches in a short time the freedom from all sorrow. Just as a man, who has known the king, confides in him and joins in his company with full vigour or fervour in order to attain the fulfilment of his desires, so also a man knows the soul—the King among things, confides in him and joins in his company in order to attain Liberation.[377]

These are a few thought-processes in which the doctrine of Deliverance of Kundakunda moves. As already said, they avoid, in contrast to Umāsvāti's, all externalities and go to the essentials. Indeed, it cannot be denied that they bring in nothing new but repeat the old widespread views. The idea that the ignorance is the cause of entanglement in the cycle of existence and that, thereby, the error about the true nature of the 'I' plays a decisive role, is already known to us from the ancient period of Indian philosophy since the doctrine of the Buddha and it again meets us in the classical Sāṃkhya where it stands in the central place of the doctrine of Deliverance.[378] Still we must say that Kundakunda has cleverly adapted it to the Jaina system and has given it an original form. He has, thereby, also not overlooked the difficulties with which the traditionally handed-down Jaina doctrine of the nature of the soul confronts him and has tried to remove them.

In the Sāṃkhya, there stands a sharp separation between the I—the soul, and the non-I—the matter and this relation between the soul and matter renders possible the proving of the doctrine of Deliverance which is given by the system. According to the Sāṃkhya system, the soul is pure knowledge and completely inactive. Every psychical occurrence takes place in the psychical organism which belongs to the sphere of matter. Only to all appearances, therefore, it is involved in the occurrences of the phenomenal world. The knowledge of this error, therefore, is enough to liberate it. The case is different in the system of the Jaina. Here the soul is considered as active and as the bearer of the psychical processes and it was, consequently, not possible, without much further ado, to prove the Deliverance in the same way. Kundakunda tried the following way out. The psychical condition depends, according to the Jaina doctrine, by far, on the *Karma*-stuff which has penetrated into the soul and exercises various influences on it. He, therefore, taught that there are different kinds of *Karma* whose difference from the soul one must know in order to attain Deliverance. The Deliverance depends, accordingly, according to this interpretation, again on a distinction between the soul different from all material things and matter which dominates the psychical processes. Indeed, the activity of the soul, itself, allows itself not to be completely explained away, and so one could easily be tempted to ascribe to it an interlocking in the occurrence of the phenomenal world which again had made impossible the tracing of the deliverance back to the removal of a mere error. Kundakunda tried to meet the difficulty as follows: He distinguished between two sorts of psychical conditions—the material condition generated by the *Karma* and the condition of the soul itself called forth therethrough. It is the material conditions which one must distinguish, like everything material in general, from the soul. Thereby, the working of these both does not encroach on each other. The soul brings forth only its own condition, though under the influence of *Karma*. The *Karma* brings forth its condition, though under the influence of the soul. When it is said that the soul brings forth the material condition and knows it also at the same time, it is to be understood as a common-place way of looking at things (*vyavahāranayaḥ*). According to the final way of looking at things (*niścayanayaḥ*), it produces and knows only its own condition.[379]

This sample may be enough in order to show how Kundakunda deals with the theory of Deliverance. With it we have also ended our short sketch of the Jaina system in the period of the classical Indian philosophy. Still it remains our task to define, on the basis of our presentation, what place and importance belong to it in the circle of other remaining systems.

The importance of the System of the Jaina: If we review, with this aim, the doctrines already described, so far as they fall in the sphere of Nature-philosophy, a certain old-fashionedness or antiqueness in them is striking. The Jaina have held fast to the old doctrine of the four elements. The space (*ākāśam*) has preserved its character and has not become the fifth element. Consequently, the sound (*śabdaḥ*) is an independent entity and not a quality of any element. The list of the qualities of the elements shows very antique features. Further it is remarkable that the system of the Jaina assumes only a single world and that it knows different world-periods, but that it has not accepted the doctrine of the periodically recurring world-creation and world-destruction. Besides, it is to be especially emphasised that one, with respect to the soul, in contrast to the ruling development, held firmly to the idea of its restricted size and its mobility and efficiency.

Besides these pronounced old antique features, later ideas also found acceptance whereby the doctrine was remodelled often in an original way, many times its original significance also being lost. One occupied himself with the problem of Time. One took over the doctrine of merit (*dharmaḥ*)and guilt(*adharmaḥ*) as world-moving forces, and made them, as the independent *Karma* doctrine was already fully developed, the bearers of movemeet and rest. It is very important that the Atom-Theory also found access in it; still, the entirely peculiar comprehension of the Jaina regarding the constitution of matter shows that here there is not the proper soil on which it has grown. According to the Jaina doctrine, the matter can be gross as well as fine or subtle. It is, therefore, not impenetrable but can contract and extend. With that the most important presupposition for the creation of the Atom-doctrine is missing. And the mechanical world-picture which has been sketched by the Vaiśeṣika is foreign to the Jaina. Characteristically missing also therein is the theory of movement and its laws. Besides the Atom-doctrine, the Jaina have also accepted the doctrine of categories—but of only the beginning ones. They differentiate between substances and qualities. They know the category of movement as little as the mechanics. They have not also shared in the further development of the doctrine of categories. In the place of all other categories they have posited only the category of condition (*paryāyaḥ*) which is best adapted to their comprehension of the manifold and changing nature of things.

Besides such doctrines which it shares with other systems, the doctrine of the Jaina exhibits also characteristic features and ideas which are peculiar to it. In the sphere of anthropology, for example, there is worked out the doctrine of the different bodies, of the two forms of sense-organs or of the different kinds of knowledge, may-be schematically but also originally arranged. Only to the Jaina, the manner is peculiar, to distribute all things in points of space (*pradeśaḥ*) and to consider them accordingly. But philosophically the most important are the different ways of consideration (*nayāḥ*) and the doctrine of relativity (*syādvādaḥ*) based thereon, which sees united in the nature of all things an alternating manifoldness.

Finally, besides the philosophical constituent parts of the system,there is also conspicuous the luxuriant growth of a sportive or playful phantasy which appears here, more strongly than in other systems. Thus for example, in the sphere of Nature-philosophy, during the consideration of the animal and the plant-world, the phantasy takes a far more share than scientific observation. But this luxuriance of phantasy shows itself strongest in the case of the world-picture delineated down to all particulars, above all, in the detailed description of the world-occurrence which happens permanently recurring, in the world-history peculiar in this form only to the Jaina.

When we summarize all this, there appears a quite variegated picture. The system appears as a motley mixture of antique and young or late doctrines and philosophical thoughts which are mostly not fully worked out and appear to be the creation of boundless phantasy.

If we ask the reason of this remarkable state of things the answer is already given in what we have already said in the presentation of the doctrine of the Jina.[380] The Jaina cherished the conviction that their doctrine depended on what was proclaimed by the omniscient one. On account of that, every development was subjected to firm restrictions from the begining. Because, the proclamation of the omniscient one cannot be changed and bettered. Doctrines, which are once uttered forth, stood firm and could not therefore be displaced. They can be interpreted and supplemented but not quashed. That explains the many antique features which the system has preserved. It also explains the half-measured and imperfect execution of philosophical thought. The thinkers of the Jaina were at every step subjected to limits which they were not to transcend. For the consistent carrying out of new great thought, for the erection of a uniformly compact doctrinal edifice, there was no room. Under these circumstances, it is also understandable, as one was cribbed and confined on all sides in the pursuit of original thoughts, that one sought for it a substitute and consequently, where the traditionally handed-down dogmatics showed a lacuna, the phantasy was allowed to have free reins without check.

The comparison with Buddhism is very instructive. While the Jaina system makes, in a great measure, an impression of backwardness and stuntedness, the Buddhists have created, on the other hand, grand doctrinal edifices which were of greatest significance for the development of the total Indian philosophy. One asks oneself involuntarily how the two doctrines, which originated at the same time and under the same conditions, could develop so differently. But a satisfactory explanation is also found at the same time. The simple doctrine of Deliverance of the Buddha had allowed a free path or course to the great philosophers of later Buddhism. They could lay hold of its thoughts unhindered and carry them through. The agreement with the few teachings handed down from old times was easy to be created. The position in which the Jaina found themselves was entirely different. Numerous aphoristic teachings were handed down to them which they were not to change. They were compelled to fill their wine in old hoses and to take great care that the latter do not burst. This could only produce a paralysing effect on philosophic thought. In spite of these things, we need not think little of the system of the Jaina. It is not only that it has enriched the general picture of Indian philosophy with independent features; it is not merely a storehouse of odd, antique ideas. The teachers of Jaina have, on the contrary, despite all difficulties, seen the things independently and comprehended them originally. And we find, among them, many earnest and deep thinkers, like Kundakunda, for example, who deserve more consideration than they have found hitherto.

9. THE MATERIALISM

It is advantageous to join the nature-philosophical schools with the description of Materialism, as the latter stands nearer to them than all other schools. By the way the Indians themselves, as a rule, speak not of Materialism but they characterize its adherents usually as deniers or negativists (*nāstikāḥ*). And it has its good ground. For the Indian Materialism the essential thing is not the denial of the soul and the exclusive restriction to matter as the cause for the explanation of the world. The decisive thing, on the contrary, is its purely negative interest. Its aim is to dispute and deny the continuance of life after death, the retribution of good and bad work and the moral claims derived out of them. It is interested in philosophical questions only so far as they serve this aim. Concerning the rest, it is indifferent to them. That distinguishes it from all others and also from Nature-philosophical schools. Naturally Materialism could reach its aim most quickly, if it denied the existence of the soul. But so far as the assumption of a soul served only the explanation of the phenomenal world, as was the case in the old Nature-philosophy, before it was connected up with belief in God and with the doctrine of Deliverance, it was also acceptable to the Materialism. As a matter of fact, there are also found given materialistic directions which recognize a soul in this sense and which have established a connection, therethrough, with the Nature-philosophical schools. But while these nature-philosophical schools were governed by the striving towards the understanding of the phenomenal world and their attempts at explanation gradually formed into the full-fledged philosophical system, the materialists satisfied themselves all the while with their positing of a purely negative aim. Therefore the Indian characterization of them as 'deniers or negativists' is appropriate. But in my presentation I will follow the usual practice for the sake of simplicity and speak of Materialism by which a man should not lose sight of the right understanding of what has been said.

Materialistic directions of the above-mentioned kind are

already found in India since early times. The old maxim, that materialism is as old as philosophy, holds good also here. And just as we hear, in the recorded oldest Vedic monuments, of believers in god, also of god-deniers, there is also information about materialistic directions standing side by side with the oldest recorded monuments of philosophical doctrine. In India, there early emerges a characteristic feature which also holds good for the later period—a close connection of materialism with political theory. The Indians had early developed a systematic doctrine of state-craft which made light of all moral scruples in the positing of its aim and of the choice of means, which, therefore, corresponds to what for us is associated with the name of Machiavelli. The embodiment of this statecraft is the legendary Minister of the King Candragupta of the Maurya family, who founded for the first time an indigenous empire on the Indian soil at the end of the fourth century B.C. The Indian tradition ascribes the merit for the success of Candragupta to this Brāhmaṇa named Cāṇakya or Kauṭilya and has always seen in him an unsurpassed master of the art of statecraft. The most famous Indian literary work about the science of statecraft is handed down under his name. This Cāṇakya, as is shown by tradition, is the prototype of the unscrupulous Real-politiker who avoids no means, if it only leads him to his goal. And his ideal as well as his theory have been much esteemed in the circles of practical Politikers or politicians.

It is now easy to understand that such a Politiker from the point of world-view supported himself on a doctrine which put out of the way or removed all moral scruples that were hindrances to his action. One such doctrine was Materialism. Its positing of the aim, as we have described above, corresponds entirely with its purpose. It was created for this circle, whether it may acknowledge it openly or secretly. It is, therefore, certainly no accident that the first materialist, whom tradition has handed down to us in living vivid colours, is a King.

King Paesi: We find, in the canon of the Jaina, as also of the Buddhists, the account of a conversation which one of their teachers had with a King who adhered to a gross materialism. The conversation ends, as it is to be expected according to the origin of the report, with the conversion of the King. But the narration is carried out in such a lively way and gives such a graphic picture of the materialistic views in the period of the Jaina and the Buddha that I cite a few pieces out of them.[381]

In the City of Seyaviyā, there rules a bad King Paesi (the Buddhists call him Pāyāsi) who believes in no God and no beyond. One day, the holy man Kesi arrives in this city. Now the King has a charioteer named Citta who was won over earlier by Kesi as an adherent and who longingly wishes that the King also should be converted. He knows how to arrange it skilfully so that the King, during his morning drive, alights down in the park in which Kesi is staying and it comes to a conversation between the King and the holy man. The King has heard that Kesi believes in a soul which is different from the body and reproaches him as follows:

"If you have the conviction that the soul is different from the body and not the same, I have, on the other hand, to cite the following. I had a godless, wicked grandfather who did not administer his Kingdom well and who, after his death, must have reached hell on account of his bad actions. If now he would come to me who am ever his beloved grandson—his joy and care—and warn me against living as godlessly as he did, in order that I should not go to hell, then I would believe that the soul is different from the body. But as he has not come to warn me, I am convinced that the soul and the body are the same."

Thereupon Kesi replied: "If you notice, oh King, that your wife has given herself up to another man, what punishment would you inflict on this man?"

"I would get him executed in any way."

"If the man were to request you that he should be given some time before his execution in order to warn his relatives and acquaintances against a similar offence, would you grant him also at least only one moment?"

"No, why should I?"

"Entirely in the same way, thy godless grandfather, who according to our doctrine, is in hell, has not come; he has, no doubt, the wish to come to thee his beloved grandson—his joy and care—in order to warn thee. But he cannot. Because there are the most diverse grounds that a being tarrying in the hell, however much he would like to come to men, cannot come. Therefore, believe, Paesi, that the soul is different from the body."

And again the King says: "What you say is merely a comparison and does not apply to the following. I had a very pious grandmother, who according to your doctrine, must have got, after her death, into a world of the gods, for her pious acts. If she would come to me who was her most beloved grandson—her joy and care—and admonish me to live piously like her in order that I should attain the world of the gods, then I would believe that the soul is different from the body. But she has not come to admonish me and I am convinced that the soul and the body are the same."

Upon this, Kesi knew how to reply. But Paesi has also made an experiment. He reports for example: "I was once in my reception-hall surrounded by the distinguished elite of my kingdom. There the city watchman brought a thief whom they had caught. I got him thrown alive into a brazen pot, with a brass lid strongly soldered laid over it, with the coppersmith watching over him. After some time, I got the lid opened and found the man dead, though there was no opening in the pot, through which the soul could have escaped. Had there been an opening in the jar through which the soul could have escaped I would believe that the soul is different from the body. But it was not the case. So I am convinced that the soul and the body are not the same."

And another experiment: Paesi had first executed one offender and then got him locked up in a jar and when it was opened after some time, the corpse was full of worms. The jar, however, had no opening through which the souls of these worms could have reached the inside. Another offender was got weighed by Paesi. Then he was killed, except that his skin only was injured and he was again weighed. But the weight was the same. Therefore, no soul could have escaped. Another offender he got hacked to pieces in order to search the soul but it was not to be found. Such other like experiments were made by Paesi. Kesi knew appropriate answers to all these arguments and finally Paesi gives himself over as beaten and converted.

This account gives a lively picture of an old Indian

Materialist on the King's throne. And Paesi was certainly not the only one of his kind. But however interesting and characteristic such accounts are, they can rarely claim a place of the same kind in a history of Indian philosophy. The Materialism gains for it an importance from the moment only when it emerged in the form of a regular doctrine and took up arms against the remaining philosophical schools. That occurred also very early. The old writings of the Buddhistic canons report that, in the time of the Buddha, a large number of teachers stalked the land and gathered students around themselves. Among them are found such as represent the materialistic doctrines.[382]

The oldest Materialistic doctrines: We hear of a certain Pūraṇa Kāśyapa who taught the following; "Anybody may do or allow to do anything, mutilate or allow somebody to be mutilated, roast or allow somebody to be roasted, persecute, plague, harass or get somebody persecuted, plagued or harassed, may rob life, steal, break into a house, drag away the loot, plunder a sequestered house, carry on highwaymanship or brigandage, commit adultery or lie; but he, with all this, does nothing bad. If any one, with a razor-sharp quoit, reduces a living creature on the earth to a heap of flesh, transforms him into a single lump of flesh, he would thereby prove himself as nothing bad; it would not appear as anything bad. If any body would go to the southern bank of the Gaṅgā,[383] murdering and allowing somebody to murder, mutilating and allowing somebody to mutilate, roasting and allowing somebody to roast, he would prove himself as nothing bad; it would not appear bad. And if he would go to the northern bank of the Gaṅgā,[383] giving gifts and causing them to be given, sacrificing and causing sacrifices to be offered, it would thereupon prove in no way meritorious; it would not appear as merit. Through presents, self-discipline, self-mastery and veracity, there arises or appears no merit."

A second teacher Ajita Keśakambala represented the following view: "There is no gift in charity, there is no sacrifice, there are no offerings. There is no fruit and ripening of good and bad actions. There is not this world or that. There is no mother nor father. There are no suddenly born beings.[384] In the world, there are no ascetics and Brāhmaṇas who have gone along the right path of conduct and follow the right conduct, who have seen this world and that world out of independent knowledge and proclaimed it. A man consists of four Elements. When he dies, earth goes into the mass of earth (*pṛthivīkāyaḥ*), the water into the mass of water, the fire into the mass of fire, the breath into the mass of air, and the sense-organs enter into the space (*ākāśaḥ*). Four men with the bier as the fifth carry forth the dead person, and they carry on their talk until they come into the place of cremation. Then there remain only white bones and all the sacrifices end in ashes. The gift of charity is, therefore, the doctrine of a buffoon; it is an empty and false talk when anybody asserts that there is something. Fools and wise men are destroyed and disappear when the body falls to pieces. They are no more after death."

A third teacher finally Kakuda Kātyāyana teaches the following :

"There are seven masses (*kāyāḥ*) which are neither created nor brought forth. They are unfruitful, unchangeable, and are firm like a pillar. They move not, nor do they change, they do not disturb each other, nor are they able to procure joy, grief or joy and grief. Which are these seven masses? The earth-mass, the water-mass, the fire-mass, the air-mass, pleasure, pain and the souls (*jīvāḥ*) as the seventh. These seven masses are neither created nor produced, they are unfruitful, unchangeable, and firm like a pillar. They do not move nor do they change, they do not disturb one another and they are not able to procure pleasure, pain or pleasure and pain. There is no murderer, nor one who allows to murder, nor any one who hears or allows to hear, no knower or one who allows to know. When anybody with a sharp sword strikes off a head, nobody robs nobody of life. The sword passes, on the contrary, through the empty space, between the seven masses."

Of these three doctrines, the first exhausts itself in mere denial of all moral obligations. The second seeks to prove it with a gross materialism. The third finally represents an ancient Nature-philosophy which explains all occurrences through the inter-play of a number of permanent factors. The souls also occur among these factors. But this doctrine also denies everything transcendent. And all the three are unanimous in the fact that they deny continuance after death and the moral consequences arising therefrom, and are, in this sense, genuine materialistic doctrines.

The old writings of the Jaina also describe similar materialistic doctrines. We, therefore, see that Materialism arose early in the form of a regular theory. But the development, thereby, does not remain stationary. It led to the creation of a fully formed materialistic system which was handed down like all other systems, in the form of a School—that of the Lokāyata.

The Lokāyata System: The Lokāyata, i.e. the doctrine which concerns this world, arose in the pre-Christian period. As a founder is regarded one Cārvāka about whom nothing further is known.[385] It is characteristic for this system that it is clothed in the same form like the remaining systems. Like these, its doctrines are written down in aphorisms which were orally handed down.[386] Further one took care to refer his doctrines to a holy seer of antiquity in the Brahmanical circles. In a similar way, the Lokāyata derived its doctrine from a higher authority. As we have already heard, the Materialism was connected most closely with the circles which taught the art of Statecraft. But as the highest teacher of the art of Statecraft and as its legendary proclaimer was considered Bṛhaspati, the teacher of the gods and besides him, there was Uśanas, the teachers of the Asuras, the demons. Accordingly, the Lokāyata traced back their aphorisms to Bṛhaspati. Besides we also hear of a school which refers itself to Uśanas.

Like the aphorisms of the Vaiśeṣika and other systems,[387] the aphorisms of the Lokāyata also begin with the words : "Now we shall explain the truth." Now the chief maxims of the system follow sharply and trenchantly.[388] "Earth, water, fire, air : these are the entities." "One designates their connection or combination as body, sense-organs and objects." "Out of them develops the mind or spirit itself." "The knowledge arises like a force of fermenting intoxicant out of a yeast, etc." "The expressions of life (*jīvaḥ*) resemble bubbles in water." "And because there is nothing that continues in the world beyond, there is, therefore, no world beyond."

With this has been said what is essential of the Lokāyata. The man consists only of four elements ; there is no soul. Therefore, there is no beyond and no retribution of good and bad actions.

These short maxims or aphorisms were explained and further set forth, first in oral and, later on, in written elucidations. For example, the question was raised by the opponents' side, why, when as a matter of fact, everything consists of the elements, the sentiency emerges only in the human body and not in inanimate things like a pot or a vessel. Thereupon, the reply was : "The sentiency does not emerge into appearance in vessels etc., because the remaining causes are missing, just as in sand, the force of intoxication or intoxicant does not appear forth."[389] Again, the force of intoxication, when it is to appear forth, presupposes not only the presence of necessary things—flour, water and molasses and the remaining ingredients but also the fact that these must be in a particular condition of mixture. So also the elements only may produce the sentiency when they appear in a particular state i.e. in the form of the body as skin, bones, flesh and blood. In the corpse already, this condition is not preserved unchanged and therefore sentiency has vanished from it." In order to derive all the psychical processes out of the Elements, one took hold of the doctrine of the three juices in the body—phlegm, bile and wind.[390] It was taught that through phlegm, there arises desire, through bile, hatred and through wind, delusion. The manifoldness of life-forces, that one experiences in incalculable alternation—now joy, now grief—was traced by the opponents of the Lokāyata to the power of good and bad actions which, according to the rigorous law of retribution, lead to joy and grief. This law was denied by the representatives of the Lokāyata and they appealed to the inculable accidental rise of bubbles in water for explaining the accidentality of joy and grief. They also asserted that natural feelings or experiences ascribe all these life-forces to no soul. Because, for example, when a man says : "I know" or when a man also says, "I am lean ; I am fat", he speaks of no soul but only of a body. Because there is no soul.

The Buddhist teachings demanded a special comment, as they assumed no soul but only a stream of consciousness i.e. a connected series of knowledge-moments.[391] What was concerned here was not the contesting of the belief in a soul—which was also denied by the opponent—but of the proof that the series of knowledge-moments does not endure uninterrupted and does not continue from one existence to another. Because that was the proof of these schools in asserting in support of a continuance after death and of a retribution of good and bad actions. Accordingly, the representatives of the Lokāyata emphasised that the coming into existence of knowledge was bound up with a body and with entirely definite prerequisites. Therefore no knowledge comes into existence in the embryo, because the sense-organs are not still developed and there is no object (for them). So also knowledge is suspended in a state like that of swoon. The knowledge in an alleged rebirth depends, however, on an entirely another body and is exactly different, like the body, from an earlier knowledge. Tbere is, therefore, as little connection as that in the knowledge of two different beings who live simultaneously near each other. It is not also right to trace back, as one does, the expression of passions and instinctive behaviour of small children to experiences in earlier births. For, then, a man must be able to remember earlier (former) births, not only in isolated cases asserted by the opponent, but in general, just as all people who were together in one village would remember about it in a similar way.

There is, therefore, no soul, no survival after death and no retribution of good and bad deeds. When one speaks of such things, it is only a misuse of words, which originally implied something quite different.[392] The 'other world' (*paralokaḥ*), which word in India denotes a peculiar meaning, is nothing else than another place, another time and another condition.[393] Hell is nothing else than grief full of agony. Deliverance is the destruction of the body. The highest god is an almighty King.

The adherents of the Lokāyata developed and proved their doctrines like this. But there were not only systematic explanations or proofs with which they met their opponents. They also knew to use especially effectually the weapon of derision and knew how to make the opponent a laughing stock. Their derision, in the first place, was directed against the sacrificial cult of the Brāhmaṇas. They said, for example,[394] "If a man after leaving the body enters into a world beyond, why does he not again come back, driven by the impulse of love or affection to his relatives ?" But the belief in the other world is meaningless. Because, if "a sacrificer would reap the reward of heaven, after the sacrificer himself, the sacrificial act and the implements of sacrifice are long gone (into the limbo of the past), the trees which were consumed by a forest conflagration would as well bear fruit." Equally meaningless it is to offer an ancestral sacrifice to the dead. "If the ancestral offering of worship would be the source of gratification to the dead, then one could as well feed the flame of a lamp which is extinguished." "Fine, indeed, would be any such effect on the things which are distant. Then a man need not provide provisions (of food etc.) to the people who go on a journey. Because, then, nothing would prevent one from satisfying him (his hunger and thirst) by an ancestral offering of worship performed at home. ! But it is all a swindle ! The ceremonies for the dead which the Brāhmaṇas performed, have been performed to provide themselves with means of maintenance. There is nothing else in that." Generally, "the fire-sacrifice, the three Vedas, the bundle of three sticks which the Brāhmaṇas carry, and the besmearing with ashes serves only as a means of livelihood for men who lack intelligence and energy for any other occupation." "The mortifications, the different self-torments, the self-discipline, the deceits for the sense-satisfaction and the sacrificial acts like the fire-sacrifice are regarded as childish play" by reasonable men. If really that would have been true, "if", really as the Brāhmaṇas assert, "the animal slaughtered in the sacrifice would go to heaven, why does not, then, the sacrificer kill his father in order to despatch him to heaven ?" But "the authors of the Vedas are none else than the three categories of the crackers of jests, rogues, and night-sneakers, when they utter their unintelligible gossip, their '*jarbharī*' and '*turbharī*' "[395] passing it for the words of wise men. That is why one should not believe in anything of this kind but should live happily, so long as life lasts. There is nothing which does not expire after death. Once the body becomes ashes, then there is no recurrence".

Thus represents itself in broad features the doctrine of the Lokāyata in the older period. Its thought-processes are simple and have rarely interfered in the philosophical development. But they have continually found adherents and their school has maintained its ground through the whole centuries. Its situation becomes more difficult at the end of the classical period of Indian philosophy, when logical and epistemological questions moved to the forefront of interest and when every system was compelled to take them into consideration, on which their systems were founded. The adherents of the Lokāyata also could not escape this demand. Originally they made light of the fact. In the *sūtras* of Bṛhaspati[396] it is said : "The inference is not the means of right knowledge." One, therefore, appealed only to sense-experience and simply dismissed the further assertions of the opponent. One could do it so long as inferences which were arrived at by the antagonistic schools were simple inferences by analogy. It was enough to show the faultiness of every conclusion, in order to decline every inference as unreliable. Things, however, were different, as the opponent developed the firmly grounded scientific doctrines forming conclusions. One had to discuss these, nay, one was compelled to establish his own doctrine differently as from what he had done hitherto and to defend it. Partly one tried to hold fast to the old line, as, for instance, when one explained :[397] "The aphorisms of Bṛhaspati have only this aim, viz. to refute the opponent". But in the majority of cases one decided to discuss the doctrine of inference and to take it over at least in parts. This desertion of the original attitude led, in no way, to the consequence of the decline of the system. The taking up of foreign thoughts and occupation with them led, on the contrary, to a regular activity and to a blossoming up of a literature richer than hitherto. We have, however, reached with it a turning point, in the development, at which we must provisionally halt.

Also among the other systems with which we have dealt, we have seen that at the end of the classical period of Indian philosophy about the middle of the first post-Christian millennium, the system-building in essentials had come to a close and had been at a stand-still. In its place there stepped in the forefront the theory of knowledge and there developed a lively and fruitful activity in this sphere for several more centuries. The presentation of this development. which appears to a certain extent as a second blossoming of the classical period, we have hitherto put in the background, in order to handle it separately as an independent section of Indian philosophy. Now we see that the Lokāyata also came round to the same path about the same time. But before we can go over to the presentation of these sections of development, there remains for us a group of systems to handle, which later sprang forth and to which we have referred up to this time, but which developed themselves to so great importance and scrambled for the lead through several centuries—namely the systems of the Buddhists.

SUPPLEMENT

Bibliography (select) and Notes[1]

General Literature (new Publications)

Ruben, W. : Geschichte der indischen Philosophie, Berlin 1954.

Zimmer, H. : Philosophies of India, ed. by T. Campbell, New York 1951.

7. The Nature-philosophical schools and the Vaiśeṣika-system

Bibliography

Faddegon, B. : The Vaiśeṣika system described with the help of the oldest Texts—Verhandelingen der Koninklijke Akademie van Wetenschappen te Amsterdam, Afdeeling Letterkunde, Nieuwe Reeks. Deel XVIII-No. 2 Amsterdam 1918.

Keith A. B. : Indian Logic and Atomism, an exposition of the Nyāya and Vaiśeṣika systems. Oxford 1921.

Chatterji, J. : Hindu Realism. Allahabad 1912.

Handt, W. : Die Atomistische Grundlage der Vaiśeṣika-Philosophie, Rostock 1900.

Ruben, W. : Zur indischen Erkenntnistheorie. Die Lehre von der Wahrnehnung nach den Nyāyasūtras III 1, Leipzig. 1926.

Umesha Mishra : The conception of Matter according to Nyāya-Vaiśeṣika. Allahabad 1936.

Sadanand Bhaduri : Studies in Nyāya-Vaiśeṣika Metaphysics, Poona 1947.

Jacobi, H. : Die Entwicklung der Gottesidee bei den Indern und deren Beweise fur das Dasein Gottes (Geistesströmungen des Ostens, edited by W. Kirfel, Band I), Bonn & Leipzig 1923.

Bulcke, C : The Theism of Nyāya-Vaiśeṣika. Its origin and early development. Calcutta 1947.

Translations

Nandlal Sinha : The Vaiśeṣikasūtras of Kaṇāda with the commentary of Śaṁkara Miśra (The Sacred Books of the Hindus) Allahabad, 1910-11.

1. When in the Notes I point out to my own presentation, it occurs merely as the statement of the volume and the page-number.

The abovementioned work of Faddegon contains also the translation of the Sūtras.

Ganganath Jha : Padārthadharma-saṃgraha of Praśastapāda with the Nyāya-Kandalī of Śrīdhara, translated into English. (The Pandit, New Series Vo. XXV—XXXVII) Benares 1916.

Ruben, W. : Die Nyāyasūtras, Text, translation, Explanation und Glossary. Abhandlungen für die Kunde des Morgenlandes, XVIII Band, No. 2 Leipzig 1928.

Ganganath Jha : The Nyāyasūtras of Gautama with the Bhāṣya of Vātsyāyana and the Vārttika of Udyotakāra, with notes from the Nyāya-Vārttikatātparyaṭīka of Vācaspati Miśra and the Tātparyapariśuddhi of Udayanācārya (Indian Thought Vol. IV-X) Allahabad 1912-20.

A presentation of the Vaiśeṣika system of the classical period confronts the following task : It has to deal with a system which has gone through a long development and has been counted for centuries as the leading philosophical system of India. Still there are no direct sources at our disposal for the history of the system, its origin and development. What lies before us as a source stems out of the last period of the system, when its development had, in the main, already concluded. The works of Candramati and Praśastapāda give short summary representations of the system in its concluding form. The Vaiśeṣika Sūtras also, in the form which is available to us, belong to the last period of the classical system. They contain, no doubt, old constituents but what can be gained out of it for the history of the system, is scanty.[1] When we, therefore, wish to write a history of the classical Vaiśeṣika system, we are thrown, for the older stages of development, on what can be inferred from the analysis of the system in its preserved form and out of it we must try to reconstruct the course of development.

The following fact forms the starting-point. The characteristic sign of the Vaiśeṣika system, as it lies before us, is its doctrine of categories. He, who studies exhaustively the work of the classical system, is forced to the observation that there is here a highly developed Nature-philosophy clothed in the form of a

1. I do not go deeper into this as I am working on a critical treatment of the Vaiśeṣikasūtras.

doctrine of categories.[1] But then the question arises : of what kind was this Nature-philosophy which lies at the basis of the doctrine of categories ? Does it deal with the views widespread in general and known also otherwise or have we to do here with a doctrine which was different from the doctrines of the remaining Nature-philosophical schools ? Now, it appears that the second is the case. It deals with an original doctrine characterized by entirely special features. For this I refer, for example, to the peculiar form of the Atomism represented by them and its shaping into a large scale atomistic-mechanistic world-picture. With that we come to the first important conclusion: The classical Vaiśeṣika is built or erected on an entirely definite original Nature-philosophy which it pursues and which it recasts in the sense of the doctrine of categories. An attempt to represent the Vaiśeṣika in its development has, therefore, as its first task to regain this Nature-philosophy as the pre-stage of the classical Vaiśeṣika. Whether we wish to name it as the Vaiśeṣika or whether we reserve this name only for the system of the doctrine of categories is an external and fully secondary question.

In the reconstruction of the old Nature-philosophy, it is seen further that it contains older and younger or later doctrines beside one another. Now, on the basis of what we know of the remaining doctrines and the systems of the ancient times, we can judge pretty exactly, how the Nature-philosophical doctrines of the ancient period look. Turning to the old Nature-philosophy of the Vaiśeṣika, we are able to docide with great probability, what constituents are old and what development is late. With that we get two stages of development of the old Vaiśeṣika—the oldest Nature-philosophy which forms the starting point of the entire later development and which by far resembles other Nature-philosophical doctrines and a later stage of deyelopment which is characterized by new thoughts showing an entirely original stamp.

In these two stages of development joins in the third—

1. B. Faddegon as well as H. Ui have seen it. I quote only the words with which H. Ui concludes his presentation. ("The Vaiśeṣika philosophy, according to the Deśapadārthaśāstra, London (917 p. 224) "The consequence may lead to the conclusion that the Vaiśeṣika system intends principally to explain things and phenomena in nature as they are. The whole system was a kind of natural philosophy in ancient India."

the shaping of the doctrine of categories. How it came about and how it ran its course in particulars, is, to a certain extent, recognizable to us through traces in the preserved system and through comparison with related systems. Thus, through the inclusion, for consideration, of old Nature-philosophy, which forms the starting point, the method and performance of its creator allow themselves to be much better assessed than hitherto. On the creation of the doctrine of categories there follows, as the next stage, its application to the old Nature-philosophy, whereby the old doctrines became clothed in the ideas of the doctrine of categories in a way characteristic for the Vaiśeṣika. Here also helps the genetic consideration towards an essentially better understanding of the doctrines in the preserved form.

With these four stages, the development of the classical Vaiśeṣika is completed in its basic features. The final fixing of the system in its concluding form by Candramati and Praśastapāda forms the conclusion.

In this way, I have tried, in my presentation, to describe the origin and development of the Vaiśeṣika system. Naturally any such attempt to infer or to conclude the whole history of the system out of the last stages of its development, is bound to work largely upon conjectures. But the attempt must once be made. Because, only in this way, much that gives an impression of being odd in the preserved system, becomes understandable and intelligible. Besides, I hope that at least the groundlines of development are drawn by me rightly and that my attempt would stimulate further labours in this direction.

Notes

1) The Vaiśeṣika-Sūtras with the later commentary of Śaṅkaramiśra are edited by Jayanārāyaṇa Tarkapañcānana, Bibliotheca Indica No.34, Calcutta 1860-61; by Dhuṇḍiraj Śāstri, Kashi Sanskrit Series No.3, Benares 1923. I quote the Sūtras more often in the wording testified to as the oldest. More exact wording about them is given by the treatment of Śūtras, prepared by me.

2) Edited by H. Ui, the Vaiśeṣika Philosophy according to the Daśapadārthaśāstra, Chinese Text with Introduction, Trans-

lation and Notes (Royal Asiatic Society, Oriental Translation Fund, N.S. Vol. XXIV.) London 1917. The text is also contained in the Taishō edition of the Chinese Tripiṭaka (T 2138, Cheng tsong che kiu yi louen). I quote according to this edition as it is more well-arranged than the edition of Ui.

3) The text was printed repeatedly. It is also contained in the quoted editions of the commentary. I quote according to the edition of the Nyāya-Kandalī.

4) The Praśastapādabhāṣyam by Praśastadevācārya with the commentaries : Śūkti by Jagadiśa Tarkālaṅkāra, Setu by Padmanābha Miśra and Vyomavatī Vyomaśivācārya ed. Gopinath Kaviraj and Dhuṇḍirāj Shāstri, Chowkhamba Sanskrit Series No. 61, Benares 1930.

5) Vaiśeṣikadarśanam, the Aphorisms of the Vaiśeṣika Philosophy by Kaṇāda, with the commentary of Praśastapāda and the Gloss of Uyadanācārya, ed. Vindhyeśvarī Prasāda Dvivedī and Dhuṇḍhirāj Shāstri, Benares Sanskrit Series No. 9, Benares 1919.

6) Kandalī is originally the name of a plant with white flowers which appear in great plenty suddenly at the beginning of the rainy season.

7) The Bhāṣya of Praśastapāda together with the Nyāyakandalī of Śrīdhara, ed. Vindhyeśvarī Prasāda Dvivedin, Vizianagaram Sanskrit Series, Vol. 4, Benares 1895.

8) The Text of the Nyāyasūtras is contained in the edition of the commentary. For the rest, compare, above all, W. Ruben, Die Nyāya-Sūtras, Text, Translation, Explanation and Glossary. Abhandlungen für die Kunde des Morgenlandes, 18. Band, No. 2, Leipzig 1928.

9) Edited by Jayanārāyaṇa Tarkapañcānana, Bibliotheca Indica No. 50, Calcutta 1864-65; by Gangādhara Śāstrī Tailaṅga, Vizianagaram Sanskrit Series Vol. 9, Benares, 1896; by Lakṣmaṇa Śāstri and Śrīrāma Śāstri, Kashi Sanskrit Series, No. 43, Benares 1920; by Nāgeśa Śāstri Joshi, Ānandāśrama Sanskrit Series No. 91, Poona 1922. I quote according to the edition of the Kashi Sanskrit Series.

10) Edited by Vindhyeśvarī Prasāda Dvivedin, Bibliotheca Indica No. 113, Calcutta 1887-1914; by Vindhyeśvarī Prasāda

Dvivedī and Lakṣmaṇa Śāstri, Kashi Sanskrit Series No. 33, Benares 1916—I quote according to the edition of the Kashi Sanskrit Series.

11) Edited by Gaṅgādhara Śāstri Tailaṅga, Vizianagaram Sanskrit Series Vol. 15, Benares 1898; by Rajeshwara Sastri Dravid, Kashi Sanskrit Series No. 24, Benares 1925-26. I quote again according to the edition of the Kashi Sanskrit Series.

12) Edited by Gaṅgādhara Śāstri Tailaṅga, Vizianagaram Sanskrit Series, Vol. 8, Benares 1895; by Sūrya Nārāyaṇa Sukla, Kashi Sanskrit Series No. 106, Benares 1934-36. I quote according to the edition of the Vizianagaram Sanskrit Series.

13) Nyāyasāraḥ of Acārya Bhāsarvajña, together with the commentary called Nyāyatātparyadīpikā by Jayasiṃha Sūri, Bibliotheca Indica No. 188, Calcutta 1910.

14) Nyāyavārttikatātparyapariśuddhi by Udayanācārya with a gloss called Nyāyanibandhaprakāśa by Vardhamānopādhyāya, ed. by Vindhyeśvarī Prasāda Dvivedin and Lakṣmaṇa Śāstrī Draviḍa, Bibliotheca Indica No.205, Calcutta 1911 ff (incomplete).

15) The Text of the Sūtras is contained in the edition of the Mīmāṃsābhāṣyam. For the rest, compare, above all, Mīmāṃsādarśanam, Jaiminimīmāṃsāsūtrapāṭha, ed. by Kevalānandasarasvatī, Wai 1948.

16) edited by Maheścandra Nyāyaratna, Bibliotheca Indica No.451, Calcutta 1863-87; by Ratna Gopal Bhatta, Kashi Sanskrit Series No.42, Benares 1910. I quote according to the edition of the Kashi Sanskrit Series.

17) Contained in the edition of the commentary cited below.

18) Bṛhatī of Prabhākara Miśra with the Ṛjuvimalapañcikā of Śālikanātha, edited by S. K. Ramanatha Sastri, Madras University Sanskrit Series No.3, Madras 1934.

19) Ślokavārttikavyākhyā (Tātparyaṭīkā) of Bhattombeka, ed. by S.K. Ramanatha Sastri, Madras University Sanskrit Series No.13, Madras 1940.

20) The Mīmāṃsāślokavārttika with the commentary Kaśikā of Sucaritamiśra, ed. by K. Sambasiva Sastri, Trivandrum Sanskrit Series No.90, 99, 150, Trivandrum 1926 ff. (incomplete).

21) Mīmāṃsāślokavārttika by Kumārila Bhaṭṭa with the commentary called Nyāyaratnākara by Pārthasārathi Miśra, ed. by Rāma Śāstrī Tailaṅga, Chowkhamba Sanskrit Series No.17, Benares 1898.

22) Prakaraṇapañcikā by Śālikanātha, ed. by Mukunda Śāstrī, Chowkhamba Sanskrit Series No.17, Benares 1904.

23) Vol. I p. (247)

24) Vol. I p. (161)

25) Thereby one thought, as also the word Vāyuḥ shows, originally of the moved air, the wind.

26) Vol. I p. (151)

27) Vol. Ip. (p. 86f.)

28) Compare below p. (79f.)

29) Compare below (p. 188)

30) Compare the presentation of the Buddhistic systems in Vol. III.

31) Vol. I (p. 97 ff.)

32) Vaiśeṣikasūtrāṇi II, 1, 1-4

33) Vaiśeṣikasūtrāṇi II, 1, 5

34) Vol. I (p. 281 f.)

35) Vol. I (p. 98 f.)

36) Nyāyakandalī p. 9, 6 f; compare also Ślokavārttikam 22 (Śabdanityatādhikaraṇam), v. 434 ff.

37) For the doctrine of the shadow and the darkness, compare, above all, Nyāyabhāṣyam p. 82, 7-14; Tātparyaṭīka p. 345, 4-16; Vyomavatī p. 46, 32-47, 10; Nyāyakandalī p. 9, 1-10, 8; Kiraṇāvalī, p. 15, 16-20, 14; Prakaraṇapañcikā p. 143, 14-145, 9; Nyāyaratnākaraḥ p. 740, 12-741, 15

38) Nyāyakandalī p. 179, 9-13.

39) About the rays of the eyes, compare below p. 52 ff.

40) The account of creation by Praśastapāda p. 48 f. is remodelled in the sense of the Atomic doctrine and points, otherwise also, to late features.

41) If one holds the view that the body is formed only out of the four elements, one could not then consider the digestive fire as a part of the body.

42) Vol. I. p. (284) f.

43) The bodies of divine beings in the other world could also be formed out of the other elements.

44) Vol. I (p. 99 f.)

45) According to the doctrine of Indian medicine, three steps of the development of the embryo following one another are not dealt with, but the first preliminary steps of the three generations.

46) What the name *kalalam* in this context implies is not clear to me (compare Nyāyabhāṣyam p. 352, 10). Hair and nails are mere attachments and are not counted in the body (Nyāyabhāṣyam, p. 342, 9-12).

47) The juice or sap of nutrition is not counted in the Vaiśeṣika among the *dhātavaḥ*. (compare Padārthadharmasaṃgrahaḥ p. 44, 17 ; Kiraṇāvalī p. 88, 13 and 273, 19.)

48) An exact rendering of the word '*doṣaḥ*' would be 'basic evil'. (compare Vāgbhaṭa's Aṣṭāṅgahṛdayasaṃhitā, translated from Sanskrit into German by L. Hilgenberg and W. Kirfel, Leiden, 1941 p. 2, Note 1.)

49) Vol. I (p. 86 f.)

50) Vol. I (p. 236)

51) Vol. I (p. 84 f.)

52) On the question of the duality of the visual organ, compare Nyāyabhāṣyam p. 236, 11-239, 6. Compare also W. Ruben, Die Nyāyasūtras, Leipzig 1928, p. 198, note 183.

53) Compare Vaiśeṣikasūtrāṇi VIII, 2, 5-6 ; Padārthadharma-saṃgrahaḥ p. 28, 6 f ; 36, 5-7 ; 39, 4-6 ; 44, 8-10 and Nyāyasūtrāṇi III, 1, 71 together with the commentaries belonging thereto. The commentaries interpret their view on the commented text partially. Both views are mentioned by Vyomomaśiva, Vyomavatī p. 233, 19-234, 23 ; 246, 3-247, 3.

54) Nyāyabhāṣyam p. 291, 9-292, 3.

55) Compare above all, Nyāyabhāṣyam p. 277, 11-17 ; Nyāyavārttikam p. 33, 15-36, 21 ; Kiraṇāvalī p. 74, 3-76, 6 ; Padmanābha, Vaiśeṣikasetuḥ p. 250, 28-253, 1 (gives important supplements). Prakaraṇapañcikā p. 44, 9-45, 20 etc. Compare further W. Ruben, Die Nyāyaūtras, Leipzig 1928, p. 199, note 188 ; p. 200, note 190 ; p. 201, note 194.

56) Compare Vasubandhu, Abhidharmakośaḥ I, v. 43 cd (translation by L. de La Vallée-Poussin p. 87 ff) ; Dignāga, Pramāṇasamuccayaḥ, I. v. 20 f., Vrttiḥ following 17 b 6-18 a 4.

57) For the doctrine of the rays of the eyes, compare,

above all, Nyāyasūtrāṇi III, 1, 33-53, and Nyāyabhāṣyam p. 258, 14 up to 274, 2, together with the later commentaries. These texts are dealt with in detail by W. Ruben in his 'Zur indischen Erkenntnistheorie, Die Lehre von der Wahrnehmung nach den Nyāyasūtras' III, 1, Leipzig 1926.

58) Nyāyasūtrāṇi III, 1, 52 ; Nyāyabhāṣyam p. 272, 8-17 ; Nyāyavārttikam p. 384, 3-15 ; Tātparyaṭīkā p. 526, 12-28; Ślokavārttikam 22 (Śabdanityādhikaraṇam) v. 183-191 ab (Another view appears in v. 180 cd—183).

59) Nyāyabhāṣyam p. 266, 3-267, 8.

60) Nyāyabhāṣyam p. 267, 1-8

61) Nyāyabhāṣyam p. 262, 5-11 and 263, 3-14.

62) Nyāyabhāṣyam p. 263, 7 f; Nyāyavārttikam p. 378, 9-21.

63) Exactly these have been held by the representatives of the Vedic auxiliary science of Phonetics (Śikṣākārāḥ), to which this doctrine is traced.

64) Padārthadharmasaṃgrahaḥ p. 287, 21-288, 2.

65) Mīmāṃsābhāṣyam I, p. 20, 5 ff; Ślokavārttikam 22 (Śabdanityatādhikarṇam), v. 122-125 and 42-45 ; Prakaraṇapañcikā p. 164, 25-165, 6 ; 166 ; 7-11 ; Nyāyamañjari p. 216, 19-217, 4.

66) Slokavārttikam 22, v. 170-176 ; Prakaraṇapañcikā p. 166, 22-167, 19.

67) Slokavārttikam 22, v. 129-130; 210 cd—213 ab ; 217 cd—221 ab ; Prakaraṇapañcikā p. 165, 6-13 ; 166, 15-21 ; 167, 20-168, 10 ; Nyāyamañjarī p. 208, 17-20 ; 209, 1-11 ; (but also the difference of the speaker 208, 13-16 and the neighbouring sounds 208, 25-27) ; 213, 22 ff; 214, 2-4.

68) Such forced explanations are found in Jayanta Bhaṭṭa, Nyāyamañjarī, p. 228, 24-229, 5.

69) Kāṭhaka Upaniṣad IV, v. 12 f ; Mahābhārata III, v. 16763 (Sāvitrī episode). Compare H. Oldenberg, Die Religion des Veda, Stuttgart and Berlin, 3-4 1923, p. 525.

70) Kāṭhaka Upaniṣad III, v. 3 ff. Mahābhārata XIV, 51, v. 1 ff.

71) Vol I. (p. 52 ff.)

72) Compare above (p. 17-18 f.)

73) There are also found the doctrines that the psychical

organ moves in the arteries (*nādyaḥ*)—(Kiraṇāvalī, p. 135, 4-12).

74) Compare the presentation of the classical Yoga System in Vol. I. (p. 328).

75) *Saṃskāraḥ* is the older designation (compare Vaiśeṣika-sūtrāṇi IX, 2, 6). *Bhāvanā* appeared to have stepped in its place, when '*vegaḥ*' and '*sthitisthāpakaḥ*' were included under the name *Saṃskāraḥ*.

76) Vol I. (p. 48 f.) and (51 f.)

77) Nyāyabhāṣyam p. 215, 5 f. '*Sadehasya ātmano manasā saṃyogo vipacyamānakarmāśayasahito jīvanam iṣyate*' ; compare also Nyāyamañjarī p. 499, 1-4 ; Nyāyakandalī p. 263, 2 f. ; Kiraṇāvalī p. 134, 5 f.

78) Compare above page (18.) In respect of the assessment of the composition of the text I agree by far with W. Ruben (Die Nyāyasūtras, Leipzig 1928, p XV f ; and above all also p. 218, note 291). According to my view, of the Chapters II-IV, only II belongs closely to the dialectical hand-book I and V, while III-IV originally form an independent unity with the sections belonging to it from Chapter I. On the other hand, I share his view also in respect of the tearing asunder of the original connection of I and V through the putting in of II and IV, as above all also, in respect of the endeavour concerned to make up or balance the length of the isolated Āhnika through an explanation put in between them. I, therefore, also, do not regard the introduced matter as an explanation in the following presentation of the Chapters III- IV, as its place in it, from the point of time and its position in the frame of the whole doctrine, is to be assessed differently from the remaining sections.

79) The old Nature-philosophy of the Nyāya knows neither the further formulation of the Nature-philosophy of the Vaiśeṣika (compare p. 81 ff), nor the doctrine of categories. In the presentation that is preserved, there have no doubt penetrated later things and, above all, the Nyāyabhāṣyam always again reckons involuntarily with the progressive Vaiśeṣika system and the doctrine of categories. But the basic features of the old Nature-philosophy are, in spite of that, rarely changed.

80) Nyāyasūtrāṇi I, 1, 2.

81) ,, I, 1, 9.

82) Nyāyasūtrāṇi I, 1, 10. They are the same qualities which the full-fledged Vaiśeṣika system ascribes to the soul and infers the soul as their bearer.

83) Compare Nyāyasūtrāṇi I, 1, 11.

84) Nyāyasūtrāṇi I, 1, 12-16.

85) ,, I, 1, 17-22.

86) Compare above p. (39-40 f.); further Nyāyabhāṣyam p. 29, 17-18.

87) Nyāyasūtrāṇi, III, 1, 19-27.

88) Compare above p. (24 f.)

89) Nyāyasūtrāṇi III, 1, 54-63. I recite in the following, as proof, a few thought-processes of the text more exactly.

90) Nyāyasūtrāṇi III, 1, 64-75

91) ,, III, 1, 64-65

92) Compare above p. (31 f.)

93) Nyāyasūtrāṇi III, 2, p. 1-56.

94) ,, III, 2, 1-17.

95) ,, III, 2, 18-42.

96) ,, III, 2, 40.

97) ,, III, 2, 43-46.

98) ,, III, 2, 47-56.

99) ,, III, 2, 57-60.

100) Compare above page (43-44 f.)

101) Nyāyasūtrāṇi III, 2, 57 and 60.

102) As already remarked, I leave out of account the interpolated excursus.

103) Nyāyavārttikam p. 510, 3-15

104) Vasubandhu, Viṃaśatikāvijñaptimātratāsiddhiḥ p. 7, 3-8 1 (by way of summary).

105) Compare below page (114 ff.)

106) The qualities of a whole are, namely, according to the orthodox doctrines of the school, basically conditioned by the qualities of its constituents. Of the two mentioned views, the first was ascribed, in later period, to the Vaiśeṣika and was named as Pīlupākaḥ (the burning of the atoms) and the second was ascribed to the Nyāya and was named as the Piṭharapākaḥ (the burning of the saucepan). Against the second view, an objection was raised that the fire does not penetrate the saucepan

as a whole and, therefore, it would not be able to change it in all its parts.

107) In contrast to the Vaiśeṣika, the doctrine of the atoms in the Jaina shows entirely different features. According to them, the matter is capable of extension and contraction and the qualities of the atoms are changeable. The basic thought about the doctrine of the atoms is, therefore, not comprehended by them. But out of that it can be deduced that it cannot be original here.

108) Vaiśeṣikasūtrāṇi V, 1. 16-18.

109) ,, V, 1, 1-6.

110) ,, V, 2, 1-18.

111) Daśapadārthaśāstram, T 2138, P. 1265 c 23 f. (in the translation by H. Ui, P. 116).

112) Vaiśeṣikasūtrāṇi, V, 2, 5 and 11

113) ,, V, 1, 14.

114) Padārthadharmasaṃgrahaḥ p. 25, 10 f.

115) Vol. I, p. (304 f.)

116) Vol. I, p. (318 f.)

117) Vol. I, p. (49 f.)

118) Vol. I, p. (330 f.)

119) Vol. I, p. (199 f.)

120) Padārthadharmasaṃgrahaḥ p. 175, 2; 177, 12 f.

121) Padārthadharmasaṃgrahaḥ p. 183, 16 f; 263, 7; 184, 8 ff.

122) Vaiśeṣikasūtrāṇi V, 2, 13; Padārthadharmasaṃgrahaḥ p. 309, 10-15.

123) Padārthadharmasaṃgrahaḥ p. 309, 10-12. Prasastapāda's supplement '*Upakārāpakārasamartham*' ('so far as it can be of advantage or disadvantage') seeks to rescue the moral character in the working of the *Adṛṣṭam*, but it can deceive nobody about the fact that, as the cited examples show, it was stretched in the cases in which there can be no talk of the reward or retribution of good or bad actions in the case of the men of best wills.

124) Compare, for the following, above all Vyomavatī p. 639, 3 upto 40,.2 and Nyāyasūtrāṇi III, 2, 61-73 with the commentaries.

125) Compare in this respect Nyāyamañjarī p. 479, 1-2;

Vyomavatī p 411, 7-12 and Nyāyakandalī p. 88, 11-16.

126) According to my view, with the change of the idea about the soul is connected the fact that in the Vaiśeṣika the old designation *jīvaḥ* is replaced by the term *ātmā*.

127) The different sort of the doctrine of the Jaina depends on syncretism. Compare note 107.

128) Compare Nyāyavārttikam p. 336, 17-337, 5.

129) Vol. I, p. (287) ff.

130) It is said, for example, in Pūjyapāda's Sarvārthasiddhiḥ on the Tattvārthādhigamasūtrāṇi VI, 1 *'ātmapradeśaparispando yogaḥ.'*

131) Slokavārttikam 21 (Ātmavādaḥ) v. 74 cd-76.

132) So far as every activity is understood as movement, the doer can only be the bearer of the movement.

133) Vasubandhu, Abhidharmakośaḥ IV, v. 1 *'Cetanā tatkṛtam ca tat* (=Karma); compare in this respect the detailed presentation in vol. III .

134) Maṇḍana Miśra, Bhāvanāvivekaḥ (ed. Gangānāth Jhā) p. 91, 8-94, 2.

135) Padārthadharmasaṃgrahaḥ p. 102, 16 f.; they work, as Udayana has exactly expressed it, only in the sphere of the body (Kiraṇāvalī p. 40, 8 *'Śarīrāvacchedena vṛttilābhaḥ'*). An interesting deviation in this respect of the memory-impressions is shown by the refuted doctrine in the Nyāyasūtrāṇi III, 2, 25.

136) Compare above page (45) f.

137) The opposing schools also placed, therefore, the representatives of the Vaiśeṣika in this respect as *'ardhavaināśikāḥ* beside the Buddhists.

138) Nyāyabhāṣyam p. 52, 8-12 on Nyāyasūtrāṇi I, 1, 29 *niratiśayāścetanāḥ, dehendriyamanaḥsu viṣayeṣu tattatkāraṇeṣu ca viśeṣa iti Sāṃkhyānām....svaguṇaviśiṣṭāś cetanāḥ iti Yogānām.'* The name Yauga or Yoga is used for the adherents of Nyāya and Vaiśeṣika not only in the later Jaina works. It is also found in the older period and can be demonstrated occasionally also in non-Jinistic works (e.g. Śālikanātha Ṛjuvimalā, p. 209, 25).

139) Nyāyamañjarī p. 473, 10 *'sakalaguṇāpoḍham eva asya rūpam.'*

140) It is characteristic, how the Buddhistic author Advayavajra in his Tattvaratnāvalī (edition of the Gaekwad's Orien-

tal Series p. 16, 11 ff) compares the state of the released man according to the Vaiśeṣika doctrine with deep sleep and places him beside the released one according to the Vedānta idea.

141) Vol. I, p. (61 f.)

142) Advayavajra, Tattvaratnāvalī (Gaekwad's Oriental Series) p. 16, 22 f. My rendering is free, as the text is uncertain. The verse was used by the Brahmanical side in which Jetavana was replaced by Vṛndāvana (Anandagiri, Bṛhadāraṇakyopaniṣadbhāsyaṭīkā) (Ānandāśrama Sanskrit Series) p. 307, 23; so also Prabhācandra. Nyāyakumudacandra (Manik Chandra Digambara Jaina Granthamāla) p. 828, 8 f. etc. Compare also: M. Winternitz, Geschichte der indischen Literatur, 3. Band, Leipzig 1922, p. 463, (note 2),

143) The following sketch of development is an attempt. Certainty cannot be reached in particulars, as the material for the old period is too scanty. Only for the idea of space, some other old information can be had from the Śūtras.

144) Vol. I. p. (48 ff.).

145) Compare, for example, Chāndogya-Upaniṣad I, 8-9. To this also properly belongs the idea of the Bṛhadāraṇyaka-Upaniṣad III, 2, 13 that the Ātmā enters into space during death.

146) Compare above p. (14) ff.

147) Among the Jainas, according to whom space has remained as *ākāśaḥ*, the world-quarters have also suffered no shifting of their importance.

148) Daśapadārthaśāstram T 2138, p. 1262 c. 22 f. (in the translation by H. Ui, p. 94).

149) Quoted in the Mahāprajñāpāramitopadeśaḥ, T 1509, p. 133 b 21 f. (in the translation by Et. Lamotte, p. 596).

150) Vaiśeṣikasūtrāṇi II, 2, 14-15; compare with it Vasu's commentary on Āryadeva's Śataśāstram, T 1569, p. 180 a 28-6 b 1 (in the translation by G. Tucci, p. 78).

151) Vaiśeṣikasūtrāṇi II, 2, 10.

152) I do not enter into details for the oldest period. Especially the speculations of the sacrificial priests in the Brāhmaṇās, which, according to my view, represent a separate development, are laid aside by me. For the doctrine of Time, compare for the older period, F. O. Schrader, 'über den Stand

der indischen Philosophie Zur Zeit Mahāvīras and Buddhas', Strassburg 1902, p. 17-30; for the further development, St. Schayer, Contribution to the Problem of Time in Indian Philosophy, Polska Akademia Umiejetności. Prace Komisji Orientalistycznej Nr. 31, Krakow 1938, which but, above all, describes the Buddhistic theories.

153) Atharvavedasaṃhitā XIX, 53, v.1, 2, 5, and 6(Translation according to M. Winternitz, Geschichte der indischen Literatur, 1, Band, Leipzig, 1908, p. 132).

154) Compare Mahāprajñāpāramitopadeśah, T 1509, p. 65b 12 f (in the translation by Et. Lamotte, p. 76); the commentary on the Sāṃkhyakārikā, v. 61; Candrakīrti, Prasannapadā, p. 386, 6 f; Haribhadra, Śāstravārttā-samuccay aḥ, v. 166; etc.

155) Haribhadra, Śāstravārttāsamuccayaḥ v, 167; etc.

156) Compare Vasu's commentary on Āryadeva's Śataśāstram, T. 1569, p. 180 a 1-3 (in the translation by G. Tucci p. 76); Mahāprajñāpāramitopadeśaḥ, T 1509, p. 65 b 17 f. (in the translation by Et. Lamotte, p. 76).

157) Vaiśeṣikasūtrāṇi VII, 2, 22.

158) Compare my presentation in Vol. III

159) Compare Vaiśeṣikasūtrāṇi VII, 2, 21.

160) Vaiśeṣikasūtrāṇi II, 2, 6; I read '*param aparam*' etc., with Kamalaśīla, Tattvasaṃgrahapanjikā p. 206, 20 f. Compare also Vasu's commentary on Āryadeva's Śataśāstram, T 1569, p. 180 a 3 f. (in the translation by G. Tucci, p. 76); Mahāprajñāpāramitopadeśaḥ, T 1509, p 65 b 18-20 (in the translation by Et. Lamotte, p. 76); Daśapadārthaśāstram, T 2138 p 1262 c 21 f. (in the translation by H. Ui, p. 93). For the kind of reading '*aparasmin aparam*' in the Sūtra compare B. Faddegon, The Vaiśeṣika system, Amsterdam 1918, p. 212, who holds this kind of reading as late.

161) About this see for great details H. v. Glasenapp, Entwicklungsstufen des indischen Denkens, Schriften der Königsberger Gelehrten Gessellschaft 15./16, Jahr, Heft 5, Halle 1940, p. 273 (=1) ff.

162) Vol. 1 p. (241)

163) Vol. 1 p. (258) f.

164) Compare Umāsvāti, Tattvārthādhigamasūtrāṇi V,

37; Vaiśeṣikasūtrāṇi I. 1, 15.

165) Umāsvāti, Tattvārthādhigamasūtrāṇi V, 40; Compare Vaiśeṣikasūtrāṇi I_1 1, 16.

166) Kundakunda, Paṃcattiyasaṃgaho v. 13.

167) On the contrary, it is characteristic that the Jaina, apart from the heretical schools, do not know these categories.

168) It shows the summary treatment of these three categories in the beginning of the Vaiśeṣikasūtras in the first Āhnikam of the first Adhyāyaḥ, while, commonness and particularity are separated from them and are dealt with in an entirely different way in the second Āhnikam. Besides, the summarizing of these three categories as *arthaḥ* is characteristic (Vaiśeṣikasūtrāṇi VIII, 2, 3).

169) Umāsvāti, Tattvārthādhigamsūtrāṇi V, 38.

170) Compare above p. (17) f and p. (20) f.

171) Compare above p. (19) f.

172) Compare above p. (14)

173) Umāsvāti, Tattvārthādhigamasūtrāṇi V, 24.

174) Compare p. (55) f.

175) Compare p. (17).

176) I again emphasize on this occasion explicitly that I cannot go here into all the details of development, how, for example, they were conditioned by the special position of sound.

177) Compare Vaiśeṣikasūtrāṇi VII, 1, 20, and Daśapadārthaśāstram, T 2138, p. 1263 a 18-22 (in the translation by H. Ui, p. 95).

178) Shortness and longness occur, therefore, only in the aggregates and are missing in the permanent substances. Indeed there were differences of opinion on this point. Compare, for example, Vyomavatī p. 474, 3 ff.

179) Compare in the Jinism the '*bandhaḥ*' (Umāsvāti, Tattvārthādhigamasūtrāṇi V, 24 ff), and in the Buddhism the '*prāptiḥ*' Vasubandhu, Abhidharmakośaḥ II, v. 36 ff.)

180) Compare the '*siṇehakāye*' in the older Jinism.

181) Compare the treatment of this question in Vol. IV.

182) Otherwise, only the qualities which change under the influence of heat form an exception. On the question of the aggregate, we shall still speak later.

183) Compare on this question p. (111) ff.

184) Compare the Sāṃkhyaikāntavādaḥ, Nyāyasūtrāṇi IV, 1, 41-43.

185) Compare p (40.) ff and p. (67) f.

186) Compare p. (84-85)

187) p. (61) ff.

188) Compare p. (36) ff.

189) Padārthadharmasaṃgrahaḥ p. 292, 10 ff.

190) I believe, that the doctrine of commonness is united herein because it was most closely connected with the question regarding the object of the word and also because the old doctrine of the grammarians was later interpreted in the sense of the theory of categories. It is also noteworthy that Praśastapāda occasionally uses in the place of the commonness (*sāmānyam*) the word foreign to the system, namely, *ākṛtiḥ* (p. 321, 16 and 19) which is at home or indigenous in the doctrine of the grammarian from whom it has been taken over also by the older Nyāya.

191) Compare Patañjali, Mahābhāṣyam (ed. F. Kielhorn), Vol I, p. 6, 8-11 and 242, 10-247, 16; translated by O. Straus, Altindische Spekulationen über die Sprache und ihre Problem, Zeitschrift der Deutschen Morgenlandischen Gesellshaft, Band 81/1927, pp. 99-151.

192) The expressions 'thing' (*dravyam*) and 'form' (*ākṛtiḥ*) were first used in the popular sense and philosophically interpreted first by Patañjali, as W. Ruben has rightly seen (W. Ruben, die Nyāyasūtras, Leipzig 1928, p. 195, note 168).

193) p. (87) f.

194) Vaiśeṣikasūtrāṇi I, 2, 3; That this Sūtra is not to be so understood, that commonness and particularity represent different ways or views in the idealistic sense, has been rightly emphasised, by H. Ui. (The Vaiśeṣika Philosophy according to the Daśapadārthaśāstra, Royal Asiatic Society, Oriental Translation Fund, N.S. Vol XXIV, London 1917, p. 173 f.)

195) This view is represented by Candramati in his Daśapadārthaśāstram. In this connection, the information about the Sixth Schism of the Jaina is interesting.

196) Taken basically, they are the same difficulties with which the Platonic doctrine of ideas saw itself confronted.

197) Exactly considered, the relation of the whole (*avayavī*) to its parts appears to have been the starting-point in the formulation of the category of inherence. Still there are details into which we shall not be able to enter here.

198) Compare p. (81-82).

199) Vol. I p. (314)f.

200) Compare p. (200) f.

201) Compare Śālikanātha, Prakaraṇapañcikā p. 110, 18-23.

202) Compare p. (98-99).

203) Compare Śālikanātha, Prakaraṇapañcikā p. 110, 8-111,3.

204) The question about this and about the position of the Sāṃkhya and the school of Kumārila on it is to be handled in Vol. IV.

205) Daśapadārthaśāstram, T 2138, p. 1263 c. 19-22 (in the translation by H. Ui, p. 100).

206) Śālikanātha, Prakaraṇapañcikā p. 81, 10-82, 11.

207) Compare Vyomavatī p. 194, 6-16 ; Nyāyakandalī p. 144, 24 upto 146, 4 ; Nyāyamañjarī 42. 2-13.

208) Daśapadārthaśāstram, T 2138, p. 1264 a 2-10 (in the translation by H. Ui, p. 101).

209) I recite here the most widespread elucidations, not the wording of the elucidation of Candramati.

210) p. (80) f.

211) p. (88)

212) Compare Anubhūtisvarūpa's Prakaṭārthavivaraṇam on the Brahmasūtrāṇi II, 2, 11 (Madras University Sanskrit Series, No. 9, p. 490, 15-17).

213) Characteristically, the Jaina, from whom such thought-processes were far off, do not know this detour about the double-atom.

214) Compare p. (59-60)f.

215) Compare Vol. I, p. (385).

216) p. (58-59).

217) They were known only as occasioning causes, as far as they are able to call forth an understanding knowledge from themselves.

218) p. (113-114).

219) p. (34) f.

220) Vaiśeṣikasūtrāṇi IV, 1, 8.

221) Vaiśeṣikasūtrāṇi IV, 1, 9.

222) *'darśanaṃ sparśanaṃ ca dravyam'* This Sūtra is missing in the handed-down text but is repeatedly quoted in the old period.

223) Compare p. (16).

224) Vaiśeṣikasūtrāṇi IV, 1, 6. I translate according to the form of the Sūtra handed down by Vyomaśiva, as it is clearer.

225) Vaiśeṣikasūtrāṇi, IV, 1, 7.

226) Compare Śālikanātha, Prakaraṇapañcikā p. 46, 6-14.

227) Compare Śāntirakṣita, Vipañcitārthā p. 35, 12 ff.

228) Vaiśeṣikasūtrāṇi IV, 1, 11 and 12.

229) Compare Śālikanātha, Prakaraṇapañcikā p, 46. 14-17, and 78, 14-81, 9 ; Kiraṇāvalī p. 281, 7-282, 14 ; Nyāyakandalī p. 194, 13-195, 7.

230) p. (107-108).

231) Vaiśeṣikasūtrāṇi VIII, 1, 9.

232) Vaiśeṣikasūtrāṇi VIII, 1, 5 and 6. In this Sūtra, the expression commonness—particularity (*sāmānyaviśeṣaḥ*) is used for the commonness. (compare p. 148).

233) Vaiśeṣikasūtrāṇi VIII, 1, 7 and 8.

234) The perceptibility of the soul is represented, for example, by Vyomaśiva, Vyomavatī, p. 391, 12-392, 22 ; compare besides, Jayanta, Nyāyamañjarī p. 429, 20 ff.

235) From the older period, Upavarṣa, above all, is named as the representative of this doctrine. Further particulars will be given in my presentation of the Vedānta. Further, on this question, compare P. Hacker, Untersuchungen über Texte des frühen Advaitavāda, 1. Die Schuler Śaṅkaras (Akademie der Wissenschaften und der Literatur in Mainz, Abhandlungen der geistes-und sozialwissenschaftlichen Klasse, Jahrgang 1950, Nr 26), p. 2037 (=131).

236) Compare Śālikanātha, Prakaraṇapañcikā, p. 151, 12-153, 25.

237) Vol I, p. (217) ff.

238) Vol. I, p. (225).

239) Padārthadharmasaṃgrahaḥ, p. 111, 8 ff.

240) p. (93-94) f.

241) p. (129) ff.

242) Compare the presentation of the theory of Nyāya in Vol. IV.

243) Padārthadharmasaṃgrahaḥ p. 112, 4 ff.

244) Padārthadharmasaṃgrahaḥ p. 164, 21 ff.

245) The Theory of knowledge of Praśastapāda is to be dealt with in Vol. IV.

246) Praśastapāda organizes his work in such a way that he first deals with the categories in general and then in particular and also in the case of particular categories, he describes first their general and then their special qualities. On account of this, the description of common qualities contains a dry compilation in the most concise form, as it is customary in India, when some matter is to be committed to memory. As such enumerations are naturally not fit for reproduction, what lies in the clue words must be, on the contrary, elucidated. I have attempted it in my presentation and no doubt, so far as it deals with the general characterization of the Categories. In doing so, I have not considered the qualities which are merely named in this Section, because they occur in the case of several categories and they appear again in the description of particular ones and have a better place there.

247) For the following, compare Padārthadharmasaṃgrahaḥ p. 16, 1 ff.

248) Behind these definitions stand problems which have been developed, above all, outside the Vaiśeṣika, in the course of epistemological discussions. We shall, therefore, come to speak of them on another occasion.

249) Padārthadharmasaṃgrahaḥ p. 20, 14 ff.

250) Padārthadharmasaṃgrahaḥ p. 27, 9 ff.

251) I cite these sections fairly exactly as they stand in the work of Praśastapāda, because the superficiality and backwardness, in dealing with things pertaining to natural science, beside the over-sharpened Scholasticism of the doctrine of categories, are characteristic of it. The commentaries awaken a favourable impression occasionally.

252) Padārthadharmasaṃgrahaḥ p. 35, 22 ff,

253) Padārthadharmasaṃgrahaḥ p. 38, 24 ff.

254) Padārthadharmasaṃgrahaḥ p. 44, 1, ff.

255) Padārthadharmasaṃgrahaḥ p. 48, 7, ff.

This doctrine shows different elements in a variegated mixture. At the basis, there lies an old myth of creation. It is remodelled in the sense of the atom-doctrine, because in place of the rising forth of the elements out of one another, their origin takes place out of the permanent elements. Further, the ideas of the doctrine of categories are employed. A later and an adventitious supplement is the intervention of God. Finally, it is to be marked that the eight conditions of knowledge (*bhāvāḥ*) also emerge out of the Sāṃkhya (p. 49, 12 and 16 f.)

256) Padārthadharmasaṃgrahaḥ p. 58, 5 ff.

257) Padārthadharmasaṃgrahaḥ p. 58, 7 ff.

258) It is produced out of the homogeneousness of the quality of sound from which it is inferred. (Vaiśeṣikasūtrāṇi II, 1, 30 ; Padārthadharmasaṃgrahaḥ p. 58, 14 f.)

259) Padārthadharmasaṃgrahaḥ p. 63, 15 ff.

260) Padārthadharmasaṃgrahaḥ p. 66, 20 ff.

261) As we have already said while describing the origination of the idea of space, the same word is used among Indians, for space and quarters.

262) Padārthadharmasaṃgrahaḥ p. 69, 6 ff.

263) p. (39-40) f.

264) p. (43-44) f.

265) Padārthadharmasaṃgrahaḥ p. 89, 8 ff.

266) Padārthadharmasaṃgrahaḥ p. 94, 6 ff.

267) I restrict myself here to the essentials and do not quote all the details and special cases.

268) Padārthadharmasaṃgrahaḥ p. 104, 1 ff.

269) Padārthadharmasaṃgrahaḥ p. 105, 8 ff.

270) Padārthadharmasaṃgrahaḥ p. 105, 23 ff.

271) Padārthadharmasaṃgrahaḥ p. 106, 8 ff.

272) This definition is connected with the perception of the substances etc. through colour and touch.

273) Padārthadharmasaṃgrahaḥ p. 106, 19 ff.

274) Padārthadharmasaṃgrahaḥ p. 111, 3 ff.

275) That is to say, there originates the quality two, which inheres, from the moment of its origination, in the commonness two.

276) Compare about this theory above, page (190) ff. Praśastapāda gives, at the conclusion of the section about the number, a defence of the 'Vadhyaghātakavādaḥ' as against the 'Sahānavasthānavādaḥ.' But we cannot enter into it, in the (defined) frame of our work.

277) Padārthadharmasaṃgrahaḥ p. 130, 20 ff.

278) Padārthadharmasaṃgrahaḥ p. 138, 5 ff.

279) Padārthadharmasaṃgrahaḥ p. 139, 13 ff.

280) Compare p. (106) ff.

281) Padārthadharmasaṃgrahaḥ p. 106, 4 ff.

282) Compare p. (192) f.

283) Padārthadharmasaṃgrahaḥ p. 164, 3 ff.

284) Padārthadharmasaṃgrahaḥ p. 171, 16 ff.

285) Padārthadharmasaṃgrahaḥ p. 183, 13 ff.

286) Compare above p. (26-27)f.

287) Padārthadharmasaṃgrahaḥ p. 259, 15 ff.

288) Padārthadharmasaṃgrahaḥ p. 260, 19 ff.

289) Padārthadharmasaṃgrahaḥ p. 261, 6 ff.

290) Padārthadharmasaṃgrahaḥ p. 262, 15 ff.

291) Padārthadharmasaṃgrahaḥ p. 263, 3 ff.

292) Padārthadharmasaṃgrahaḥ p. 263, 25 ff.

293) Padārthadharmasaṃgrahaḥ p. 264, 23 ff.

294) This noteworthy comprehension is proved on the basis of the fact that another cause is not ascertainable and that, for example, fluid salt is seen to be becoming solid under the influence of fire.

295) Compare p. (156)

296) Padārthadharmasaṃgrahaḥ p. 266, 16 f.

297) Padārthadharmasaṃgrahaḥ p. 266, 24 ff.

298) Padārthadharmasaṃgrahaḥ p. 267, 2 ff.

299) Padārthadharmasaṃgrahaḥ p. 267, 13 ff.

300) Padārthadharmasaṃgrahaḥ p. 272, 8 ff.

301) Padārthadharmasaṃgrahaḥ p. 280, 20 ff.

302) Padārthadharmasaṃgrahaḥ p. 287, 17 ff.

303) It is a forced and very questionable theory which was formulated, because no other way out was known.

304) About this theory, compare p. (35) ff.

305) Compare page (113) f.

306) Padārthadharmasaṃgrahaḥ p. 290, 1 ff.

307) Compare about this, p. (113-114).

308) In this connection, one compared the description of the process above on p. (87) and considered, how Praśastapāda during the description of the same process introduced, step by step, the idea of the doctrine of categories, the qualities of the soul, wish (*icchā*) and effort (*prayatnaḥ*), the common qualities connection (*saṃyogaḥ*) and swing (*vegaḥ*) etc.

309) Compare page (232).

310) Compare the corresponding Sāṃkhya doctrine, Vol. I, p. (287-288).

311) Padārthadharmasaṃgrahaḥ p. 311, 13 ff.

312) This interpretation of the word *Svarūpābhedena* (=*abhinnātmakam*) appears to me the most probable.

313) Padārthadharmasaṃgrahaḥ p. 321, 11 ff.

314) Candramati restricts its occurrence to the substances which exist only in number one.

315) Padārthadharmasaṃgrahaḥ p. 324, 18 ff.

316) Vol. I, p. (315) f.

8 The System of the Jaina

Bibliography

Glasenapp, H. v. : Der Jainismus, eine indischen Erlosungs-religion, Berlin 1925.

Schubring, W. : Die Lehre der Jaina, Grundriss der indoarischen Philologie und Altertum-Skunde III 7. Berlin & Leipzig 1935. (It should be mentioned of this work that Schubring brings in Umāsvāti again and again to supplement the lacunae in the canonical information.)

Translations

Jacobi, H. : Eine Jaina Dogmatik, Umāsvāti's Tattvārthādhigamasūtra (translated and explained), Zeitschrift der Deutschen Morgenlandischen Gesellschaft, Band 60, Leipzig 1906. p. 287-325 and 512-551.

Faddegon, B. : The Pravacansāra of Kunda-kunda Ācārya, together with the commentary Tattvadīpikā by Amṛtacandrasūri, English translation, edited with an Introduction by F. W.

Thomas (Jain Literary Society Series, Vol. I), Cambridge 1935.

With the older Jinism, the position with respect to the tradition as well as the state of research is more unfavourable than in Buddhism. The available information about the original canon, its handing down (tradition) and the loss of holy writings appear to me untrustworthy. In every case, however, the canon in its handed-down form is composed of constituents from different times. A comparison with the canonical writings of the Buddhsits is instructive. A work like the Thāṇaṅgam corresponds somewhat with the Saṃgītiparyāyaḥ which forms the transition to the Abhidharma literature. The Jinacariyam of the Kalpasūtra stands about on the level of the Lalitavistaraḥ. The cosmographical texts Sūrapaṇṇatti and Jambuddīvapaṇṇatti correspond to the Lokaprajñaptiḥ of the Abhidharmapiṭakaṃ. Especially important appears to me the proof of L. Alsdorf that the cosmography of this text depends on the Bṛhatkathā.[1] The fiction Bṛhatkathā, although it is placed in pre-Christian times, requires to be put still much later with regard to its estimate of time. The works[2] of W. Kirfel and J. Fr. Kohl have enabled us to know the stages of development of the cosmographical texts—which again remind us of the Lokaprajñaptiḥ whose recasting and further development can be pursued by us in historical times. But apart from such younger or later texts, there stand also, in the oldest layers of the canon, the late beside the old.[3] Under these circumstances, in the position today of research in the fields of the Jaina canons there is no appropriate or proper basic foundation to build a historical presentation on it.

Further, completely unsatisfactory—at least for the ancient period—are the preliminary works in the sphere of commentarial literature and independent doctrinal writings. Unreliable definitions of chronology on the basis of questionable evidence and superficial statement of contents are of no use. But only in rarest

1. Alsdorf : Zur Geschichte der Jaina-Kosmographie und-Mythologie, Zeitschrift der Deutschen Morgenlandischen Gesellschaft, Band 92/1938 p. 464-493.

2. W. Kirfel : Studien zu Texten des Jaina-Kanons Zeitschrift fur Indologie und Iranistik, Band 3/1924 p. 50-80, J. Fr. Kohl : Die Sūryaprajñaptiḥ, Versuch einer Text-geschichte, Bonner Orientalische Studien, Heft 20, Stuttgart 1937.

3. This is strongly emphasised by Schubring, 'Die Lehre de Jainas' p. 55.

cases, more of that period will be found at present.

Under these circumstances I have decided in favour of getting out of a necessity or an emergency and build my presentation on a few isolated sources. How I think of the historical position of the cited doctrines, is hinted in the presentation itself. I have, however, absolutely held fast to one thing. I have endeavoured to reproduce in pure form the doctrines from the chosen sources. I intended to avoid, in every case, the popular joining together or collection of information from various sources and times. Because thereby, one only dims or blurs the picture and blocks the way of further knowledge.

NOTES

317) Compare E. Leumann, Die altern Berichte von den Schismen der Jaina, Indische Studien, 17, Band, Leipzig, 1885, p. 91-135.

318) Compare on this, above all, the works of L. Alsdorf : Harivaṃśapurāṇa, Alt-und Neu-Indische Studien, Band 5, Hamburg 1936; Zur Geschichte der Jaina-Kosmographie und-Mythologie, Zeitschrift der Deutschen Morgenlandischen Gesellschaft, Band 92/938, p. 464-493 ; Further contributions to the History of Jain Cosmography and Mythology, New Indian Antiquary, Vol. IX, Bombay 1947, p. 105-128.

319) Vol. I, p. (195) f.

320) Above all, E. Leumann makes a beginning in his 'Übersicht über die Āvaśyaka-Literatur, Alt-und Neu-Indische Studien, vol. 4, Hamburg 1934.

321) Tattvārthādhigamasūtra, with a bhāṣya by the author, ed. M. K. Premchand, Bibliotheca Indica, No. 159, Calcutta 1903-05. Further, numerous editions with different commentaries.

322) Sri Kundakundācārya's Pravacanasāra, a Pro-Canonical Text of the Jainas, ed. by A. N. Upadhye, Śrī Rayacandra Jaina Śāstramālā, Bombay[2] 1935.

323) Śrimatkundakundasvāmiviracitaḥ Pañcāstikāyaḥ ed. by Manohar Lal, Rayacandra Jaina Śāstramālā, Bombay[2] 1914, and other editions.

324) Śrīmadbhagavatkundakundācāryaviracitaṃ Samaya-

prābhṛtam, ed. by Gajadhar Lal Jain, Sanātana Jaina Granthamālā 3, Benares 1914, and other editions.

325) The contrast to the infinitely great substances of the Vaiśeṣika is characteristic because therein it is shown especially clearly that for Jinism the philosophical thought does not stand in the forefront but that it starts from the world-picture.

326) Compare Tattvārthādhigamasūtrāṇi V, 22 and 38-39, and above all Pavayaṇasāro II, v. 43-52 and Paṃcatthiyasaṃgaho v. 23-26 and 100-102. I stick here only to Kundakunda ; I do not take later views into consideration. It appears to me also doubtful whether the distinction between '*vyavahārakālaḥ*' and '*niścayakālaḥ*' can or need be already traced back to Kundakunda.

327) This must have been originally the only definition *Pariṇāmaḥ kriya paratvāparatve ca*' are considered by me as a later enlargement.

328) Tattvārthādhigamasūtrāṇi V. 21.

329) The following is according to Kundakunda, Paṃcatthiyasaṃgaho v. 27 ff.

330) Kundakunda, in the work quoted above, v. 56-68.

331) Vol. I, p. (199) f.

332) The corporeality or limitedness (*mūrtatvam*) was, according to the Vaiśeṣika, conditioned by impenetrability which depends on the quality of touch. For the Jaina, this interpretation was impossible, as according to them, the matter, at least in the condition of fine material particles, is not impenetrable. They were, therefore, compelled to seek another definition for the corporeality and found it, for example, in the sensuous perception (Paṃcattiyasaṃgaho v. 99).

333) Tattvārthādhigamasūtrāṇi V, 19-20.

334) Tattvārthādhigamasūtrāṇi V, 32-36; Pavayaṇasāro II, v. 71-74.

335) The word '*snigdhaḥ*' in Sanskrit implies both glossy as well as sticky.

336) Tattvārthādhigamsūtrāṇi V, 37, 40 and 41.

337) Paṃcatthiyasaṃgaho v. 8-21 ; Pavayaṇasāro II, v. 3-19.

338) Paṃcatthiyasaṃgaho v. 16-21 ; compare Pavayaṇasāro II, v. 20. ff.

339) Tattvārthādhigamasūtrāṇi III and IV.

340) Tattvārthādhigamasūtrāṇi II, 10-25. Paṃcatthiya-saṃgaho v. 109-117.

341) Tattvārthādhigamasūtrāṇi II, 32-36.

342) A natural-scientific explanation, worth consideration of the expression '*potajaḥ*' is given by J. Fr. Kohl, 'Zur Deutung des Begriffs '*potaja*' in der Zoologie der Jainas, Zeitschrift der Deutschen Morgenlandischen Gasellschaft, Band 103/1953, p. 151-155.

343) Compre Tattvārthādhigamasūtrāṇi II, 37-49

344) Vol. I, p. (287) ff.

345) Vol. I, p. (113) and (142)

346) The description which Umāsvāti gives of these wonder-powers, resembles strikingly the wonder-powers (*ṛddhi-prabhedāḥ*) which are enumerated by older Buddhism. Compare Vol. I, p. (143).

347) Pavayaṇasāro II, v. 53-55 ; Paṃcatthiyasaṃgaho v. 30 ; according to other treatises, these life-forces are reckoned under Karma.

348) Tattvārthādhigamasūtrāṇi II, 16-19. I follow in my presentation the Digambara commentators Devanandī (Pūjya-pāda) and Akalaṅka, by whom the subject is better thought out than by Umāsvāti.

349) Devanandī and Akalaṅka on the Tattvārthādhigama-sūtrāṇi II, 11 ; Compare also the commentary of Siddhasena.

350) Tattvārthādhigamasūtrāṇi I, 9—33.

351) The self-willed and, many times, not a very happy terminology of the Jaina is especially difficult to render. I rely, during the rendering, on the usual translations, so far as they, otherwise, do not contradict the terminology used by me.

352) Tattvārthādhigamasūtrāṇi I, 5.

353) Vol. I, p. (315).

354) Tattvārthādhigamasūtrāṇi I, 34-35. I cite the doctrine of Umāsvāti intentionally, in its obscure form, without supplementing it. The different later interpretations will be given in their proper place.

355) Vol. I, (199) ff.

356) Tattvārthādhigamasūtrāṇi VIII, 1.

357) Tattvārthādhigamasūtrāṇi VII.

358) Vol. I, p. (201) f.

359) Tattvārthādhigamasūtrāṇi VI.

360) Tattvārthādhigamasūtrāṇi VIII.

361) Tattvārthādhigamasūtrāṇi II, 1-7.

362) Compare W. Schubring, Die Lehre der Jainas, Berlin and Leipzig 1935, p. 28 and 127. About Maskari Gośālīputra, see Vol. I. p. (270) ff.

363) Tattvārthādhigamasūtrāṇi IX.

364) Vol. I, p. (202) f.

365) Vol. I, p. (203) f.

366) Tattvārthādhigamasūtrāṇi X.

367) The Samayasāro which is considered as the best work of Kundakunda contains the detailed presentation of the doctrine of Deliverance. Therefore, I have taken it as the basis in the following treatment.

368) I believe that here, as also in the following, the influence of a Buddhistic prototype is at work.

369) Samayasāro v. 8.

370) Kundakunda employs the expression *'āsravaḥ'* for the three passions. He is, therefore, in contact, in this respect, with the linguistic usage of the Buddhistic Dogmatik.

371) These are in contrast to the triad of right belief, right knowledge, and right conduct, together with the idea of activity in general.

372) Samayasāro v. 25-29.

373) Compare p. (186)

374) Compare Samayasāro v. 41-43.

375) A mixture of water and milk is well quoted as an example of a special inner connection.

376) Compare Samayasāro v. 55-62.

377) Compare Samayasaro v. 11 ff.

378) Vol. I, p. (152) ff. and (298) ff.

379) Samayasāro v. 80 ff.

380) Vol. I, p. (195) f.

9 The Materialism

BIBLIOGRAPHY

Hillebrandt, A. : Zur Kenntnis der indischen Materialisten. Aufsätze zur Kultur und Sprachageschichte vornehmlich des Orients, Ernst Kuhn gewidmet, München 1916, p. 24-26.

Tucci, G. : Linee di una Storia del materialismo Indiano. Memorie della R. Accademia Nazionale dei Lincei, Serie V, Vol. 17-Fasc. 7/1923 and Serie VI. Vol. 2, Fasc. 10/1929.

Ruben, W. : Materialismus im Leben des alten Indien, Acta Orientalia XIII, Leiden 1935, p. 128-162 and 177-225.

Dakshina Ranjan Shastri : Short History of Indian Materialism, Calcutta 1930.

Translations are not mentioned; apart from a few concise works recently found, in later times, the literature of the system is lost. Nothing much is to be remarked about my presentation. In a history of Indian Philosophy, the systematic materialism of the Lokāyata must naturally stand at the middle point or centre. A grouping of scattered utterances of materialistic views has no value, because therethrough no essentially new features come forth. For the systematic Lokāyata, the most important thing is the assembling and making use of the available fragments. It is still, upto this time, not performed in a satisfactory form but is not difficult for the older times. Difficulties present themselves only in the post-classical times, where the thought-processes become complicated and isolated authors and works become available for consideration. But it falls already out of the limits of the present volume.

NOTES

381) This deals with the second Uvaṅgaṃ of the Jaina, the Rāyapasenaijjaṃ, to which from the Buddhistic side Dīghanikāya XXIII (Payāsisuttantaṃ) = Dīrghāgamaḥ 7 corresponds. Of both the versions, the Jinistic one is, according to all appearances, the original one. Compare E. Leumann, Beziehungen der Jaina-Literatur zu andern Literaturkreisen Indiens. Actes du sixieme Congrés International, des Orientalistes tenu en 1883 à Leide, Troisiéme Partie, Section 2, Leiden 1885, p. 467-564. I closely follow, in the following, the translation by E. Leumann, though in doing so, I have made it more smooth and short.

382) Compare Dīghanikāya II (Sāmaññaphalasuttaṃ) = Dīrghāgamaḥ 27

383) The northern bank of the Gaṅgā was considered at that time as an old Brahmanical holy land in contrast to the southern bank.

384) The beings in the hell and the world of the gods are not produced but they originate suddenly and directly [compare p. (41) f and (267)]. The belief in such suddenly originated beings is, therefore, of importance for the doctrine of the rebirth and of the retribution of good and bad actions in the world beyond.

385) The word Cārvāka holds good partly as the name of the founder of the system but is also explained in a different way.

386) The aphorisms of Bṛhaspati are not preserved to us but are only known from quotations. And as the remaining literature of the system is lost and besides, the works and the authors, about whom we hear, belong to a later time, I have not further gone in this place into the literature of the Lokāyata.

387) The beginning of the Vaiśeṣika-Sūtras runs originally: *Yad iha bhāvarūpaṃ tat sarvam abhidhāsyāmi* (compare Vyomaśiva, Vyomavatī p. 47, 13 f. and 492, 25).

388) The quoted Sūtras are often quoted in an isolated manner. In the cited order, they appear in Prabhācandra, Nyāyakumudacandra, Māṇikacandra Digambara Jaina Granthamālā vols. 38-39, Bombay 1938-41, p. 341, 17 ff. I follow it here.

389) Prabhācandra, Nyāyakumudacandra p. 343, 9 f.

390) Compare p. (27) f.

391) For the following, compare Śāntirakṣita, Tattvasaṃgrahaḥ, Gaekwad's Oriental Series No. 30-31, Baroda 1926, v. 1857 ff.

392) Compare Sāyaṇamādhava, Sarvadarśanasaṃgrahaḥ, Ānandāśrama Sanskrit Series No. 51, Poona[2] 1928, p. 2, 23 f. and 3, 1-4.

393) Śāntirakṣita, Tattvasaṃgrahaḥ v. 1874.

394) The verses employed for the following are found in their largest number in Sāyaṇamādhava's Sarvadarśanasaṃgrahaḥ, p. 5, 1 ff.

395) *jarbharī* and *turpharī* are antiquated obsolete Vedic

words which become unintelligible in later times and appear to the sceptics as a senseless Abrakadabra.

396) *Pratyakṣam eva pramāṇam anumānam apramāṇam.* Compare Abhayadevasūri, Tattvabodhavidhāyinī on Siddhasenadivākara's Saṃmatitarkaprakaraṇam, Purātattvamandira Granthāvalī No. 10, 16, 18, 19 and 21, Ahmedabad 1923-30, p. 70, 18 f and 73, 14 ff.

397) *Sarvatra paryanuyogaparāṇi eva sūtrāṇi Bṛhaspateḥ.* Compare Abhayadevasūri, in his above referred-to work, p. 69, 39.

I. INDEX OF NAMES

Ajita Keśakambala 12, 219
Akṣapāda 8
Ātreya, Ātreyabhāṣyam, Ātreyatantram 4
Aviddhakarṇa 8, 126

Bhartṛhari 101
Bhāsarvajña (Bhāvasarvajña) 9
Bhāvivikta 8
Bhṛgu, dialogue between Bhṛgu and Bharadvāja 14
Bṛhaspati 221, the aphorisms of B. 221ff.
Bṛhatī (Nibandhanam) 10

Candramati (Maticandra) 4, 109 ff 133 ff.
Cārvāka 221

Daśapadārthaśāstram 4, 134
Digambara 182

Jaimini 9
Jayanta Bhaṭṭa 9

Kakuda Kātyāyana 12, 220
Kaṇāda 4
Kāśikā 11
Keśi 217 ff.
Kiraṇāvalī 5
Kumārila 10ff, 21, 68, 84, 99, 108
Kundakunda 183 ff

Laghvī (Vivaraṇam) 10
Lokāyata 221 ff.

Maṇḍana Miśra 10, 68
Maticandra see Candramati
Mīmāṃsābhāṣyam 9
Mīmāṃsā-Sūtras 9

Nyāyabhāṣyam 8
Nyāyabhūṣaṇam 9
Nyāyakandalī 5
Nyāyamañjarī 9
Nyāyaratnākaraḥ 11
Nyāyasāraḥ 9
Nyāya-sūtras 8
Nyāyavārttikam 9
Nyāyavārttika-tātparya-pariśuddhiḥ 9
Nyāyavārttika-tātparya-ṭīkā 9 ff (Tātparya-ṭīkā)

Padārthadharmasaṃgrahaḥ (Praśastapādabhāṣyam) 4, 111, 134 ff
Paesi (Pāyāsi) 216 ff.
Pakṣilasvāmī (Vātsyāyana) 8
Paṃcatthiyasaṃgaho (Pañcāstikāyaḥ) 184 ff.
Pañcaśikhī 3
Pārthasārathi Miśra 11
Pavayaṇasāro (Pravacanasāraḥ) 183
Prabhākara 10, 99, 108 ff, 126 ff, 128, 132 ff.
Prakaraṇapañcikā 11
Praśastapāda (Praśastadeva, Praśastakāra) 4 ff, 111, 134 ff
Praśastapādabhāṣyam, see Padārthadharmasaṃgrahaḥ
Purāṇa Kāśyapa 219

Rāvaṇa, Rāvaṇabhāṣyam 4

Śabarasvāmī 9 ff.
Śālikanātha 11.
Samayasāro 183
Śaṅkarasvāmī 8
Ślokavārttikam 10 ff
Śrīdhara 5
Sucarita Miśra 11
Śvetāmbara 182

Tātparyaṭīkā see Nyāyavārttikatātparyaṭīkā
Tattvārthādhigamasūtrāṇi 183
Trilocana 8

Udayana 5, 9
Uddyotakara 9
Ulūka 3
Umāsvāti (Umāsvāmī) 183
Umveka 11
Uśanas 221

Vācaspati Miśra 9 ff.
Vaiśeṣika-sūtras 4, 133 ff, 140, 221
Vātsyāyana, see Pakṣilasvāmī
Vṛttikāraḥ 10
Vyomaśiva 4
Vyomavatī 4

II. SUBJECT INDEX

Accumulation Theory 16, 25, 85
Action (*karma*) 61 ff., 222 cf. also Invisible (*adṛṣṭam*)
Activity (*upayogaḥ*) 186, 209
Aggregate (in the Vaiśeṣika, cf. also the whole) 54 ff, 85, 86, 115-119; (in the Jaina *Skandhāḥ*) 187 ff.
Air (*Vāyuḥ*) 145 ff.; nonperceptibility of air 16, 126 ff., 145 ff.
Ātmā (world-soul) 3, 11, 41 ff.
Atom-doctrine 53-57, 115 ff, 187-188, 212; atoms (*aṇavaḥ, paramāṇavaḥ*) 55, 159, 187; double atoms (*dvyaṇukāni*) 115, 159.
Aversion (*dveṣaḥ*) 42, 96, 167

Basic Truths (*tattvāni*), seven 202.
Bhāsa 183
Body of man 24, 48; body that accompanies beyond (*ātivāhikam*), the transmigratory body 67, 175; five bodies according to the Jaina 194
Bondage of Karma (*bandhaḥ*) 202, 203, 205
Brightness (see Light)
Buddhism 7, 14, 16, 19, 28, 32, 35, 39, 42, 73, 88, 126, 181, 214; Logical schools 83, 131, 132

Cancellation of Karma (*nirjarā*) 202, 206
Categories (*padārthāḥ*) 141
Categories-doctrine—of the Jaina 189-190, 212; of the Vaiśeṣika, its origin 79; its formulation 112; its final form 133
Causality-doctrine of the Vaiśeṣika 59, 119-122, 142, 143; *ārambhavādaḥ* 59; *asatkāryavādaḥ* 119.
Causes-material or positive (*kāraṇam*) 59, 119; occasioning (*nimittam*) 59, 119; inhering (*samavāyikāraṇam*) 120; noninhering (*asamavāyikāraṇam*) 120
Causes of action, four (*pratyayāḥ*) 209
Change or transformation (*pariṇāmaḥ*) doctrine of change (*pariṇāma-vādaḥ*) 59 cf. 118, 188
Colour or form (*varṇaḥ rūpam*) 86, 156, 188
Colours of Souls (*leśyāḥ*) 205
Commonness (*sāmānyam*) 101, 108, 175-176.
Perception of Commonness 129.
Commonness-particularity (*Sāmānya-viśeṣaḥ*) 104
Conditions of the soul (*bhāvāḥ*) 186, 210-211
Conditions of things (*paryāyāḥ* also *pariṇāmāḥ*) 81, 189, 199
Conduct, fivefold (*caritram*) 206
Connection (*Saṁyogaḥ*) 88, 105, 160; connection according to Jaina (*bandhaḥ*) 188
Considerations twelve (*anuprekṣāḥ*) 206.
Corporeal winds (*prāṇāḥ*) 26-27
Cuṇṇi 183.

Darkness (*tamaḥ* or *andhakāraḥ*) 19, 188.
Deliverance (*Mokṣaḥ*) 201, 207; Deliverance-doctrine of the Jaina 201, 207-210; of the Nyāya 47, 52; of the Vaiśeṣika 140, 170.
Desire (*icchā*) 42, 96, 167.
Discipline, three kinds of (*guptiḥ*) 206.
Disposition or preparedness (*saṁskāraḥ*) 98, 168.
Distance, distantness (*paratvam*) 92, 139, 164.
Duties, ten (*dharmāḥ*) 206

Ear (*śrotram*) 31, 36.
Earth (*pṛthvī*) 143.
Effort (*prayatnaḥ*) 68, 96, 167.
Elasticity (*sthitisthāpakaḥ*) 98, 169.
Elements 14, 17, 22, 84.
Ether (*ākāśaḥ*) 15, 31, 35, 84, 147.
Existence (*sattā* or *bhāvaḥ*) 103, 176, 189.
Extension (*parimāṇam*) 87, 102, 115, 159.

Fire (*tejaḥ*) 145.
Fluidity (*dravatvam*) 14, 57, 84, 96, 168.
Force or capacity (*śaktiḥ*) 109.
Form or shape (*ākṛtiḥ*) 102.
Form (*rūpam*) 19, 85, 156.

Genus (*jātiḥ*) 104.
God-idea 140.
Grammarians 36, 68, 101.

Grossness or largeness (*sthaulyam*) 19, 188.
Guilt, demerit (*adharmaḥ*) 62, 98, 169.

Heat (of the Sun) radiation of warmth (*ātapaḥ*) 20, 188.
Heaviness (*gurutvam*) 57, 97, 167.
Hindrance (*adharmaḥ*) 62, 184, 212.

Ignorance (*ajñānam*) 209.
Impressions, psychical (*saṁskārāḥ*, *bhāvanāḥ*) 44, 98, 168.
Impulse, movement (*dharmaḥ*) 62, 184, 212.
Inherence (*Samavāyaḥ*) 105, 108, 177, nonperceptability of I. 128, 178.
Instreaming of Karma-matter (*āsravaḥ*) 202, 203.
Invisible, the (*adṛṣṭam*) 62, 98, 169, 175.

Jinism 8, 13, 16, 19, 67, 73, 81, 84, 88, 108.
Juices or saps, the doctrine of the three saps 27, 166, 222.

Karma, according to the Jaina 186, 203-205, 209.
Knowledge (*jñānam*), five sorts of, 197.
Knowledge, instrument of (*buddhiḥ*) 42, 51, 96, 165; observing knowleage (*apekṣā-buddhiḥ*) 94, 137, 157, 160, 164. means of right knowledge (*pramāṇāni*) 199, 225.

Life (*jīvanam*) 47, 174.
Life-forces (*prāṇāḥ*) 195.
Light (*ālokaḥ* or *uddyotaḥ*) 20, 188.
Linguistic Philosophy 101.
Living objects or creatures 23, 193.

Man, the doctrine of, 24-47.
Masses of existence (*astikāyāḥ*) 184.
Materialism 12, 215.
Matter (*pudgalāḥ*) 185, 187-188.
Mechanics 57-58.
Meditation (*dhyānam*) 206.
Merit (*dharmaḥ*) 206.
Merit (*dharmaḥ*) 62, 98, 169.
Mīmāṃsā 8, 17, 21, 37, 84, 126, 132, 200.
Moistness, humidity, stickiness (*snehaḥ*) 14, 84, 96, 168.
Moral commands or vows five (*vratāni*) 202.
Movement (*karma*) 57, 81, 99, 114, 171-175; causality of movement 172; Perception of movement 128.

Nearness (*aparatvam*) 92, 139, 163-164.
Nijjutti 183.
Non-existence (*abhāvaḥ*) 110.
Number (*saṃkhyā*) 93, 109, 116, 136, 138, 157.
Nutrional juice or sap (*rasaḥ*) 26, 156.
Nyāya 5, 12, 180; the Nature-philosophy of N. 47-53.

Organ, psychical (*manaḥ*) 43, 45, 46, 52, 66, 83, 151, 174, 196.
Origination, new composition or synthesis (*ārambhavādaḥ*), the doctrine of O. (*ārambhavādaḥ*) 59 cf. 118.

Passions (*kaṣāyāḥ*) 203.
Peculiarity or particularity (*viśeṣaḥ*) 103, 108, 176; ultimate peculiarities (*antyāḥ viśeṣāḥ*) 103, 176.
Penance (*tapaḥ*) 206.
Pleasure (*sukham*) 42, 96, 166.
Points of space (*pradeśāḥ*) 212.
Points of view, four 200.
Preparedness, see Disposition.

Quality, category of, (*guṇaḥ*) 80, 84-99, 152-171, 188; characteristic qualities (*vaiśeṣikaguṇāḥ*) 85, 87, 96, 142, 153; Common qualities (*sāmānyaguṇāḥ*) 85, 87, 142, 153; changeable quality through heat (*pākajaḥ*) 56, 156; Causality of quantities 153-156; Perception of qualities 123, 127, 153.
Qualities of the Elements 14-21, 50, 84, 188; old series 14, 17, 24, 84; later series 14, 17, 25.
Quarters (*diśaḥ*) 73.

Relativity, doctrine of (*syādvādaḥ*) 108, 189, 200.

Sāṃkhya 15, 28, 41, 59, 61, 66, 70, 79, 108, 118, 180, 210.
Scholastics, nature of Indian 112; Its deterioration in Praśastapāda 135.
Sense-organs (*indriyāṇi*) 27-38, 49, 196.
Sense-perception 31-38, 49, 123-132, 196.
Separateness (*pṛthaktvam*) 108, 135, 160.
Separation (*vibhāgaḥ*) 90, 162-163; Separation according to Jaina (bhedaḥ) 188.
Shadow (*chāyā*) 20, 188.

Shape or form (*saṃsthānam*) 86, 102, 188.
Similarity (*sādṛśyam*) 109.
Sleep 46, 166.
Smell (*gandhaḥ*) 19, 85, 156, 188.
Sorrow, pain (*duḥkham*) 42, 96, 167.
Soul (*jīvaḥ or ātmā*) 3, 11-12, 24, 38-47, 48, 64-71, 84, 150, 184-187, 198, 202, 215; proofs for the existence of the soul 40, 49, 150; Its size 38, 39, 65, 187; perception of the soul 131; denial of the soul 215, 217, 222; the qualities of the soul 39, 68-69, 95, 209; momentariness of the soul (*Kṣaṇikatvam*) 70; the activity of the soul 42, 47, 67.
Sound (*Śabdaḥ*) 15, 19-20, 31, 35, 86, 113, 170, 188, 211.
Space (*ākāśaḥ*) 16, 72, 184, 211.
Space (*dik*) 72-74, 84, 147, 150.
Speech 36.
Stains, three (*āsravāḥ*) 208.
Stickiness, see moistness.
Substance (*dravyam*) 80, 83, 141-152, 189, 199; causality of substance 143; perception of substance 125-126
Subtleness, fineness or smallness (*Saukṣmyam*) 19, 188.
Suffering or enduring of miseries (*pariṣāhaḥ*) 206.
Swing, impetus (*vegaḥ*) 57, 98, 114, 168.

Taste (*rasaḥ*) 19, 85, 156, 188.
Time (*kālaḥ*) 75-78, 84, 147, 149, 185.
Touch or contact (*sparśaḥ*) 19, 85, 156, 187

Upaniṣads 3, 11, 41, 46, 70

Vaiśeṣika 3, 12; the nature-philosophy of the V. 14; Its further formulation 53; the categories-doctrine of the V. 79; the world-picture of the V. 59, 118; Its realism 81; the importance of the V. 179.
Vedānta 132.

Warding off of new Karma (*saṃvaraḥ*) 202, 206.
Wariness, fivefold (*samitiḥ*) 206.
Water (*āpaḥ*) 144.
Ways of consideration (*nayāḥ*) 199-201, 208.
Whole (*avayavī*) 117.
World-ages and world periods 192.
World-construction 22, 190.
World-creation 21, 147.
World-history 192.
World-soul; see Ātmā.

III. INDEX OF INDIAN TERMS

ajñānam	ignorance
aṇavaḥ	atoms
adṛṣṭam	invisible
adharmaḥ	hindrance and guilt
anuprekṣāḥ	considerations
andhakāraḥ	darkness
aparatvam	nearness
apekṣābuddhiḥ	'observing knowledge
abhāvaḥ	nonexistence
avayavī	a whole
asamavāyikāraṇam	non-inhering cause
astikāyaḥ	mass of existence
ākāśaḥ	ether and space
ākṛtiḥ	shape, form
ātapaḥ	radiation of heat
ātmā	soul
ārambhaḥ	composition, origination
ārambhavādaḥ	composition, the doctrine of the composition or origination.
ālokaḥ	light
āsravaḥ	instreaming of *karma*-matter.

āsravāḥ	stains or taints.
icchā	desire
indriyāṇi	sense-organs
uddyotaḥ	light
upayogaḥ	activity
karma	movement and action
kaṣāyāḥ	passions
kāraṇam	material cause
kālaḥ	time
gandhaḥ	smell
guṇaḥ	quality
guptiḥ	discipline
gurutvam	heaviness
cāritram	conduct
chāyā	shadow
jātiḥ	genus
jīvanam	life
jīvaḥ	soul
jñānam	knowledge
tattvāni	basic truths
tapaḥ	penance
tamaḥ	darkness
tejaḥ	fire
dik	space
diśaḥ	quarters
duḥkham	sorrow
dravatvam	liquidness
dravyam	substance
dveṣaḥ	aversion
dharmaḥ	motion and merit
dharmāḥ	duties
dhyānam	meditation
nayāḥ	ways of consideration
nimittam	occasioning cause
nirjarā	cancellation of *karma*
padārthāḥ	categories
paratvam	distance
paramāṇavaḥ	atoms
pariṇāmaḥ	change and condition
pariṇāmavādaḥ	doctrine of change
parimāṇam	extension
pariṣāhaḥ	suffering miseries
paryāyaḥ	condition
pudgalāḥ	matter
pṛthaktva	separateness
pratyayāḥ	causes of actions
pradeśāḥ	points of space
pramāṇam	means of right knowledge
prayatnaḥ	effort
prāṇāḥ	corporeal winds and lifeforces
bandhaḥ	connection and bondage of *karma*
buddhiḥ	knowledge
bhāvanāḥ	psychic impressions
bhāvaḥ	existence
bhāvāḥ	conditions of the soul
bhedaḥ	separation
manaḥ	psychical organ
mokṣaḥ	deliverance
rasaḥ	taste and sap of nutrition
rūpam	form and colour

leśyāḥ	colours of the souls
varṇaḥ	colour
vāyuḥ	air
vibhāgaḥ	separation
viśeṣaḥ	particularity or peculiarity
vegaḥ	swing or impulse
vratāni	moral commands.
śaktiḥ	force
śabdaḥ	sound
śrotram	ear
saṃyogaḥ	conneotion
saṃvaraḥ	defence against or warding off of new *karma*.
saṃskāraḥ	disposition
saṃskārāḥ	psychical impressions
saṃsthānam	form
saṃkhyā	number
sattā	existence
samavāyaḥ	inherence
samavāyikāranam	inhering cause
samitiḥ	wariness
sādṛśyam	similarity
sāmānya	commonness
sāmānya-viśesaḥ	commonness-particularity
sukham	pleasure
sauksmyam	fineness, subtleness
skandhāḥ	aggregate
sthitisthāpakaḥ	elasticity
sthaulyaṃ	grossness
snehaḥ	humidity or stickiness
sparśaḥ	touch
syādvādaḥ	doctrine of relativity.

ERICH FRAUWALLNER

Born on 28.12. 1898 in Vienna. Admitted in 1928 as University lecturer for Indian Philology and Ancient Cultural Sciences. From 1939-45, Professor for Indology and Iranistik. Since 1945, when the Faculty in the University was closed, he lived as Private Professor in Vienna. He is the corresponding member of the Austrian Academy of Sciences.

Publications : A long series of papers and articles on Indian Philosophy. The present work represents the summing up of the thirty years' preparation.